85 Days in Cuba

Jerry

Kindest

Regards

Walt V

85 Days in Cuba

✦

A True Story about Friendship and Struggle

Brandon Valentine

iUniverse, Inc.
New York Lincoln Shanghai

85 Days in Cuba
A True Story about Friendship and Struggle

iUniverse books may be ordered through booksellers or by contacting:

iUniverse
2021 Pine Lake Road, Suite 100
Lincoln, NE 68512
www.iuniverse.com
1-800-Authors (1-800-288-4677)

ISBN-13: 978-0-595-39335-0 (pbk)
ISBN-13: 978-0-595-83732-8 (ebk)
ISBN-10: 0-595-39335-7 (pbk)
ISBN-10: 0-595-83732-8 (ebk)

Printed in the United States of America

For MaryAnn Anderberg and Don Dernovich
Who opened me to the world of art

For Mark Gabel and Steve Anderson
Who opened me to the world of natural science

For all of my teachers, in and out of school,
Who opened me to the world

Contents

Author's Note

The story contained within is true. Names have been changed to protect the privacy of my friends. Ricardo (Days 64-75) was created from a composite of men I have known. The conversations actually happened although not on the days indicated in the book. I did not keep a diary, so the days were recreated from my memories which are often as hard to grasp as smoke. The spoken words, colors, sights, and smells were not from a video. Others at the same time and place would remember them differently. However, I know the most unbelievable parts of the story are absolutely true.

The most unbelievable things to me are that a wonderful friend like Carlos wanted me to visit him and opened his home to me. A beautiful woman like Carmen loved me for a time. The people of Cuba, full of life, music and generosity, welcomed me and made me feel as though I was one of them. These things are true.

Things the reader may find unbelievable are also absolutely true. Looking back, I wonder at my choices, but at the time, the choices I made always seemed the best thing to do.

This book would not have been possible without my parents. My father has much more skill as a writer than I do. As editor/ghostwriter he managed to rearrange my words and add some of his own so that they sounded right. The result was always just what I was trying to say, but clearer and more entertaining. My mother worked much harder than my father or I worked. She spent endless hours, proof-reading and correcting, over and over and over.

I hope that the story is enjoyable to read and that I portrayed the strength, generosity, and vitality of the Cuban people in a way that makes the reader appreciate their struggle.

Carlos

✦

Day 1
Friday, August 15, 2003

Carlos said, "*Everting chris*," but the ache in my stomach wasn't listening. This was the day I would fly to Cuba; paradise with Carlos after three years of rarely feeling safe in Jamaica. In the fifteen-by-fifteen house I had lived in for those three years, I paced back and forth, like swimming laps in a kiddy pool. I knew Eve would come late because everyone in Jamaica came late. Would we make it to the plane on time? Would I be arrested by the U.S. before I got to Cuba? If I get there, would I get thrown in jail for being in Cuba? Carlos said everything would be fine but the unknown scared me. I focused on the home I was leaving before my nerves exploded.

The big bed grabbed me as it had so many times during the past three years. It had been much kinder than the wobbly, paint-spattered table that I had borrowed from the art classroom and never returned. Since the legs on the table are all different lengths, the hours I spent writing grants at this table made me feel like Chris Columbus making journal entries on the high seas. The two gray and rust folding chairs were just hard and boring. Since that was all my furniture, the bed was clearly my best furniture, and it had been so kind after some of those long rum and rain-soaked days I'd spent hearing about Cuba from Carlos.

I counted goats and parrots (few sheep in Jamaica) for almost an hour with the cool morning air drifting in through the louvered windows. Finally, I gave up on sleeping. The nervousness about this day had been keeping me awake a lot for two months.

At four o'clock, nervous and frustrated, I grabbed my yellow pitcher like the one my family in Nebraska uses for orange juice. Here, it was my bathing pitcher. I lowered the pitcher into the fifty-gallon drum which sat directly below the end of my bamboo rain gutter. I tapped the bottom of the pitcher against the surface of the water. This was to scare the mosquito larvae to the bottom of the tank. I

1

waited about ten seconds and then submerged the pitcher. I really do not mind having a bathing partner but the larvae are not my first choice. I carried the pitcher inside and placed it next to the drain in the middle of the concrete square that is slightly raised above the level of the floor. I undressed, stepped into the square, and plunged my two hands into the pitcher for a breath-stopping dose of freezing-cold rainwater.

During my first few months here I realized how precious water is. There was no running water and what you could buy from the Rapid Response water truck, when it did happen to come by, was very expensive. Therefore, I allotted myself one pitcher of water for bathing. I remember a Lever 2000 soap commercial that said the body has over 2000 parts. However, if you only have a pitcher of water to wash and rinse, you soon determine there are only about four important ones.

Clean and dressed, standing in the kitchen that was just big enough to turn around in, I started to laugh. Peeling a banana, I thought about a time when Carlos and I decided to go exploring for fruit on a Saturday morning. With our machetes and empty backpacks we set off through the mountainside in search of fruit, oranges mostly, since it was orange season. After crossing a cane field behind teacher housing, we followed a steep path down into a narrow river valley. There were large stands of bamboo on both sides of the valley, with dense vegetation crowding the meandering dry-season stream.

Looking up at the giant branches covered with epiphytes, I imagined us swinging on the large vines like George of the Jungle. Epiphytes live on trees like parasites but do no harm. Orchids of every possible variety are the most common, sharing space with another less common epiphyte, pineapple-like bromates. Loud green parakeets flew in tightly-formed groups through the tiny points of light that penetrated the canopy and reached the ground. Doctor birds, bright long-tailed hummingbirds pictured by Air Jamaica on the sides of their planes, rose from the heliconia in waves as we chopped our way through a grove of the tropical plants. Some of the heliconia were six feet tall with massive orange and yellow flowers as long as my arm. In the states these plants would sell for at least twenty dollars a piece, and here we were chopping them down like weeds.

Suddenly, a giant orange popsicle appeared across the stream. We jumped and slipped, laughing, from stone to stone across the tame stream that had been a deadly rush of water during Isabelle, the last hurricane. The giant popsicle seemed to be set in orange sherbet because the ground was orange too. Then some of the ice cream moved. Five-inch Anole lizards, enjoying the feast, puffed out their radiant orange throat pouches to frighten us away.

We didn't turn back so the lizards scurried to the far side of the gigantic, forty-foot orange tree. Clouds of fruit flies hovered around us as we placed our machetes in the crook of a lower branch and hung our bags from a limb. Some oranges were easy to reach, but the child within us said, "Climb." We made our way to a large branch about eight feet above the ground. I sat down first and then Carlos settled in beside me. Resting our feet on another branch only a few feet below, it reminded me of a porch swing back home. Within easy reach were more oranges than Carlos and I could ever eat.

I grabbed a large one and ripped off the skin. The taste was like biting into a bottle of honey. Carlos said this was the best way to eat an orange, when the fruit is so ripe that it is ready to fall from the tree. I told him that this was a luxury that I never had growing up in Nebraska. Carlos and I ate until we were ready to burst.

Carlos said when he was a boy, he was always sick during mango season. Every day after school he would climb his neighbor's eighty-foot tall mango tree and eat until he could not eat anymore. He said there were always mangoes in that tree, each weighing at least four pounds, and they were so ripe they would explode when they hit the ground.

I was explaining about Newton and gravity when he told me to listen. I stopped talking but I did not know what I was listening for. "*Shet up an cum dung from outta eh tree.*" Carlos and I spoke a mixture of English, Jamaican patois, and a little Spanish. When Carlos used Spanish, he explained quickly when I looked puzzled. I never attempted to speak Spanish.

Following Carlos's patois instructions, I shut up and climbed out of the tree. Carlos stalked a giant guango tree, staring up into the dark green. Once again, I was lost, but I stared too. Yes, it was the middle of the day, but I felt like Carlos was an astronomer, keenly picking out constellation after constellation when all I could see were a bunch of stars.

Finally, through the foliage, he pointed out a few birds squawking and squabbling. He then pointed out the fact that beside me was a banana tree, but the leaves were barely visible almost thirty-five feet up due to the surrounding vegetation from other trees. He told me that there were ripe bananas up there. I thought, "Is this the Crocodile Dundee of the Jamaican outback?"

Unwrapping a knife from some Kingston newspaper, he told me that he was going to climb the guango tree and then cross over to the banana tree on a branch directly below the leaves. I knew from previous excursions that he wraps the knife in newspaper so that he can stick it along the inside of his waistband without jeopardizing his chance of having more children. "Brandon," he said, "these bananas will be ripe so you will have to catch them. Wait right here."

As he climbed, I marveled as his double-jointed athletic frame snaked effortlessly up the tree. I was still trying to figure out how he reached the first branch when he shouted down, "Yuh ready? It's not too big." The foliage obscured the view, but I knew Carlos was working because the banana tree started to shake as he hacked at the stem. When he yelled that he was almost finished, I heard limbs breaking and looked up at a yellow Volkswagen rushing toward me. I attempted to break its fall but my attempt was futile. Flat on my back, struggling with more over-ripe bananas than we could eat in a month, Carlos was standing over me laughing until his wonderful yellow eyes filled with tears.

"It's not funny. You could have killed me."

"Wouldn't that be funny?" Carlos laughed. "The Peace Corps director has to call your parents and tell them you were killed in Jamaica by a seventy-pound bunch of bananas." I started to laugh as I wiped the banana goo from my face. He helped me up and we stuffed our backpacks with bananas.

On our way back I asked Carlos where he learned so much about climbing trees and how he knew what type of birds make so much noise fighting over fruit. Born a few years after the revolution, he grew up in the countryside. His parents worked on a farm near the town of Banes (pronounced BONN—ace) in eastern Cuba. He spent much time hunting the *jutia*, a large rat-like rodent that lived in the trees. If he shot one that didn't fall, he would have to climb the tree to retrieve it.

"Why did you hunt a big rat?"

"In Cuba it is a delicacy."

I was not surprised. A few days before I had eaten chicken-foot soup and pigs' tails with rice and beans. "*Thas chris*," I said, and everything was okay. I was going to Cuba to live with Carlos and learn Spanish.

Air Jamaica

♦

Day 1
Friday, August 15, 2003

I finished my banana a little before five. In three years I had learned much about "Jamaica Time" so I was not really expecting Eve to come pick me up until six. I began my pacing again and running everything through my mind to ensure I had all I needed. I realized that all I really needed was my passport, ticket, and money: check, check, check. Time drug on. It reminded me of sitting in a political geography class I took at Black Hills State. It was a Friday night class and I looked at my watch every few minutes. By nine o'clock I knew that the rest of my friends were working on their third beer. I knew for sure it was a Friday night class since college students wouldn't drink during the week. Right.

Vibrant pinks and gold crested over the Blue Mountains in the distance around five-thirty. During my first year living at St. Faiths, I cycled to the top of our mountain every morning to catch the sunrise out of the ocean before the lights were turned out in Kingston.

God and Air Jamaica willing, I would be able to watch the sunset in Havana. I smiled at the thought, and smiled, and smiled. At about fifteen 'til six a blue 1998 Toyota Corolla came rolling down the driveway. Eve pulled up to the house and popped the trunk. "*Yuh waan nuh elp?*" She smiled and got out to help with my bags. Eve is vibrant, about five-foot-five, a rich milk chocolate brown, and might weigh 100 pounds. Although old enough to be my mother, she looked more like she could be my sister, a very pretty sister. If she had been the one trying to stop the falling bananas with Carlos, she would have been seriously injured.

Over the loud gospel music, as I put my two bags into the trunk, she explained that Heavy D would drive me into Kingston because she had to open up the clinic in Spanish Town. Heavy D is a friend of Eve who drove a mini-bus taxi up here in the country. Fitting his nickname, he is a little over six feet tall and weighed 300 pounds. He lived just up the road from me and I had known him as long as I had been in-country.

I met Eve only about three months ago. I met her at the Spanish Town clinic when I went there; holding my hand over my eye, hoping that all this blood didn't mean I would never see again. I received a little gash cutting cane when the sweaty wooden handle of a very sharp machete slipped from my friend's hand. The blade grazed my forehead. Eve sewed up my eyebrow with six gentle stitches, and I had worshipped her hands since.

We arrived to pick up Heavy D at about six o'clock. As he drove the forty minutes down to Spanish Town, I was taking in the sights one last time. We traveled down the school road to the crossroads, a route I had taken countless times on my bicycle. Most of the time it was to go to the old wooden shop at the crossroads to buy rice, band-aids, cigarettes, salted cod, a cold beer, toilet paper, or paint. Bud's shop was almost as small as my apartment, and I don't know how he had such a variety of items, but to me, it was better than Wal-Mart.

We turned right and headed toward Spanish Town, past all my favorite watering holes, where many nights were filled with the rubbing alcohol taste of shots of white rum and conversation in the deep rural language of Jamaican patois. Now the domino tables sat outside empty, still moist from the morning dew. However, this was Friday. By nine o'clock this morning they would be covered with cornmeal to smooth the turning of the dominoes. We passed the old market women waiting for a taxi by the side of the road. They carried worn plastic bags stuffed with oranges, green bananas, plantain, pumpkin, or grain. I hoped that all of them would return that evening with empty bags and wads of money stuffed in their bras.

We reached a place called Pedro's Hill where the children were lined up with their old vegetable oil drums to catch water from an old tank. Then we reached Copper Turn where the death-defying turn allows you to see a panoramic view of the orange fields and the karst topography of the land. Karst is a word I learned in geology, which Webster describes as "an irregular limestone region." An egg container turned upside-down looks similar to karst topography.

Descending into the valley, past cane fields and orange groves, the road improved and Heavy D let it roll. Spanish Town was just starting to wake up, the streets and sidewalks still mostly empty. In a few hours this local trade center would be full of people lining the streets, items laid out on blue tarps or placed neatly in wooden displays—clothing, food, CDs, vegetables, shoes, perfume, and sunglasses.

With our professional driver, we made the trip to Eve's clinic about twenty-five minutes faster than usual. Heavy D tackles the roads like he tackles a plate of food, extremely well.

"*No watch, no face,*" I told Eve along with a hug. This patois phrase means something like, "I'll see you when I see you."

The rest of the way to the airport was a blur. It was as if my mind was retracing the last three years in twenty-five minutes. I remembered being robbed a couple of times at knife point. I remembered threats and nasty names. I remembered strange things, like turning goat intestines inside out with a stick and throwing them in a pot to cook, and taking the toenails from chicken feet before making soup.

I remembered too, the grants I wrote that brought things to the District of Browns Hall. Grants that helped make the area a little better place for medical care, more computers at the school, more flowers. Students learned about the beauty in their world and helped save orchids from fallen timber.

I remembered wonderful things. Smiles. Children playing. Friendly farmers with enthusiasm toward change. Sunsets and winding mountain roads. A small group of farmers were at the end of one such road. Many times I biked to a house made of sticks and mud with a small bar. The farmers, dragging in from a long day in the field, would each push a twenty dollar coin, worth 60 cents American, across the bar in exchange for a shot of white rum. The first shots they would pour into their hands and splash onto their faces, rubbing their faces before placing their hands over their mouths and noses, and inhaling deeply. Thereby invigorated, we would drink and laugh until early in the morning.

Jamaica had bad times, but many more good times. The struggle and hurt make the good times better. As we cruised the Mandela Freeway between Spanish Town and Kingston, the cool morning air pouring into the window was helping the bad stuff drift away, leaving me with the clean pain of leaving family and friends. Goodbye, Jamaica. Hello, Cuba. I knew leaving Cuba in six months would feel the same. I had to focus on keeping the good stuff.

My flight was scheduled to leave at seven o'clock. I checked my baggage and handed my ticket and passport over to the airline agent. "Twelve dollars, please."

I handed him the money for the Cuban visa, scanning the area, waiting for the agents at Delta and American Airlines to rip off their airline agent uniforms, jump over the counter with their CIA badges in hand, yelling for me to put my hands up. I felt like the world's largest drug dealer making the largest transaction of my career. It turned out to be as exciting as a pizza delivery. I smiled. "Thanks."

Security took a few seconds and I made a beeline for the Coffee Mill. I was tired and I needed a pick-me-up. I grabbed a large coffee and went to the smoking lounge to have a cigarette. My first drag tasted too good. It felt as though Carlos was already by my side helping to fill the room with smoke.

The purple hummingbird on the Air Jamaica plane looked especially pleased with himself, maybe herself, this morning. I watched through the window as the aircraft arrived. Shortly, the announcement was made that Air Jamaica Flight 367 to Montego Bay was now boarding. I strolled down the long tunnel, the security rechecked my carry-on, and I boarded the plane.

The things I like best about Air Jamaica are the service and the flight attendants, not necessarily in that order. While in Jamaica I judged a few beauty competitions. The winners always said that they wanted to be flight attendants, and today I was grateful for such aspirations. I could tell that we had some past beauty contest winners serving pretzels and tuna fish sandwiches aboard this plane. The flight to MoBay took a little less than an hour. My eyes were eagerly scanning below, searching for familiar landmarks. The Rio Cobre River snakes south towards Spanish Town where the traffic stops as it takes turns crossing Flat Bridge. The bauxite plant is a horrible scar. The land was stripped of vegetation so that the red clayish dirt could be processed into bauxite so that Canadians could have aluminum cans.

I pulled my eyes away from the ground and focused on the beautiful Jamaican scenery floating in the sky. Each attendant gracefully refilled the glasses with Coke and handed out more pretzels. Suddenly my lifetime aspiration was simply to be a beverage pushcart.

The Sangster International Airport in MoBay is a little nicer than the airport in Kingston. The clear Caribbean water of Montego Bay borders the airport and hotels sprawl from the airport in both directions. It was a little after nine o'clock and my flight to Havana was scheduled to depart at eleven o'clock. My job now was to wait. I thought about buying a *Time* or *Newsweek*, but they both had Howard Dean on the cover, so I bought a local Jamaican paper instead. I had waited for three years; what was another two hours? After 20 minutes and three cigarettes I was ready to chop down a tree, hollow it out, and canoe the ninety miles across the Sea to Santiago de Cuba. I paid for a sandwich and water. But damn, I didn't want water in Montego Bay; I wanted rum in Havana.

I could tell that I was getting a little crazy. I took deep breaths, ate my sandwich, drank my water, and tried to figure out how much wood would a woodchuck chuck. I almost had the answer when they announced the flight to Cuba

They didn't announce it was loading. They announced it was rescheduled until four in the afternoon.

"*Bumba! Rass! Blood clot!*" To an American tourist it may have sounded like foreign medical terms, but the Air Jamaica travel agents recognized the words of a pissed off Jamaican, a Blue Mountain dude who just found out someone had pissed in his coffee.

Still smoking, I went back to the lounge for another cigarette. I offered a cigarette to an older man who seemed to be waiting for the same flight. "Are you headed to Cuba?"

"Yes. I'm from Miami and travel to visit my parents whenever I can." His eyes were warm and friendly, somehow reminding me of Eric Estrada, from the old TV show with the motorcycle cops.

"Why not just fly from Miami?"

"I can only fly from the U.S. to Cuba one time each year. I go back every month by passing through Jamaica."

We introduced ourselves and lit up our cancer sticks, perhaps hoping to die calmly before they could announce that our flight had been canceled. "Are your parents ill, that you come so often?"

"No, they are fine. I think I come so often just to get out of Miami. I own some apartments and make a good living, but it is hard to relax. Everything is so busy you have to schedule stuff a month ahead. Somehow, it's just being in Cuba, friendly and relaxed. I love my beach in Cuba."

"Doesn't Miami have beaches?" I laughed.

"Sure, but I can't relax there. The differences are hard to explain, but Cuba just feels better."

Smiling, thinking about the differences, we boarded the smaller plane, with the same purple hummingbird. A different, but equally wonderful, ex-beauty pageant winner greeted us as she fulfilled her dream. I was on the way to fulfill my dreams too. As the plane took off, I had a strange sensation of going to the Garden of Eden to partake in the forbidden fruit. Would they serve apples?

José Martí International

✦

Day 1
Friday, August 15, 2003

There were no apples, just pretzels. Looking down as we flew over the Cayman Islands and the shimmering Caribbean Sea, the wondrous blue carpet changed suddenly to Astroturf. The forests and irrigated circles of western Cuba soon became an ocean of lights as we approached Havana.

The large words "José Martí International Airport" on the terminal proclaimed that I was finally in Cuba as the landing gear deployed with a jolt. It was not as new as the airport in Denver but it appeared to be fully modern, much nicer than Kingston. The door to the airplane was opened like the lid to a treasure chest. I was not sure what was inside, but I was excited to find out.

We hopped onto a bus that took us the two hundred yards to the terminal. Day was slipping away and so were my chances of getting a bus for the ten-hour ride to the eastern part of Cuba. Carlos had told me that a tourist bus called Viazul leaves Havana at nine o'clock in the evening. If I was not on that one I had to stay in Havana and leave in the morning.

The immigration officers were led around the terminal by beautiful Cocker Spaniels meandering through the luggage, sniffing for drugs. In front of me was a row of fifteen doors, each with its own booth and immigration officer. I felt like Neo in the movie *The Matrix*, except I was choosing a door, not a pill. Joining the line headed toward door number three, I was soon face to face with the immigration officer. I gave him my passport and visa. He asked me where I was coming from and where I was staying in Cuba. I told him that I was coming from Jamaica and that I was staying with my friend in Holguin. He wanted an address and I gave him Carlos's. In Cuba, they did not stamp my passport, only the visa form that I had purchased in Jamaica. No record of my Cuban visit would appear in my passport. With a double bang, my visa was stamped and the door was buzzed.

I gave the door a push and revealed, presto, the baggage claim area. I went through a metal detector without a beep, collected my carry-on, and was off to collect my baggage. The floors were shiny but littered with cigarette butts as nervous Germans waited to see if their bags had made it from Europe. As other people from my flight started to grab their bags off the carousel I threw my butt on the floor too. Finally, everyone else was gone and I stood alone like a ray of light refusing to give way to darkness. Darkness crashed in as the carousel came to a halt.

The signs identifying the desk for missing luggage were in seven languages. The desk was surrounded by a glass box and you had to talk through a microphone. Evidently I wasn't the first passenger to arrive in Havana without luggage. I slowly walked up to the window and was spoken to for the first time by one of the beautiful Cuban women Carlos had always told me about.

I returned her "*hola*" and asked if she spoke English. I was frustrated that I didn't have the nerve to try sticking to Spanish, but I knew I would have many opportunities during what I thought would be six months. I was told they would be on the next flight from Jamaica. I was disappointed but reminded myself how much practice I had the last three years waiting. I knew that when I asked Eve to be at my house at five o'clock this morning, she would not arrive until six. I spent three years scheduling events around the fact that people always arrive at least forty-five minutes late to everything except their own funeral.

"Quit worrying and celebrate," I told myself. "You are in Cuba." Four big-screen TVs were all showing Cuban boxers beating people up in the Pan-American Games. The customs officers were describing the hooks, jabs, and footwork in animated Spanish that sounded like music, but I couldn't understand a word. I collapsed on one of the benches next to the wall and sat there in a daze. The traffic fluctuated those two hours as planes arrived and departed.

During the two hours that I sat there, I shared my bench with people from all over: Europeans, Asians, and Africans; but I might have been the only one from the United States. Finally, it was my cargo plane, Flight 376, from Montego Bay. The television screen above carousel number two flickered on and there were the three lucky numbers. The carousel, slowly turning, reminded me of an injured moose surrounded by a pack of hungry wolves. My bag appeared and I headed for customs.

Many, many cans of corned beef and salted cod had drawn the attention of customs to the young man in front of me. He spoke in Spanish to customs but under his breath he was mumbling the same words I had used in Montego Bay. This was a Jamaican.

"Da people dem wicked, eh?"

"Boy, yah dun kno breden." After he responded, he looked at me, puzzled. It was a look I had seen many times. It said, "How did a white guy like you learn patois?"

I explained my three years in St. Faiths and found out that he was studying in Camagüey. Camagüey was in the center of the island, half-way to Holguin. Stranded in Havana, I asked him if he knew any place I could stay because I missed my bus to Holguin.

"Come with us," he said with a sincere smile. "We have room. I have a friend, no problem. You can catch a bus to Holguin from Camagüey in the morning."

"Bwoy, nuff respect, Star." I thanked him in patois.

Architecturally beautiful but dilapidated buildings lined the road from Havana as we made our way to the autopisto from Havana to Camagüey. There were numerous checkpoints along the way. Police officers at the regular checkpoints stopped traffic to ask questions. My new friends had good answers and we were soon into the countryside. We met and passed large trucks with people standing in the back of them, packed like sardines in a can. At many intersections along the highway large groups of people were sitting, apparently waiting for a ride. I learned many things in Cuba, but I never did find out how long they had to wait or where they were going.

Carlos's House

◆

Day 2
Saturday, August 16, 2003

An island, carved out of the road by two meandering soapy streams, provided a place for me and my luggage. Carlos had taken pictures of his house from this exact spot so I knew I was in the right place. A picture speaks a thousand words but I was speechless. The morning sun warmed my skin; children played in the street.

I was soaking in the sights and sounds when the wooden door to the house opened and Belicia came outside wearing a nightgown and a smile, more beautiful in person than in Carlos's pictures of her. With an enthusiastic hug and a kiss on the cheek, I had arrived and I was welcome. The next few minutes were filled with my very bad Spanish and her melodic Cuban Spanish. I carried my bags inside and sat down on the nice red leather couch. Every house in this part of Holguin would have been torn down in the bad parts of most American cities. The couch would have looked fine in any house in my hometown. The contrast was startling.

"¿Quieres un cafecito?"

I hesitated for a second, translating everything in my mind.

"Sí." I smiled and Belicia smiled back. I knew that she asked me if I wanted coffee and right now I felt pretty good. I was batting a thousand. However, my average would decline sharply in the following moments, filled with numerous strikeouts. Mostly, I was just swinging at the air. When she returned with the coffee, she asked me how the trip from Havana to Holguin went. I was sipping on a thimble-sized cup of very potent and very tasty coffee. My other cup, a cup of nervousness and anxiety, was bigger than their little house.

I wanted to tell her that when I arrived in Havana my bags were still in Jamaica so I had to wait for a long time at the airport. "Bueno, cuando yo…." I thought to myself, "Crap, how do you say 'arrived'?" Belicia helped me out by

13

forming a plane with her hand and landing it softly with the word "Havana" flowing out of her mouth as her hand became parallel with the ground.

"*Sí*." I paused. I thought about what to say and was nervous about saying things correctly. The verbs should be in the past tense, but I'd just go for the present and let her figure that out. I knew a word for luggage was maletas. "*Sí, yo in Havana pero maletas es in Jamaica.*" Belicia looked at me funny and I tried to rephrase. "*Cuando yo Havana no maletas, so yo waito por my maletas.*" Once again she looked lost, but then she said everything back to me, probably using correct Spanish, and using lots of hand signals. She understood. She started saying Carlos and "*bus*" (rhymes with moose) so I figured that Carlos was down at the bus place waiting for me. She hardly ever pronounced the *s* in words so what little Spanish I could understand when Carlos talked slipped by me when she talked.

Suddenly Belicia interrupted our attempts to talk. "*¡Vaya rápido a la cocina! ¡Vaya rápido! ¡Esconde! ¡Rápido!*" Belicia whispered urgently. I knew I should do something rapidly but I had no idea what I was supposed to do. She grabbed my arm and pulled me into the kitchen and pushed me behind the refrigerator. I got the idea. She had heard Carlos greet a neighbor so she knew he was coming in and wanted to surprise him.

He walked in and spoke sadly. I couldn't understand but I caught the words "bus" and "family" and "United States." He must have thought that I had changed my mind about Cuba and gone to Omaha.

Belicia, a little shorter than Carlos, with the lean and tight body of a long distance runner, could hardly control her excitement and didn't keep him in suspense very long.

"Yes," she said, "maybe he isn't coming, but perhaps he is behind the refrigerator."

Carlos took a second to understand and then raced in whooping and grabbed me. He is a very demonstrative, huggy kind of guy. "You hadn't called. I was afraid you'd changed your mind."

"No." I smiled. "It's just hard to get through."

"What bus did you come in on, Viazul?"

"No, I took one of the other buses from Camagüey to here."

"One of the other ones?" Carlos looked a little confused.

"The white buses with the red stripes down the side."

"But those aren't tourist buses. Those are mainly for Cubans."

"I know, but that was my only option." Then I told him about my flight and how I had gotten to Holguin.

Cruising down the nearly empty four-lane highway from Havana to Camagüey, the sleepless nights caught up with me and I soon started to drift in and out of consciousness. I tried to sleep, but the questions I wanted to ask everyone, but hadn't asked anyone, kept going off loudly enough to keep me awake. What if you had a best friend who invited you to come live with him and his family for six months? Do you take advantage of the opportunity to learn a new language and experience a new culture? How many times in life do you have a friend that helps you survive three years of the "Hardest Job You'll Ever Love"? Carlos taught Spanish in the school where I was assigned by Peace Corps to do Environmental Education. We lived next to each other in school housing. A little older than me, he was a new big brother whom I could go to for advice, encouragement, and laughs. He invited me often, almost daily, to come see his country after Peace Corps. Therefore, what do you think, would you go? I had saved enough money to live comfortably and study in this country. So what is the answer?

These were the questions going through my head as I tried to sleep. However, the big thing I left out was that this friend lives in Cuba. Then all of these new questions come into play. The writers of the *Declaration of Independence* said that I have the right to pursue happiness. My travel to Cuba wasn't some kind of threat to American security. Was the constitution any good if laws make it illegal to go visit a friend? When I took my seat on the plane in Kingston, I wasn't worried about turbulence on the flight; I was worried about the turbulence it would create if I was arrested for trying to go to Cuba. I fastened the seat-belt and ended up in Cuba because I knew it was something I had to do. Carlos had invited me every day to come live with him and his family. In a few hours, I would be with Carlos again.

Then I started to worry about my family back in Omaha, Mom, Dad, three brothers and sister, Megan. I had told my parents of my plans and they were worried but understood it was something that I wanted to do. My mother was the one that worried the most. She is the type of person whom I consider the perfect law-abiding citizen. She will not start the vehicle until everyone inside is wearing his or her seat belt and she never breaks the speed limit. Heck, she never even bends it. The only time she got a speeding ticket was twenty-one years ago when I was four and had a Mastermind game piece stuck up my nose. She got the ticket speeding to the hospital, but she could blame the ticket on me. When I am driving, she constantly makes noises that sound like in the next few seconds we could meet our death. She is protective, but she is a mother and that is her job, and I am lucky to have a mother who takes her job seriously. In addition, it is because she takes her job seriously that I take my role as a son seriously. I often think things out, trying to realize what could go wrong and plan accordingly, a trait I picked up from my mother. My father is more relaxed and will deal with the problems as they come. I cannot think of a better combination of parenting and I am grateful to have what I have.

I slept then, until my courteous host pulled up behind an old white bus with strange letters on the back door. I found out later that it was Russian. The Viazul tourist bus had already left but he knew that a little cash would get me on the regular bus.

"Thanks for the ride," I said in Standard English. Then in patois I told him, *"Bwoy mi wuld ah appy fi use one ole dankey as long as it can caaw mi go ah olguin."* The driver of our car flagged down the bus and asked if I could go with them. The driver looked back at the packed seats with some people sitting on luggage in the aisle and shook his head until he saw that I had real dollars and not peso dollars. Then he remembered that a window seat was empty. I gave the man five dollars, his helper threw my luggage on top, and I squeezed and excused myself back to the seat that had suddenly become available. I was too tired to sleep. I smiled and smiled, listening to the music of Spanish all around me and getting closer to Holguin every minute.

As the sun chased away the night, any doubts about my choice to come to Cuba went with the darkness. We entered the province of Holguin at around eight o'clock and although I couldn't see a line on the ground marking the boundary, I knew I was almost to a new home and I nearly cried. An interstate, straight out of the Midwest, was full of bicycles, mounted riders, horse carts, and walkers, but few cars or trucks. An hour later we were at the bus terminal. Carlos wasn't expecting me on this bus so I grabbed my luggage and found a taxi. It took awhile to find the address but the driver used my address and asked people on the street until we found it. Third-world housing is difficult to explain to Americans that think housing in the inner city or on the reservation is bad. Compton would look like Beverly Hills compared to the houses here. The unfinished houses, made of boards, unfinished brick, or concrete blocks, were packed together on dirt roads and narrow paths. Carlos's was a little bigger and nicer than the other houses in the area and I recognized it from pictures Carlos had shown me in Jamaica when he had first found a way to get the bricks and cement he needed. He had talked and talked about the struggles of building a house in Cuba.

Each of the three pictures of the house he showed me in Jamaica had a long story behind it. The first picture was the old wooden house before he started the reconstruction. The house was made of wooden boards thrown together to give some privacy and some relief from the elements. The house looked like a little wolf-sneeze would bring it down without any huffing or puffing.

The second picture showed the beginning of the present house, mostly just the cement floor and materials. Belicia and their son, Galeno, lived with his parents while the house was being built.

The third picture was of the finished house, the way it looked when the taxi dropped me off and Belicia greeted me. Now I was here, in this house, ready to be a part of Carlos's family for awhile.

After the story about my travel adventures, I asked about taking a shower. Carlos showed me the bathroom that was outside. It reminded me of the outhouse at my grandpa's ranch in Western Nebraska. Carlos's bathroom was about a five-foot by five-foot square made of boards thrown together like a jigsaw puzzle. It had a wooden door and the toilet was a stool cemented into the ground. In front of the stool was a concrete slab with a drain. The roof looked like an inverted back of an old pickup. There were vines which grew through the cracks and the openings near the roof. I dipped water from one of the fifty-gallon metal drums outside the kitchen into two buckets. Carlos apologized for the conditions, but I reminded him that this was the way we had bathed ourselves in Jamaica. The bathroom had a metal tube running from the drain in the bathroom to the street.

After my shower, we talked through the afternoon. Carlos told me that his house used to resemble the wooden jigsaw puzzle that was the bathroom but he sent a part of the money he was earning from Jamaica to start building his new house. The house was currently an unfinished ten-foot by twenty-foot rectangle. A wooden door opened to the street at one end and a narrow hallway to the kitchen at the other end. The kitchen was small, but it did contain a refrigerator and an electric hot plate. The hot plate, or burner, is illegal in Cuba, but common.

As we talked, I met his brother, Pedro, who lived on top of Carlos's house with his wife, Juanita, and son, Salvador. They had been visiting Carlos's parents and had Galeno, Carlos's son with them. The boys were very excited about my visit but were too shy to talk to me. They climbed metal stairs, hooked onto the side of the house, to a small room, built of brick, above Carlos's kitchen. Their room was divided into a sleeping area and kitchen by a wooden cupboard. The sink had no drain. Just a radiator hose that led to a bucket that they dumped out into the street when it was over half full. They had a legal kerosene burner, which made their place always smell like kerosene. The fan they used for cooling looked like a car fan attached to a motorcycle engine. It was started by twisting two wires together. Salvador was six and slept in a baby crib because they didn't have the room, or probably the money, to buy a regular bed. The other half of the second level had walls but no roof so it had become the laundry room with a clothes line. Carlos was anxious to get enough money to finish the house.

I also met Miguel, the next-door neighbor, that afternoon. He talked rapidly without s's, "*Buena tarde. Con mucho gusto conocerlo. Bien venido a Holguin. Si necesita algo…*" He was a funny little man, balding and skinny, but with a round little gut that made me think he had eaten a beach ball for lunch.

"*El no habla Español,*" Carlos interrupted him. Miguel slowed down and spoke louder but I still had no idea what he was saying. This continued for several minutes. He would talk, I would smile and nod and Carlos would interrupt him, which he ignored. Finally Belicia saved us by telling us to come eat. I shook Miguel's hands, which seemed to be put on his arms backward, and went in to eat.

While we ate supper around the round wooden table, Carlos told me that he had talked with his cousin a week before about my Spanish class. He said that everything would work out. We just needed to go to the university on September fifth to do the paper work and settle everything. Belicia's congri, a mixture of rice and black beans, fufu, chicken, and avocado was delicious. Fufu is made from a starchy banana called plantain, which is boiled and smashed. Belicia talked about the congri but I understood little. Carlos told me that she said, "Cuban cuisine is ruled by rice and kept afloat by beans, forming the staple of the Cuban diet."

Then he asked what I wanted to watch on TV. We had our choice of three channels. We watched the early evening news and then found a movie. Belicia went to bed around nine o'clock while Carlos and I continued to talk and watch the movie. Galeno had gotten friendlier and had fallen asleep on the couch with his head on my leg. Luckily, the movie was in English with Spanish subtitles. At around ten o'clock I heard a whistle outside the house. It sounded like a referee blowing a whistle during a basketball game. Carlos got up and went to the kitchen and got a metal pot. He came back, unlocked the door, and went outside. A few minutes later he came back into the house with the pot full of milk. He went to the kitchen and put it in the refrigerator. He explained that it was the man that brings milk to the community for the government. Most of the time he comes at about six in the morning but today the milk truck broke down on its way to Holguin. Galeno and Salvador are entitled to one liter of milk each day until they are seven years old.

After the movie I went to bed. The two beds were next to each other. They let me sleep in Galeno's small, squeaky, but comfortable bed and Galeno was happy to sleep with them. On my back, hands folded together beneath my head, I stared upward into the darkness. A large smile formed on my face. I didn't know what the next few months would bring, but I had a new home.

Dollar Stores

◆

Day 3
Sunday, August 17, 2003

Like the shower the night before, much of Cuban life is like Jamaican life. Riding on the bar that connects the front fork and Carlos's seat, I looked like a *paisano*, a citizen, because on Sunday morning on the main road downtown many adults were using the same transportation. Adults in Jamaica often ride the same way.

"First thing, let me show you downtown," Carlos said earlier that morning as I drank, again, the sweet strong coffee from the thimble with a handle. Along with the coffee we had milk and crackers. Before I had a chance to roll out of bed and rub the sleep out of my eyes, I knew that we were having galletas for breakfast. I didn't know what time it was, but I think it was still dark when I started to hear the voices from the street. First there was the panadero selling bread, then there was a guy selling eggs, and then the galletero. There may have been more vendors as I continued to flow in and out of sleep. I was the most awake when I heard, *"Ga...lletas! Ga...lletas!"* I knew that galletas were crackers because Carlos and I had galletas and coffee together numerous times in Jamaica. I heard Carlos scramble out of bed. Then I heard some pesos hit the ground and Carlos cuss. The kitchen door opened and a few minutes later I heard the bag hit the table.

We walked his bike the one hundred yards along the rocky, uneven dirt road to the main road and headed toward Parque Central. Holguin is called the "City of Parks," and we passed several small parks on our way to the main park at the center of Holguin. I deal with new places by comparing them to old places. The bicycle traffic was similar to the traffic in Jamaica, only in Cuba there were more bikes and less cars.

Carlos stopped at a sight familiar to me from Jamaica and asked, *"Yuh waan some'n fi drink?"*

"Sure," I laughed. "What do they say in Cuba?"

"*¿Quieres un guarapo?*" I practiced saying Carlos's line as we watched the *guarapero* prepare our drink. Better than Gatorade, the *guarapo* is sugar cane juice on ice. There were numerous *guarapo* stands along the road. The smell made me think of moist brown sugar. The cane is stripped of its outer layer and then run through a machine that has two large drums that grab the cane and crush it. The *guarapero* folds the crushed cane in half and the process is done all over again until the cane is juiceless. The juice is strained through a cloth and then poured into the bottom half of a Coke or rum bottle that has had the neck removed.

Some people were selling pizzas out of cardboard boxes with plastic over the top. Others sold ice cream straight from the hand-cranked machines. In Jamaica food was rarely sold on the street. Snacks or in-season fruit were sold along the road, but the only food that was prepared and sold on the street were soup and jerked chicken. The jerked chicken was prepared in old oil drums that were cut in half vertically and then had legs welded to the side. It opened up like a grill. They used charcoal (slow-burnt wood) to heat the chicken. The soup was sold from large pots along the road.

About six blocks later we passed a plaza where there were bicycles with side-carts, known as bici-taxis, to take people around town. The side-carts were made from old barber chairs. Unlike Jamaica, there were also horse-drawn carriages of two types. The most common was an old metal cart with a tarp for a roof with enough room to fit about ten adults. There were also smaller carriages with a seat for the driver and another for two or three people under a canopy. Cars and these carriages were both called "*coches.*"

People sat on their doorsteps watching the traffic go by or conversing with their friends. As we approached the central park there were people with pushcart ovens selling pizzas, and people with buckets with the word "*granizado*" written on them, sitting on the back of their bikes. They sold cups of crushed ice with syrup poured over the top, the Cuban version of a sno-cone. Peanuts were sold in paper funnels from a two foot by two foot metal box kept warm by burning coal contained in the bottom of the box.

We parked the bike in one of many bicycle parks. These are often in people's houses, with the front living room designated for the parking of bicycles and motorcycles. In Jamaica, we locked our bikes to racks similar to those in the states. Carlos told the man his name and Carlos was handed a number signifying what spot the bicycle was parked in.

Carlos showed me all of the stores and I was surprised that he had never mentioned that there were two completely different types of stores in Cuba. Dollar stores only took dollars, either U.S. dollars or dollars *convertable*. *Convertables* are

Cuban money that is exchanged for U.S. dollars, one for one. In 1993 Cuba had legalized the U.S. dollar. This was done to soak up the estimated hundreds of millions of U.S. dollars floating illegally around the country, usually as aid sent from relatives abroad or as tips from foreign tourists. The government needed desperately to get a hold of this currency that floated around the black market. You can buy anything from electronics to toothpaste in the Dollar Shops, and all of the change is in pesos or dollars *convertable*.

To shop in these stores, Cubans, paid in pesos, had to buy dollars of one kind or the other on the street. In the center of the city there are numerous dollar shops and only a few peso shops. The peso shops sell some of the same types of goods as the dollar shops, but of dramatically less quality. Carlos was angry about the dollar stores and felt that they divide the people. Those people with access to dollars are able to buy nicer clothes, electronics, new bicycles, and a higher quality of food items, which are unavailable in the peso shops. For instance, if a Cuban smokes cigarettes and doesn't have access to dollars, then he can only smoke cigarettes without filters. Cuba does produce cigarettes with filters, but they are only available for U.S. dollars.

There were lines to enter the dollar shops. I asked Carlos, "In general, what are these people buying?"

He said, "Soap, toilet paper, shampoo. Maybe slippers." Carlos took me to a clothing store that had second-hand clothing that was sent from another country or sold to the store by Cubans. As we looked at a few clothes, Carlos said that a lot of the time it was difficult to find his size. He was interested in a jean jacket that cost the equivalent of two U.S. dollars.

He said, "Could you imagine that someone would be able to buy this jacket if they are making fifteen dollars per month and have a family to feed?" I could tell already that life here was tough, but I could also see the love and pride Carlos had for his country.

"Remember our last meal together in Jamaica was at Burger King?" I asked Carlos as I washed down perhaps the toughest hamburger I had ever eaten.

"Yes. Yes. And this is a little more like leather than meat. This stuff they use for cheese, what is it?" Hungry from touring, we had been lured by the bright blue corner shop that advertised, "*Hamburguesa Super*."

I countered, "I like this burger better than that Whopper we had because this one has the taste of my new life. And besides, those Whoppers were more than three dollars and this *Hamburguesa Super* is only five pesos, less than an American quarter."

Relaxing and chatting, I found myself drifting away in the short breaks in conversation, envisioning what the next six months were going to be like. I saw myself cruising down to this spot on my new bicycle, maybe meeting Carlos in this same spot four months from now to share a super burger. English would be a language I would seldom use. Maybe I would use it when I called my parents and that was it. I would probably throw in some patois once in awhile when I talked to Carlos. "Carlos, *yuh tink me can married yah so?*" He would laugh and probably answer, "*Yuh prably affi ask yuh president fuss.*"

It was difficult not to think about the future. I would be spending Christmas, and perhaps my birthday, here in Holguin. Holguin and everything I was seeing was now a novelty, but in a short time this would be my home. Much like how it was in Jamaica when I first arrived. Everything was strange. The language, the food, the culture. I knew that the newness would wear off and soon it would become mundane, but for now everything was magical.

I remember one of my first days at Tacius Golding High School in Jamaica. A teacher had called in sick and I was asked to sit with a class. I was nervous, but thought, "How bad could it be?" I would go into the classroom, take attendance, and then probably answer a million questions about why I was there and what I was planning on doing at the school.

When I entered the class, there was dead silence. I introduced myself and said that I was going to be filling in for the teacher because she was sick. I noticed that a couple of students had their heads down on their desks and weren't looking at me. I asked what was wrong and a girl mumbled something to a boy sitting next to her. The young boy looked up at me and smiled.

"Sir, she said that she can't look at you because you're a '*duppy*.'"

Since I knew what a "*duppy*" was, I told the student that I wasn't a ghost. I was a human just like all of the students.

"But sir, she wants to know why you are so white."

I took a deep breath. I realized that this was going to be a little more difficult than I had first anticipated. After questions about my red hair, my blue eyes, and where I came from, the bell finally rang.

I knew Cuba was going to be the same way; everything would seem strange. Small children probably wouldn't want to touch my hair or my skin to see if they were real the way they did in Jamaica, but I knew I would encounter awkward situations. It would take a while to get used to everything, but just like the Jamaican experience, I would survive everything and leave, just the way I had left Jamaica, a changed person. I loved the way that type of change felt.

Carlos and I picked up a large bag of crackers from a man that was selling them on the street. It was starting to get late so we headed back to get the bike. When we were traveling back along one of the main roads, I noticed the construction of make-shift food stands and drink stands. Carlos said that Tuesday was the beginning of Carnival in Holguin, which would last until next Sunday. There were large metal kegs which would be filled with over 500 gallons of cold beer.

We stopped to buy a giant avocado from a man selling along the street. The streets were lined with Ixora, which look much like the lilacs in Nebraska, and Oleander, beautiful pink, puffy flowers perched on the top of smooth glossy green stems. The contrast was breath-taking, but so was the beginning of this experience. I enjoyed the beautiful flowers next to the street with horse-carts and bici-taxis. I was thankful for being here and having a friend share his life with me.

Back at his house, we sat on the steps by the street and shared a giant avocado with Galeno and Belicia. It was bigger than Galeno's head and was eaten in long thin strips. Across the street a family was also sitting, watching the neighborhood. The children played a game: climb a tree, pull off leaves, jump down, and count them. When the avocado was gone, Galeno and I played catch until it got dark and Belicia called us in to watch TV.

Tomas and Santiago

✦

Day 4
Monday, August 18, 2003

The beautiful little girl, with long straight black hair nearly to her knees, laughed happily because she had three more mango leaves than her big brother. I thought maybe he was letting her win. The *chica* scrambled back up the mango tree to pull off more leaves. Big brother followed. "*Uno, dos, tres.*" They jumped down together and counted again. This time big brother won by one leaf.

"What are you smiling about?" Carlos asked as he came into the living room from the kitchen.

"The two across the street are playing their climb, pull, jump, and count game. They are cute. Plus, I just can't believe I'm here, here in Cuba," I answered from the couch.

He paused with the lighter just in front of his cigarette and looked over at me. "You've been saying that since you first got here."

"I know, but...," I paused as I leaned over to light my cigarette. "But, I just can't believe that I'm here. I mean, we talked about it for three years and I'm finally here. I'm here with you, in your house in Cuba."

"Are you glad you're here?" He said with his warm, teasing smile.

"I know I'm acting like a little girl who just got the new Barbie for Christmas."

He laughed. "I'm glad you're here too."

"Carlos, I was wondering if we could go downtown and buy a phone card. I haven't called since I arrived and I know that my mom is sitting by the phone."

"Yes, let's go. I need to buy some crackers for breakfast tomorrow and I need to go to the immigration office to buy an application for a new passport."

"Oh, Carlos, that squeaky cheese we had for breakfast, could we get some more of that?"

"Squeaky cheese." He laughed. "That's a good name for it. Sure, we can buy some, I just don't know when. I bought it from a friend who works in a factory that makes the cheese. The cheese can only be sold to dollar restaurants and others in the tourist business. My friend takes some home when he can."

"What about some more butter?" I asked Carlos, as he rolled his bike out the kitchen door.

"Yes. There's none in the peso stores, but we can get it in the dollar stores. We don't have to have a friend that churns it." Carlos walked the fifteen feet to the wooden fence that ran parallel to the house. He grabbed the white sugar bag, filled with trash, from one of the posts and set it along the road. An old used-to-be green John Deere Model B was slowly chugging toward us pulling a flat-bed trailer loaded with garbage. "I guess that today is trash pickup day," I mused.

We walked to the paved road that went toward the center of town. I sat side-saddle in front and Carlos pedaled. He soon groaned, "We need to get you a bike."

"Why? I'm not as light as Belicia?"

"No, and you're not as pretty. Besides, I don't want anyone thinking that you're my girlfriend."

I laughed. "Would it help if I shaved my legs?"

We arrived downtown and went to the DHL office next to the Calixto Garcia Park. DHL is an international version of UPS or FedEx. They only had twenty-dollar phone cards. Twenty dollars wouldn't allow me much talk time, but I just needed to say that I was alive and everything was fine. We tried all three of the blue payphones around the park, but when we dialed, the little screen said, "*Servicio Prohibido*," so we couldn't call.

"*No te preocupes.*" Carlos told me not to worry. "It does that sometimes. You can try tomorrow."

Later, we sipped beer at the *Pico Cristal*, a downtown bar and restaurant. The walls of the restaurant were giant tinted windows and we watched the endless stream of beautiful women walk by on the sidewalk just outside the restaurant. Carlos laughed at me as he did his oscillating fan imitation. I felt like a tiger being taunted by the trainer, dangling fresh meat just beyond the bars. I was thinking of how I could pounce when Carlos jumped up and went outside. Part of me was hoping he'd gone out to bring me back one of those beautiful ladies. That day I never dreamed that within a month I would have one more beautiful than any of these, for myself.

Instead of a "*señorita guapa*," he returned with a pudgy forty-something hombre with a sweat-drenched T-shirt and wind-blown hair perched on a worn exhausted face. Carlos introduced us and I was able to put a face with a name. In Jamaica, Carlos had told me that Tomas, his cousin, worked as an accountant at the University of Holguin. This was the man that was going to secure a course at the university for me. Carlos and Tomas chatted as I drank my beer. Carlos motioned for another beer and a maroon *Bucanero* can was placed in front of Tomas. Carlos would stop talking in Spanish and ask me questions about what type of course I wanted at the university. I had transcripts sent down from the states to show that I had graduated from a university. The Spanish course I was going to take was graduate level and I needed proof that I was a graduate. Tomas said that he needed to get back to the university. He turned the pirate on the can upside down, shook my hand, and left.

Carlos translated a few things for me. He said that the university was closed until the second of September. Then the staff and administration would meet and discuss the school year. After that meeting we could go and find out about the course. I was pleased. In the middle of a sentence, Carlos bolted for the door again. This time he returned with a younger, slimmer man. Santiago was deeply serious, and when Carlos mentioned that I needed a bike, he looked like it was a challenge to battle. Carlos offered him a beer, but judging from the hand motions, he had a sore throat. He did look like he was slightly ill. He looked at me, serious, and said, "*Mañana.*" Leaving with a firm handshake and a smile, he headed for the *farmacia*. We would go tomorrow.

Carlos leaned across the table, nearly forcing my pirate overboard. "Santiago and I went to school together. He knows a lot of people in the *Candonga*. We can probably get a good bike at a good price."

I smiled. "You guys went to school together? He looks like he could be your son."

Carlos smiled and threw his lighter at me. I always troubled Carlos about his salt and pepper hair. He was only thirty-two, but he said that the Special Period aged him; the Special Period and marriage.

We left the bar and walked down to the corner. Carlos handed a man, who was screaming "¡*Pizza, Pizza Caliente!*" loud enough he could have been selling pizzas to people in downtown Miami, ten pesos. He opened his blue metal box and pulled out a cookie tray stacked with pizza. He folded over the seven inch round pizza in half with his tongs. Cheese and a couple of one-fourth inch square pieces of *jamón* oozed from the sides. The dough was spongy and barely warm. The light coating of tomato paste and cheese added little flavor, but it was filling. We got Carlos's bike from the *bici*-park and headed for the immigration office where Carlos was starting the process to move more permanently to Jamaica.

"The immigration office isn't far from here, maybe five minutes. You will need to go to the same office to renew your visa. You will have to stay outside with the bike because there are no *bici*-parks around there." Carlos parked the bicycle in the shade of the two-story white adobe building with red trim that was used for immigration business in a residential area. I sat down on the curb next to the bicycle. Children chased each other in the park across the street while I thought about the enjoyment of coming to the immigration office. I thought I would come six times, once a month for six months. I was very wrong about enjoying the immigration office and the number of times that I would return.

After about twenty minutes Carlos came back out of the office holding a paper.

"Do you know how much I paid for this application?" I looked at him dumbfounded, waiting for an answer. After a short pause, he answered his own question. "I paid fifty-four U.S. dollars for this piece of paper. I will have to pay more if the application is accepted and I have to buy the passport."

"So you want to go back to Jamaica?"

There was a short pause. "I love Cuba. I love the people. But life is tough, and if I can create a better life for my family and friends, I will leave…Something needs to change."

I didn't know what to say, or if I should say anything at all. Silence followed us all the way back to the corner across from where we bought the pizza. Carlos stopped and handed me twenty pesos at the cracker table. I stood in line between an ice cream vendor and a pizza vendor. When it was my turn, a large man grabbed the pesos I held above the hand-painted wooden sign advertising crackers and cigarettes, "*Galletas y Cigarrillos.*" Sitting in an old wooden folding chair, he stuffed the money into his blue jeans, under his faded green dress-shirt. I grabbed a bag of crackers which was about a fourth the size of a fifty-pound sugar bag, but not nearly as heavy, and got back on the bike. There were no words spoken for five minutes. The only sounds were the ringing of bicycle bells and the occasional call of a carriage driver to his horses.

"Carlos, you know that if you need money, all you have to do is ask. I have a check from Peace Corps at home. My parents can send me the money." After a pause, the answer I expected came.

A soft sincere, "Thank you, Brandon. I'm okay," flowed out of Carlos's mouth.

It was the response I had expected. I knew that he would never ask me for money, even for a seven peso pack of Popular. This was Carlos. I had never known someone like Carlos. While in Jamaica, he went back to Cuba to visit four times. Each time he took back clothes, toys, medical stuff, and even a VCR to his mother-in-law, whom he hated. Why, because he gets joy out of people being happy. After three years in Jamaica, he could still fit all of his clothes in one small bag. For three years he had thought about everyone except himself. Carlos's self-lessness, with his smile and chatter, carried me through the three tough years in Jamaica.

While in Jamaica, he asked me if I could get a baseball glove for his son. Jamaica, being a cricket crazy island, had no baseball gloves. My father sent down a leather Spaulding glove and two official major league baseballs. Carlos almost cried and tried to give me money. I told him it was a gift from my father to his son. Carlos said he wanted to pay me back. As the sun began to set over the town, and the sky filled with a brilliant red, I wish he knew how I felt about being here in Cuba at this very moment. Then he would know that any debt he would ever owe me had already been repaid a million times over.

The Candonga

✦

Day 5
Tuesday, August 19, 2003

My butt was happy to be sitting on a nice flat surface instead of a skinny bar. Since my arrival in Cuba, (*el sabado, el domingo,* and *el lunes,* those three days) Carlos had wanted to show me everything, so I had spent hours on the bar between his seat and the handle bars. Now the three of us were headed for the big bike buy. I was sitting on a steel grill behind Carlos on Santiago's faded blue Chinese bike. His bike had every possible attachment except a stereo and he was talking about adding a Sony. Santiago was riding Carlos's pink mountain bike from Europe in front of us. Carlos was keeping his bike simple. The small mountain with the cross on top just outside of town, La Loma de la Cruz, rose above the buildings crowding the street from Calixto Garcia Plaza to the *Candonga,* where bicycles were sold. Even higher was the transmitter tower on top of the ETECSA building, the town's tallest. I was going to get a bicycle and I was floating, floating higher than the telephone tower. However, I had to stay focused. We were warriors headed for battle.

Earlier, I felt like I was a sixteen-year-old girl at a college party. Carlos tipped his beer and offered a toast to the bike I was about to get. The view from the air-conditioned bar was great. It was located on a corner just across from the main park, Calixto Garcia. Two of the walls of the bar were made of glass and you could see the park and the human traffic walking on the crowded sidewalks. The occasional sun-burnt, short-wearing tourist from Germany or Canada would walk into the bar. They would come in to rent a car from the car rental booth in the corner of the bar or just come in to get out of the heat. I was glad Carlos was with me to get this bike and Carlos's friend Santiago was going to arrive at the bar in about an hour. He had a friend in the *Candonga.*

I was glad to have help. The truth was that I didn't know anything about bicycles. Sure, I knew how to ride one, but when it came to maintenance, it was a language I didn't understand. In Cuba bicycles were life. There were bicycle garages and places where you could buy air for your tires or fix your punctured tire. Some of these were actually garages in the town center or wooden structures as you got away from the city center and out where Carlos lived. We shared another *Bucanero* before Santiago arrived about ten.

"Feeling better, Santiago?" Carlos asked as he raised his glass of beer.

"Yes, a lot better," he responded with a smile to Carlos as if saying that it was all right to buy him a beer.

Carlos raised his hand and motioned to the waitress to bring one more beer.

When we finished the beers, we walked to a dollar store at the opposite corner of the park and picked up a fine Cuban rum for two dollars and fifty cents. Dramatically, Santiago broke the seal and splashed some rum onto the sidewalk. "To the Saints." He followed the little toast with a long swallow from the bottle.

"To the Saints," Carlos and I repeated.

Santiago looked at me and raised his eyebrows, as if saying, "What do you think?"

"*Suave*," I replied. I was actually surprised how smooth it went down. "Great rum for only two-fifty."

Carlos looked at the bottle and nodded. That was all the body language Santiago needed to put a big smile on his face. He said something to Carlos that I didn't understand. I looked at Carlos with a confused, "please translate" expression on my face. He held out the bottle and said, "It will help you get a good bike at a great price." Santiago laughed along with Carlos and me. I could tell by Santiago's laugh that that was the main reason for buying the rum. And I could tell that it was definitely a main ingredient in any Cuban business transaction.

Santiago, Carlos, and I headed down to the *bici*-park to get the bicycles. Santiago mounted Carlos's and I got on the back of Santiago's. Santiago's bike had a grill welded over the back tire. Riding on the grill was easier for the driver and passenger of the bike than if the passenger had to ride on the frame, and it was easier on my backside. We headed down to the *Candonga*. The *Candonga* was the area where food was sold in the Calixto Garcia Stadium parking lot. But it was also the place where you could get anything, if you had the money and the trust of one of the head guys of the Candonga. This was the black market.

As I rode on the back of Santiago's bike, Carlos went over the rules I was to follow at the *Candonga*. "Rule number one: Don't talk. You have red hair and blue eyes, however, you could pass as a Cuban, so don't talk. If you talk they will know you are not Cuban. Don't talk. That is rule number one. Don't talk. That is the first and most important rule. Don't talk."

About the tenth time he told me not to talk, I asked, "This rule number one, I don't quite get it. Could you tell me again?"

"Yes, I will tell you again. Don't talk. You can nod your head if you are sure the answer or situation calls for a yes or no headshake, but do not talk." He laughed to himself and said, "You have laryngitis or something."

"Rule number two: Drink rum when it is passed to you. This is very important. Never turn down a drink. Rule number three: This is my bike we are buying, not yours. I will do all of the test driving and inspection of the bicycle. I will look at you to see if you like the bike that I am riding. We have already talked about the bike that you would like to have and I will know which one is best for you."

Carlos was a trusted friend, but he also has been around bicycles, worked on bicycles, all of his life. The way Carlos was making it sound was that we were going to try to buy a Lamborghini, but there were going to be several Lamborghinis to buy and several crooked salesmen selling them. We had already agreed on a price. I was going to spend $200. No more.

Probably 100 bikes were parked beneath the large orange flowers and shade from the gigantic African Flamboyant. There were new mountain bikes made in Mexico with springs all over the frame. There were many Chinese bikes that have been in Cuba for thirty years and rebuilt and repainted over and over. Some bikes were stripped, just frame, seat, and wheels. Others were so loaded they had a car battery behind the seat to run the electronics. Vendors walked through and around the area selling bicycle parts, stickers for bicycles, and pigs on ropes. Santiago rode ahead of us and parked Carlos's bike next to a guy with a large mustache and beard. The man stood straddled above his bicycle with his arms folded. In his mid-thirties, he wore a black tank top stretched around his well-maintained pecs and enormous shoulders. Santiago shook hands and handed him the bottle of rum. We parked Santiago's bike next to Carlos's. By the time he'd shaken our hands and consumed half the rum, we were surrounded by about thirty bike salesmen. I looked around at the way the men looked to this man for what to say and what to do. I thought that not much got sold here without his permission. Santiago's friend was the Godfather of the Holguin Bicycle Market.

Santiago was also aware of what I had in mind for a bicycle. He talked to the large man and the man relayed the message to the guys huddled around him. Almost instantly twenty bicycles formed a semi-circle around us. They were all large, new mountain bikes. Many of them had springs below the seat and on the upper portion of the front fork. After Carlos and Santiago shook the tires inspected the chains, gears, and brakes for about ten minutes, they had narrowed the field to two.

I felt like I was watching a dog contest, because I have never been able to figure out what the judges are looking for when they rub their hands all over the dogs, check the teeth, watch them run, and then pick the winner. I also had no idea what Carlos and Santiago were looking for. The *vendadores* rode their bikes in a circle, changing gears and talking to Carlos and Santiago.

Carlos preferred a new shiny blue bike with the springs under the seat and beside the front forks, but before he could inspect it everything stopped suddenly. No one said anything and my first thought was about police and jail. But then I looked where everyone else was looking. A beautiful young woman in a light, expensive pantsuit and great hair was walking up to the group like she owned them. She smiled, greeted the crowd, and walked up to the Godfather with a boy about the same age as Galeno. I couldn't hear, nor understand if I could have heard, the conversation, but I could see the roll of bills, both U.S. dollars and peso dollars, almost as big as his biceps. He smiled, handed his lady a few bills, and kissed the boy. It was silent as the crowd admired her as she walked away. Then back to business.

The salesman of the bike Carlos liked was tall, lean, and powerful. He enjoyed showing off the bike and his skills. The price was $150. We made a deal, shook hands with the large man and started following the bike owner back to his house to get the papers on the bike. Carlos was riding alongside the owner when Santiago, who was riding behind us, said something. Carlos said a few things to the owner and he started peddling faster to move out in front of us. Santiago rode up beside us and continued to talk to Carlos. I had no idea what was going on.

Carlos whispered to me on the back of the bike. "Look at the frame. Look at the front and back tire."

I was still confused when I looked over to Santiago. He had his arm straight, then bent it slightly inward toward his chest. I finally got it. He was saying that the frame was bent. I glanced back in front of us and I could now see the front tire was slightly to the right of the back tire when you looked down the middle of the bicycle. Carlos and Santiago said something to the owner of the bike and he vanished. Carlos now spoke a little louder to me.

"I knew that something could be wrong with the bike because he was selling it for only one-fifty. Sometimes it's difficult to see the bent frame. You wouldn't have noticed it even by riding it. But if you tried to sell it later, when you leave Cuba, you might only get fifty bucks."

We went back to the *Candonga* and talked once again with the brawny man.

"I'm sorry, Santiago. You are my friend and I don't want you to be disappointed. I have a friend with a special bike. I'll get you a good deal. New paint. Shimano gears."

"How much?"

"It's worth $300. How much can you pay?"

"Two hundred dollars."

"He will do that. *Esperen aquí.*" Telling us to wait, he went to find his friend with the bike.

We waited at a small open-air bar in sight of the man who ran the shade tree bicycle store. Santiago and I sat down while Carlos went over to the bar and brought back what looked like three Bloody Marys. As he got closer I could see some white things at the bottom of the glass.

"*Oistiones.*" Carlos looked at me and smiled. "Oysters," he translated for me.

I grabbed my glass and drank it down. "Carlos, what's in this?" I asked, raising my empty glass.

"Air," he said, laughing.

"Alright, what was in my glass before I drank it?"

"Tomato juice with a little bit of minced peppers, salt, lemon juice, water, and of course, oysters. Do you want another?"

"Yes, how much are they?"

"Well, these were doubles. A single is two pesos and a double is five."

I reached into my pocket and pulled out a twenty peso bill and handed it to Carlos. I looked over to Santiago. "*Tú quieres uno más, ¿verdad?*" He smiled and looked shocked that I could ask him if he wanted another.

"*Sí, mi amigo,*" he grinned.

As we knocked back our second glass of oysters and our cups hit the table, the Godfather pulled up alongside the railing to the bar. He pointed to where we had first arrived that morning. We walked over to the man sitting on another blue mountain bike that looked much like the first, but a little paler shade of blue. He looked like he might be a brother of the big man. Santiago took it for a test drive. I could tell that Carlos and Santiago were both pleased with the bike. As a result, I was pleased. Carlos had the money. He glanced at me, smiled, and gave me his "What do you think?" look. I nodded. It really wasn't an approval of the bicycle. It was approval of my friend.

Next, the paperwork. First, documentation of ownership was signed. Next, a statement was signed by both the previous owner and Carlos, giving the date, time, and location of the sale. The numbers on each of the one hundred dollar bills was registered. Carlos and the seller exchanged national identification cards and those numbers were written down with telephone numbers and addresses. I stood there in awe. In the States bikes were sold as easy as baseball cards.

Hands were gripped and one last, small drink for everyone finished off the rum. Santiago rode my new bike and I rode Carlos's until we were out of sight. As he handed me the bike, he spoke slowly to Carlos, holding back his laughter, hoping I would catch on. He pointed at the front shocks and then made two women figures in the air. One small, and then a large one, as he pointed at me. "Why does Brandon need shocks in the front?" he was asking.

Carlos laughed and said, "Because Brandon's going to be here six months and he likes his women large." I laughed and shook my head. Santiago and Carlos were a comical tag-team when they were together, and I loved it, even if I was the occasional victim of their jokes.

It was mid-afternoon and crowds were forming around the large green vats which were housed in make-shift wooden beer stands. I asked Carlos if he wanted to stop, but he smiled and shook his head. "I've had enough to drink for today and the Carnival lasts for a week. Tonight we need to go home and rest."

Street Madness

♦

Day 6
Wednesday, August 20, 2003

I grabbed the large clear plastic bottle, tilted my head back, and poured more ice-cold beer down my throat. The beer ran down my esophagus and joined gallons of beer already in my stomach. This was insane. The sun was still just getting up and I was well on my way to painlessness.

Carlos woke me up and asked if I wanted to bike to the market out on the main road. Now we had our small bag of garlic, onion, and peppers in the middle of a drinking frenzy. As we snaked through the people congregating on the left-hand side of the road, we stopped often to allow the people to run to the right-hand side of the road. There were numerous beer stands along the right-hand side. I couldn't see what they looked like due to the wall of people standing in front of them. Everyone wore faded clothing and a bright smile. There was no segregation. It was different from what I remembered the States to be. I think we divide ourselves as much as possible, whether it is politically, based on income, sexual preference, race, political or religious affiliation, or what activities one is involved in. These people standing on the left-hand side did have a common binding thread. They were Cuban and they intermingled with Cubans and they shared everything. There were no divisions. Carlos saw my bewilderment and pulled me away from the throng that had gathered at a beer truck.

"Brandon, this is Carnival." He paused and then started over. "Brandon, this is part of Carnival, people getting drunk on cheap, cold beer. The next four days are wonderful. Great music. Dancing in the street. Rides for Galeno. On Saturday, in the stadium, you will see the most beautiful girls in the world dancing on wonderful floats. A sight no man will ever forget. This is Carnival. Come on. Let's drink some more beer. Always take at least a little from everyone who offers."

The funny thing was that we didn't have anything to hold any beer. Every three feet, as we pushed our bikes through the thick crowd, the name "Carlos" would be shouted loud enough for the whole town to hear. We would stop and there would be no time for formal introductions. Just a bottle, or any plastic or metal container filled with beer, was held in front of us. That was the, "Pleased to meet you." It didn't matter if you were drunk, on medication, or had no hands to drink with. They would pour it down your throat for you. When we got out of the crowd, we were in no shape to ride the bikes, so we walked slowly home, enjoying the morning sun and the warmth of Carnival.

"That was certainly a happy crowd." I was wondering if Carlos could explain why we had just been given so much beer.

"For that crowd," Carlos said, "it was a rare opportunity to give something. *La lucha*, we call it. "Life is a struggle." You know how little we have, not just compared to the United States, but to other countries around us. You can't walk by and pretend you didn't hear them call your name. It is a rare opportunity to give. If you do not respond with a sense of celebration you rob that person of the opportunity to receive joy from giving something. That opportunity for them may only come on one occasion a year. That occasion is this week. Carnival."

Belicia smiled at our condition and gave us *cafecitos*. Then she took the vegetables to put with eggs for breakfast.

That afternoon I was sitting on the couch smoking a cigarette when Galeno placed the ball in my right hand. He folded my fingers around the ball and then grabbed my wrist. "*Brandon, vamos afuera*," he said as he tugged at my wrist.

I knew that he wanted me to go outside and I gave in. Once I was on my feet he ran to the kitchen for the bat. With the red bat now in hand we both went through the kitchen door. Galeno stood almost under the metal stairs going up to the second floor, with his back facing the house. I stood beside the bathroom. The distance between us was maybe twenty feet and I was hoping he wouldn't hit a line drive. The red bat made of hard plastic Carlos had bought in Jamaica, and the ball was sent down from the States. Galeno stood ready after slightly tapping the bat against the ground. He took a practice swing and I could tell I was in trouble.

"*¿Listo?*" I asked, as though I didn't know he was ready.

"*Sí.*" He took his stance and tapped the bat on the ground one more time. Then he cocked back the bat. I pitched a nice underhand pitch and he swung and missed. I breathed a sigh of relief. When Galeno would swing, he would twirl around. I pitched a few more and then decided I would impart some of my own little league knowledge.

"*Mire, Galeno.*" I paused, fishing for the words in my mind. Let's see, ball is *pelota*, bat, I have no idea, and eyes are *ojos*. Okay. I grabbed the bat from Galeno and showed him what I hoped he would understand. I held the bat with my right hand and brought the ball against it with my left.

"*Tus ojos. Mire la pelota aquí,*" I said, as I tapped the ball against the bat.

"*Sí,*" he said, as he grabbed the bat. As I walked back beside the bathroom I thought to myself that he just wants to swing the bat and maybe I should let him without confusing him. For all I know I told him to try to get hit in the head with the ball, and then when you're lying on the ground, hit yourself in the eyes with the bat. I took my stance and he tapped the ground with the bat.

"*¿Listo?*" I asked.

"*Sí.*" One last tap and he put the bat in the ready position. I pitched the ball and he watched the ball and then hit a line drive that whizzed past my waist line. Galeno laughed and tapped his bat against the ground. I walked back to the bathroom and grabbed the ball that was sitting just outside the wooden door. After the next three pitches I was wishing I had a little protection from the barrage of balls, the air between provided an insignificant barrier. It reminded me of my grenade training in Fort Sill, Oklahoma. The drill instructor was kneeling beside me and I had the blue M-60 fragmentation grenade in my hand. I looked into his eyes, waiting for the nod. I pulled the pin and tossed the grenade over the four foot concrete wall in front of me. The spoon from the grenade landed beside me and I cowered to the ground. A wave of dirt blanketed me. I wish that I had the four foot wall to crouch behind after pitching to Galeno. It was like showing someone how to shoot and then taping a target to your chest. After he was tired and I was bruised and had probably lost the ability to produce offspring, it was dinner time.

Carlos and I sat down at the table and started eating. Galeno was being force-fed the chicken Belicia had prepared. Belicia finished shoving the food in Galeno's mouth and sat down to eat.

Later Belicia and Galeno rested up for the next three days. Carlos and I went back out to the main road and gave more people the opportunity to give. I once again found myself tipping back an old coffee can filled with beer. I was in a group of people and I looked at Carlos for the cue to nod or laugh or drink. Jokes were told and I rarely understood, except when they were about Fidel. Fidel's name was never mentioned, instead, the stroking of an imaginary beard was the cue that the joke was about him. I was enjoying everything, but frustrated with not having the ability to speak. I wanted to speak, to joke, to talk about the weather. But I knew that it would come and I just had to be patient. I worked on drinking beer, and was happy that I could at least fit in this way. I didn't know what time it was, but I remember walking down the rocky road trying to maintain my balance.

Struggling to put the key into the lock, Carlos looked back and asked, "Did you have fun tonight?"

"Yeah, I had fun, but I wish that I could speak more Spanish. I think I would have had more fun, sharing jokes and trying to converse."

"*No te preocupes.* You are dong fine. Remember, you don't learn a language overnight." He smiled and patted me on my back.

"So what do you learn overnight?"

Carlos paused for a moment, glancing away, trying to think what to say. He then turned back to me a few seconds later with a smile on his face.

"Well, I think that your first night in Cuba you learned that you can't learn Spanish overnight." He laughed and gave me another playful slap on the back. "So are you ready for Carnival?"

"Why, what's happening during Carnival besides drinking beer and having fun?"

"You will see the prettiest girls in the world moving like a blender on 'puree.'"

I laughed. "Do you think that I could take one home with me? I want to make a milkshake."

"Well, you could, but they don't come with a lifetime guarantee."

"Few things in this life do."

Dancing in the Barrio

✦

Day 7
Thursday, August 21, 2003

I felt a tug on my toe and then heard my name being called. I didn't want to open my eyes, but wanted to continue to sleep. I slowly opened my eyes and Galeno stood at the foot of the bed with his bat, staring back at me. I didn't want to get up but I did. I slipped on my sandals and went outside. I tossed Galeno his glove and picked up the ball. He shook his bat and said something to me that I didn't understand.

"*No, es demasiado temprano.*" I hoped he would understand that I thought it was too early to play "Let's hit line drives at Brandon." He finally put down his bat and picked up his glove. We played catch for a little while and then I let him practice pitching. Belicia came to the kitchen door. She had been in the kitchen preparing coffee and milk. She told Galeno to get ready to take a shower. I went inside, where Carlos now sat drinking his coffee and milk. I joined him. Exhausted from the night before, there was little conversation.

Belicia wrapped Galeno in a towel and sent him inside for Carlos to dress him while she showered. After clothes were put on and doors locked, we walked about six blocks from Carlos's house to an open area with a stage. It was a place where small performances were held. The ground was covered with new gravel and metal food and beer stands were now erected, forming a semi-circle around the stage. The first thing I noticed was the man selling *oistiones*. Carlos, Belicia, and I each downed our first cup and got another one.

An old white Russian tractor squatted next to us. It made me think of the tall, lean FarmAlls I drove harvesting hay on my Grandpa's ranch. Carlos walked over to the driver. His plump belly hung over the top of his grease-stained pants and nearly touched the steering wheel. He had on dark glasses and a cowboy hat. The foam from the beer stuck on his mustache as he took the cup away from his mouth, but soon disappeared as it was soaked into his thick, black whiskers.

Merengue music blared from the old car speakers by his seat, dangling like ripe fruit ready to fall from the tree. I walked over to a lady selling aluminum cups for five pesos. The cups looked like aluminum origami, welded together to maintain their shape.

As I was getting beer from a man sitting beside the spigot of a large green tank, Miguel walked up. I did not recognize the large pale-faced woman with black hair who was with him. At first glance she could have been Michael Jackson's mother. He shook my hand and introduced the woman. It was Belicia's mother. She did not look anything like Belicia, or rather Belicia didn't look anything like her. She had on black knee-length tights that showed off her many curves. She had enough curves she could have shared them with a few other women. I handed one of the cups to Miguel and we walked back over to where Belicia and Carlos were sitting. Once Miguel got near the tractor and heard the music, the dancing started. I was pretty sure that Miguel and Belicia's mom had already begun drinking. I kept watching Miguel's hands as he chattered, trying to understand what was strange about them. They seemed to be twisted inward, with his pinkies, not his thumbs, breaking the air in front of him when he walked. Belicia's mother grabbed my hand and pulled me to the gravel dance floor in front of the tractor. Although Miguel looked silly trying to recreate Michael Jackson's dance moves to Merengue music in front of an old tractor, I felt like a zebra among Clydesdales. Jeers from the peanut gallery came in full force.

"Come on, Brandon, show us some moves." These words came from Carlos, a man who admits he has no rhythm. I don't know how you grow up in Cuba without rhythm, but he's accomplished it. I broke into the robotic man. My motto in this situation was, "If you feel like a zebra, why not play the part of a jackass. It's a lot more fun." It's hard to try to fit in, but I always try to spend less time thinking about it and more time just being a little crazy. The drinking extended well into the night.

Galeno was playing with other children whose parents were glad they were able to enjoy a night of drinking and dancing. There were only about forty people sitting and buying beer at the gravel parking lot with a stage. Carlos and I took turns making beer runs over to the green containers that looked like giant propane tanks. Carlos showed me how to figure out what tank had the freshest, coolest beer. It was an easy concept. Go to the tank that has the longest line. Two men were huddled over a large metal pot which caught the overflow from the spigot on the tank. They would dump a large, what looked like a metal Irish mug, into the pool of beer that was forming in the pot. They would shovel the beer into a container that was then full to the brim with foamless beer.

As we headed home, Belicia's mother said that we needed to come over for supper one of these nights. It was one o'clock, so we followed Belicia's mother the extra five minutes past Carlos's turn off to her home. I pushed my bike along the deserted road, balancing my bike and Galeno against my side as I walked home. Galeno was straddled along the frame with his hands and head resting on the handlebars. I loved these moments because it was during these times I felt like part of Carlos's family and part of Carlos's Cuba.

While Belicia took another shower I helped Galeno get ready for bed. He had a long night and I could tell that he was tired. It was like trying to put clothes on a large sack of sugar. I was happy to help and I was happy to be a part of this family.

Carnival Rides

✦

Day 8
Friday, August 22, 2003

As we passed through the main transportation depot for the city I saw more of the trucks that had puzzled me my first night in Cuba when I was riding to Camagüey with the Jamaican. They were large old trucks with bubble hoods common to the fifties. Large metal compartments were welded onto flatbeds. Neither the trucks nor the metal boxes had been painted for years. There were two metal benches along the back walls and everyone else had to stand. When the trucks were full with up to fifty people, arms and heads hung out of the slot cut below the roof. Names of surrounding cities were written on the back of the truck, along with the fares. I wondered if this system was more efficient than Greyhound.

Carlos said that during the Special Period his friend would walk to this terminal from the teachers' college, a twenty minute walk northeast of the stadium. Sometimes he would wait two days to find a ride toward Banes. Often he would just give up and walk back to the college. It didn't matter if you had two hundred pesos in your pocket. During the Special Period there were no vehicles to take you, because there was no fuel.

Today, horses with carriages were lined up along one side of the station. The carriages each had a long front seat and two seats that ran along the side, which could hold ten to twelve people. A tarp served as a roof to keep the passengers cool or dry, depending on the weather.

Carlos was riding his bike with Belicia riding on the bar between the seat and the handlebars. Galeno had a similar seat on my bike. As we eased up to the stop sign, ready to cross one of the main roads that dissected the city, I could feel Galeno getting antsy. He kept pointing to the rides across the parking lot of the stadium.

43

"Mire, mire, Brandon." Galeno pointed to the rides, telling me to look at the machines that were set up on the east side of the stadium. Galeno had waited 365 days to enjoy this moment. Now, he couldn't wait another minute to feel his stomach turn sideways.

"Sí, Galeno, sí." We crossed the street and parked our bikes in a bici-park that was open for the Children's Carnival. Galeno was as excited as a pack of dogs outside of an open meat-packing plant. As we walked toward the rides, Galeno kept grabbing Belicia and Carlos's hands and tugging them toward the Carnival as if it would soon vanish if we didn't reach it in time. Wanting to try everything, he was distracted by a vendor with *chicharones de harina. Chicharones* are fried pork skins. These were simply bits of wheat flour deep-fried in pork grease, with a texture similar to Cheetos.

As we approached the rides, there were people with novelty items neatly arranged on tarps. There were so many silver necklaces, rubber alligators, noisemakers, slingshots, and such, that it looked like the island of Taiwan had exploded and landed in Holguin. The first ride Galeno would conquer, after he finished his *chicharones de harina*, would be a ferris wheel with airplanes. Well, not really airplanes. In fact, they were old, crude metal boxes with airplanes painted on the sides, but Galeno sat in his seat and became an aviator.

Galeno was like a humming bird at the peak of the blooming season, buzzing this way and that, sucking up all the fun at one ride before darting to another. Some rides were obviously sweeter than others. The ride that he seemed to enjoy the most was the one with cars that were attached to power cables, which enabled you to drive it around a small square area. There were pony rides and tricycles that you could ride to the end of a section of street and back.

While Galeno was riding, the food vendors entranced me. There were popcorn and cotton candy, just like at any carnival in the States. A browned crispy pig's head sitting on a table was a sign that *puerco asado* was available. The cotton candy machine was particularly inventive. An old washing machine tub had been hooked up to spin. The operator used the main vein of a palm leaf to spin the sugar on. Carlos smiled and said, "There is always a way to cut back on operating costs. Necessity is the mother of invention and in Cuba that is our motto."

Then a shower stopped the rides and sent everyone to huddle along the stadium walls where the awning protected most from the rain. We stood packed together with several hundred people, half of them children with blue, cone shaped noisemakers. The noise was deafening. The only creature impervious to the noise was the roasted pig, sitting on the table next to me, attempting to stay dry. When the rain quit, Belicia said something about *Díos* that Carlos translated

"She said that the noise must have been so bad that God stopped the rain so the children could get back to the rides." Belicia took Galeno back to the rides and Carlos and I went to the front of the stadium where an old white boxcar with windows and a door was sitting. It was a mobile dollar store that could be moved around for events like the Children's Carnival. Carlos and I bought a beer and a pack of cigarettes.

"Look down there." He pointed to a row of twenty stalls, side by side, extending about fifty yards, with green tanks at the back of each stall.

"What's that?"

"That's the part of the Carnival the adults enjoy. By this afternoon, each one of those tanks will be filled with ice cold beer."

"Is the beer expensive?"

"Well, for about a liter of beer it's about fifteen pesos. So to us it's cheap and the beer is good."

I was wondering what Carlos meant by "So to us it's cheap," but he soon responded with the answer. "You know, Brandon, some people can't even enjoy Carnival. Sometimes they have to decide who is going to enjoy Carnival. Is it going to be me or my children? Each ride is one peso, each snack is one peso. Drinks, toys, it can cost a lot to someone making two hundred and fifty pesos a month. That's why there is so much 'illegal' business in Cuba." He looked down at the ground and then took a drag of his cigarette. "I mean, people aren't selling drugs. They're selling eggs or the pigs that they've raised. I wouldn't have made it through the Special Period if I wouldn't have broken the law. Very few people would have."

I didn't know what to say. When Carlos told me these things, I went numb. I could pretend I knew what struggling or pain was because I went through basic training, but there was really no comparison. This was just something that I had to realize that I never would understand.

"Do you want another beer?" I said in an attempt to break the awkward silence.

"Sure, I'll take another."

I handed Carlos a cold *Bucanero*. I could tell that Carlos was still pondering the past. "Carlos, do you remember that time in Jamaica when I woke up in the morning and was still drunk from the night before."

Carlos finally smiled. "Yes, I remember. You came to my house and your face was white and it looked like you were going to puke. You asked me to ride your bike out to the shop to buy you some orange juice."

"Yah, you asshole. I asked you to buy orange juice and you came back with a bottle of white rum," I said, laughing.

Carlos quickly said, "I bought you some orange juice too."

We both laughed. Belicia and Galeno came walking up the steps. It looked like Galeno was starting to wear down. "Belicia, do you want a beer?" I asked in Spanish, badly mispronouncing the word for "want."

"*Sí, gracias.*" She warmed me with her smile.

"And Galeno, do you want a soda?" He understood and nodded. I bought the beer and the soda and we started to walk back to the bicycles. Galeno was still blowing away at the noisemaker.

Woman Power

✦

Day 9
Saturday, August 23, 2003

I was mesmerized by the most beautiful woman I had ever seen. My blood pounded to the salsa music which was moving her in her tight red top and short skirt. Jennifer Lopez or Selma Hayak is great on screen, but the girl on the first float was more beautiful and more alive than any movie star I had ever seen. Her body was a force of nature, a feather in the wind. Her dark hair flowed around her beautiful brown shoulders as she smiled at me. Yes, she smiled directly at me. A smile better than the best smile Julia Roberts ever smiled.

I'm sure the floats had themes and sponsors but I can't remember anything but the women. Dancing, moving, strutting, laughing, on float after float, "the most beautiful woman I had ever seen" was on every float and each one smiled at me. About one out of four was very dark skinned, a few were light enough to be from my hometown, but each was beautiful. I understood why Carlos had always told me that the parade at the Carnival in Holguin was something no man in the world should miss.

On the way downtown that morning Galeno rode on the frame of my bike and kept changing the gears and pressing the brakes. Belicia, riding with Carlos, told him to quit, but he laughed and braked hard. I laughed too.

Galeno was hungry. He was still chewing on the last piece of an ice cream cone, ice cream dripping from his chin, when he pointed to the blue metal ten-by-ten box that had "Pizza" written on it.

"Pizza does sound good," I said. "I'll get it." I stood in line, waiting for four pizzas. The line crawled along, stopped, and started again. Listening to the Spanish chatter of the crowd, I watched the band set up on a large stage at the far end of the stadium parking lot. There were long lines in front of the large green tanks containing either *Mayabe* or Tiananmen beer. People, trying to maneuver their way back out of the crowd, raised their containers high above the heads of the people waiting behind them. Everyone was wearing their Sunday best. For most men, that was blue jeans and a polo shirt. The women, young and old, were prepared for a fashion shoot. I was wearing something I had tried to discard since arriving in Cuba, the smile a person wears when he doesn't understand what is being said or what is happening around him.

I got far enough forward in line that I could see inside of the blue pizza house. Black metal pans were stacked eight layers high. All the pans contained dough spread to the edges and smeared with a small helping of tomato paste and cheese. I motioned to Carlos when the money had been paid and my pizzas were in the oven. I handed Carlos the pizzas as they came to me and he passed one each to Belicia and Galeno. They came folded with a small piece of paper to hold them.

Carlos and I had our welded aluminum cups and went to the big green tanks to fill them up. The pizza was warm and spongy and I knew that in the next few hours we would fully test its ability to absorb beer.

We ate the pizza slowly as we enjoyed the beer and the crowd. We had arrived at the stadium early to make sure we would have a good spot to watch the parade. After the pizza, we bought some warm peanuts stuffed into a paper funnel. I noticed Santiago with a very polite woman. I told Carlos that I wanted to thank him again for helping with the bike.

Carlos called to Santiago and the two walked over. The woman had a very familiar smile and the twinkle in her eyes reminded me of Carlos, because as it turned out, the girl was Carlos's sister.

Santiago, sporting his trademark smile, patted me on the back. I left Carlos's family to keep our spot and went with Santiago. We strolled along through the crowd as Santiago pointed out possible women for me. There was enough food to feed an army. There were sandwiches made of chicken and pork, hot-dogs, banana chips, popcorn, goat steaks, and of course, whole roasted pigs. Carlos explained that you could choose what part you wanted and they would chop off that piece. Most of the time the pork was served with *congri* and *fungo* chips. *Fungo* looks like regular bananas, maybe even a bit skinnier, but are heavy and starchy like *platanos* (plantains). They seem to be uniquely Cuban, cheaper than *platanos*, and more readily available.

My bladder felt like it was nearing the point of rupturing. I was standing next to Santiago. I asked him if he knew a place where I could go to the bathroom. We looked around but I couldn't see any place that even resembled a portable toilet. We walked toward the place were Carlos and I had left our bikes. He saw two portable toilets, but they looked like they sat on deserted islands of gravel, surrounded by a sea of urine. Santiago looked back at me as if to say, "Those aren't going to work." He grabbed my arm. "*Vamos.*"

We walked under the road inside a tunnel that extended from the stadium parking lot to the bus terminal across the road. The tunnel smelled like the urine saturated walls of downtown Kingston. Santiago and I quickly moved through the tunnel and came out taking in a large breath of air. We walked over to a small unpainted building beside the terminal. We went inside and there were about forty people in old wooden pews watching an old western on television. I guessed they were waiting for the next bus out of Holguin. We walked to the back of the room and there, sitting next to the restroom, was a lady at a table. She had yellow peso coins setting in front of her, along with a few silver centavos. I dug around in my pockets. Santiago grabbed my arm and motioned for me to enter. I looked back and he dropped a yellow coin on the table and started to chat with the woman. I drained the *Mayabe* out of my bladder and Santiago and I headed back to the Carnival.

Galeno wanted to ride some more of the rides that were still set up, so we walked over by the stadium. Four rows, consisting of maybe ten large green tanks, ran the length of the parking lot. We stood at the end of one of the rows and watched Galeno ride the carousel a few times. While we were standing there, Carlos's other sister arrived with her daughter. Her daughter rode on the rides with Galeno. As we stood there, Carlos's name began being yelled again. Once again, I was drinking more beer than I should have. At about eleven o'clock everyone was gathering around the main road that runs in front of the stadium. There were bleachers set up to accommodate the judges that would evaluate the floats that would soon be passing by. As the floats started to come by the stands, Carlos led us down to the road going to the university and the Plaza de la *Revolución*. We got a good spot and waited for the floats to come by. Then I was mesmerized by all those wonderful women in their brilliant costumes and enveloping smiles. They were dancing to upbeat salsa music and their bodies were, like Carlos so eloquently put it, moving like a blender. Santiago and I continued to walk back and forth to get beer, hurrying so we wouldn't miss another float. I looked over at Carlos. Carlos was smiling in between playful slaps on the back from Belicia.

"Carlos, you said during the Special Period they had to cut back on electricity, right?" I asked as the last float went by at one o'clock.

Carlos looked at me, wondering why I was bringing up something as harsh as the Special Period at a time like this. He responded hesitantly.

"Yes, we had large blackouts." He paused and looked over at me, wondering where I was going with this question. He smiled as I took another drink from my beer.

"Well, I think I figured out how Fidel could have not only maintained the electricity provided to the country, but produce so much that he could have exported it."

Carlos smiled and shook his head. He was probably ready to grab the beer away from me. He nodded to me, indicating that he wanted me to tell him this grand plan that was formulating in my mind.

"Well, if you could hook up some cables to the bodies of these women and have them jiggle for a while, we could light Cuba up like Las Vegas."

Carlos laughed and told Belicia what I had said. She laughed and shook her head.

Galeno was asleep, sitting on Carlos's shoulders, resting his head on Carlos's head. We walked back, got our bikes, and headed to the central bus station. Carlos probably figured that Galeno or I would fall off of the bike if I tried to pedal home, so he sent us home in the back of a horse carriage.

Recovering from Carnival

◆

Day 10
Sunday, August 24, 2003

Plunk. The red plastic bucket hit the water. Seconds later, plunk again, as the red plastic bucket hit the water. I lay in my bed as the rhythmic plunks repeated over and over. I found myself counting to twenty before I got up and joined Carlos at the well. Between plunks, Carlos fed more rope through the pulley so that the heavy knot on the bucket handle sank into the water. Then the bucket tilted and followed the knot, filled up with water, and started to sink. Then Carlos would pull the bucket just above the surface of the water to straighten it, and then released enough rope to let the bucket go underwater again. This ensured the bucket was completely full. Carlos did this without looking. I figured that he had done it so many times that, to him, it was like tying his shoes.

"*Buenos días*, Belicia. Yo carry agua." Belicia understood that I would take over the water-carrying task. She greeted me and returned to the living room. "This must be the only house in the world built so that a well is really in the house but not in the house."

"We had to build the house around the well," Carlos answered.

The house was shaped like a "C," with the well in the mouth of the letter. The kitchen was on one side of the well and the bedroom/living room was on the other. A narrow hallway connected them.

Carlos lifted the bucket onto the window ledge and then poured the water from the red bucket into the white bucket at my feet. I carried the bucket out of the kitchen door and poured the water into the metal drum that sat next to the bathroom. We had two drums to fill up and the process took about twenty minutes. Carlos's kitchen did have running water connected to a city system that worked part of the time, but for the last few days the water was filled with sediments. Carlos thought it was because there was a drought around Holguin and the dam was low. This morning about fifteen people stood in line, in the narrow

51

walkway between Carlos's and Miguel's house, waiting to get water. Most of them had a coffee can with a metal wire tied to it and they fished for water right along Carlos's bucket. The well was probably eight feet in diameter and about twenty-five feet deep, fifteen of that filled with water. I could tell that the rock walls were very hard. Based on my college classes in geology, I guessed that it was some type of igneous rock. The water was cold and clear.

"Carlos, do you drink this water?"

"When there are no trucks to provide drinking water, yes."

"Have you gotten sick?"

"I never have and we don't boil the water."

We had finally filled the two tanks. Carlos untied the bucket and pulled the rope through the pulley and put it under the sink. We shut the grill to the opening of the window and sat down for a cigarette.

"Did you ever see a well in Jamaica?" I wondered aloud.

Carlos thought about this as he took a drag on the cigarette. "No, I never saw one."

"Maybe it was because of the type of rock that was in certain areas in Jamaica."

"Or maybe it was so the government could charge the people for the water." Carlos was always cynical about governments, including his own.

Although some Carnival activities continued downtown, we stayed home and recovered from the last four days. Belicia returned to her mother's house right after breakfast because her mother had been ill lately and the dancing and drinking of Carnival had put her back into bed.

Through the afternoon, Carlos and I played catch with Galeno and talked about Carlos's job as principal of three elementary schools. He was starting back to work the next day and wasn't excited. "I feel like a slave. For 500 pesos a month, about $18, I work like a donkey. I have to plan out the duties for all of those teachers, evaluate how they teach, give ideas to improve their teaching, and make sure that all of the students are learning. I work every weekday and one Saturday a month. They will all be looking at me to make changes because I have been abroad. But I will say nothing. They will ask me for ideas and I will say that the system is great the way it is. I have a lot of ideas how things could be changed but some of them might be thought of as counter-revolutionary, so I will keep my mouth shut. I want to go back to Jamaica, so I have to be a perfect employee and not ruffle any feathers."

"Do students skip school here like they did in Jamaica?" I asked.

"No. Education is very important and children never miss school. If a child misses three days of school without a good excuse there is the possibility that the parents could be sent to jail. That never happens because education has been so important here. Everyone realizes how important education is. I keep thinking how ironic it is that we export doctors, nurses, and teachers, but can't afford decent food."

"I know how hard you worked in Jamaica, even when no one really paid attention. Did you ever get evaluated?"

"Twice during the three years the principal spent about ten minutes in my classroom. No one ever looked at my lesson plans. I will try to do better for my teachers, but there are so many of them and so little time."

"Do all the teachers in Cuba work as hard as you?"

"No one works as hard as I do. You know that." Carlos's yellow eyes twinkled. "Really, the teachers try hard, but so many are new. I think I'll be starting with some untrained substitutes because of the number of teachers being sent to Venezuela."

"Will the teacher shortage reach up into the university? Will they have enough teachers for a gringo?"

"*No te preocupes.*" He gently put his hand on my shoulder and said in English, "Don't worry, my friend."

The World from a Coffin

◆

Day 11
Monday, August 25, 2003

Carlos had to start work today. I think he told Belicia to keep me busy and try to get me to talk as much as possible. After I ate the crackers and finished the milk and coffee, Belicia came into the kitchen.

"Do you want to help me?"

I smiled and said, "*Siempre*: always."

She smiled and handed me the two empty white cooking oil drums that were under the counter. She gave me twenty centavos and showed me the white water truck at the corner of the road.

So that is how I found myself standing among half a dozen housewives filling buckets from the spigot on the back of this water truck. Smiling children with freshly-ironed uniforms walked to school. The younger students wore short-sleeved white shirts with maroon shorts or mini-skirts. The secondary students wore white shirts with ochre yellow pants or mini-skirts. Being in rural Jamaica for three years, I felt I had learned to blend in. That's pretty good for a red-haired blue-eyed man with a complexion that, when placed beside a snowball, could make it appear to have a golden tan. But standing here in my shorts and sandals, holding two large drums, I felt out of place, like a Snoop Doggy Dog CD among classical ones. I tried to pay somebody the centavos, but no one was there to collect the money. I brought back the water and placed the drums back under the counter beside Miguel's box of rum. Miguel lived next door, but for some reason, he left his rum under Carlos's counter. Carlos said that he bought it cheap, by the box, and then resold it. Sitting on the box was a bunch of *fungo*. I set the centavos on the table and sat down. Belicia looked up from a piece of paper she was reading. She pointed at the coins and furrowed her brow.

"No one," I responded. She shook her head and continued to read the paper.

"Look." She handed the paper to me. She ran her finger down the long list of items.

"Galeno, *escuela.*"

When talking to me, Belicia only used the nouns of her sentence and hoped I could figure out what she meant. If she put in all the words I didn't understand any of them. She reached inside a bag that was sitting on the table and started pulling things out of the bag. She pulled out about ten vials, a cloth hair net, an apron, and about five other things. I thought to myself, "Is Galeno a lab technician or is he a first grader?" I could tell that Belicia was feeling pressured, having to get all of these things for school. And like the uniform and backpack, she had to buy them. The school provided the books and writing utensils.

Putting the school items back in their sack, she pointed at some rice on the table and said a couple more words, accompanied by hand signals. I started cleaning the rice. She smiled and nodded. The rice grains were smaller than the ones in Jamaica and there were a lot more husks and other foreign materials mixed in with them. I think Belicia enjoyed having me help her prepare lunch. I cleaned the garlic and took the seeds out of the peppers she had placed in front of me. Belicia washed the rice and put it into the pressure cooker. When the rice was about done, she heated up some leftover chicken from the refrigerator. I sat down and ate. Then I went and sat down on the bench by the front window. I lit a cigarette and relaxed. My daydreaming was interrupted by squeaking noises coming from the backyard of the house beside us. It was a kid, probably my age, doing lat pull-downs while sitting on a log. I laughed. I remembered Carlos saying that in Cuba people lifted weights, but most of the time those weights weren't made by Olympus. They were either made by Ford or Chevrolet. He was pulling down a straight metal bar. Attached to the bar was a cable that ran over a pulley attached to a tree, and at the end of the cable were assorted car parts. He was sweating, so I think the contraption was working.

Miguel came by the house wearing the same attire I had seen him in most days I was there: shirtless, a baseball cap, black shorts, and heavy work boots. And like most days, he wanted a cold glass of water. I soon came to the conclusion, after five different people came to the house for a cold glass of water and to store meat in the freezer, that Carlos was one of the few, if not the only person, to have a fridge. Miguel would often come in with a piece of chicken or pork or other meat to put into the freezer. But before placing it in the freezer he would show it to Carlos. They would hold it in their hands, weighing it, and then poke and inspect it before placing it into the freezer. This was done with everything Miguel brought to the house: rum, flowers, car parts, ropes, clothes. I guess you needed to be an expert in the quality of everything because you had little money to make that right purchase. Unlike Wal-Mart, you couldn't take your receipt back and ask for a refund.

I was sitting at the table when Galeno ran in, coming from school. He was trying to rip the buttons off his shirt so I told him to come to me. I had seen Belicia and Carlos undress Galeno quite a few times so he could go outside and play. This was a phrase that I picked up quite quickly in Carlos's house and his neighborhood. It could be heard in the streets, in the houses, in the day, and in the night. Anywhere there was a child and a parent, "*Ven aquí*" was frequently heard. He came over to me and I undid his white short-sleeved shirt and hung it over the chair. He was kicking off his shoes as I was working to undo his belt. He was as fidgety as the man who tried to make it into The *Guinness Book of World Records* by drinking the most cups of Colombian coffee in twenty-four hours. I finally pulled off his shorts and he immediately reached down and ripped off his socks. He put on his slippers and ran outside in his underwear. I had wondered why all of the children in the neighborhood played in their underwear. But the reason was as obvious as the answer to the following question, "If you made ten dollars a month would you let your child wear a two dollar shirt to go play in the dirt?" Some people probably would, but if you were constantly thinking about where every peso is going, you would definitely pinch every single yellow coin you could.

"Brandon, do you want ice cream?" Belicia looked through the kitchen doorway at me sitting on the bench.

"Yes, thank you."

She came in with some rich creamy orange-flavored ice cream. I had seen a man go by yelling, "*Helado!*," pushing what looked like a metal coffin perched on top of a motorless lawnmower. I learned not to judge the ice cream by its container. Belicia and I sat at the table savoring our ice cream.

When Carlos came home, Belicia gave him a cup of ice cream with a strong hug and a kiss. I was wondering what that was for, but I soon remembered the last couple of weeks. It's the great feeling of giving that made her happy, and giving Carlos a cup of ice cream, in Cuba, was like handing him the world.

Killing a Chicken

✦

Day 12
Tuesday, August 26, 2003

Belicia had left me "the man of the house." I sat on the bench near the window, trying to study a little Spanish. I would occasionally glance next door and watch Miguel feed the pigs he kept in square brick pens. I sat daydreaming on the bench when a man walked by with two chickens dangling upside-down. Their two feet were tied together with a string. The string was draped around the man's neck. I remembered that in Jamaica I had about twenty stray chickens that would roost in an Ackee tree behind my house. Carlos had always complained about them shitting in front of his door and I had the same grumble about these indecent fowl. I also remembered when Carlos and I decided to do something about it.

I think it was in the early part of May, 2002. Hurricane Isabella or Iris or Ingrid, maybe it didn't start with an "I," but whoever the hurricane was, it was inflicting the island of Jamaica with heavy rains. The rains lasted for eleven straight days. The first day that Isabella was dumping rain on the island, school was let out early. Then later that day school was canceled until further notice. I had experienced cancellations and closures due to snow, but rain? This was because the majority of the teachers were unable to leave Spanish Town or Old Harbor due to flooding of the low-lying roads and bridges. Unlike Carlos and me, some teachers lived close to the beach, while we were stuck next to the school, on the mountain. But the good thing is, during the rainy season, we didn't have to swim to get to the grocery store. Carlos and I sat in his house watching the news on TV. We laughed as we watched a news item from Old Harbor, where fishermen brought their boats into town and were charging people to take them places. Yes, we laughed and enjoyed the rain those first few days, but as the days went by, our high spirits were washing away. During those days I would make daily trips out to the road to get supplies and just get out of the

57

house. I would stop by Carlos's house and ask him if he needed anything. Most of the time it was just cigarettes.

It was probably day nine of the deluge. I found myself bored out of my water-logged mind. I stared at my mold-covered walls and my mildew-stained sheets. Right now I would have loved to get out my basins and do some stress-relieving hand washing, but I didn't want to try to dry the laundry with the flame of a candle. I was boiling some water for some coffee and I glanced out my kitchen window. There, sitting in my backyard, perched in an Ackee tree were my twenty sopping-wet friends. Apparently my water-saturated brain worked faster than a dry one. I saw the boiling water and the chickens and automatically thought about my Grandma. When our family traveled up to Nebraska from New Mexico each summer, it was guaranteed that we would have fried chicken. And I would always be the lucky one who would help my Grandma kill the chickens. I did most of the killing. I'd place a head between two nails on a stump. Then with an ax-blow across its neck, I'd grab the flailing body and throw it so they could flop around and bleed on everything until it died. Grandma was the one who would place the chickens in the boiling water. Then she and I would strip off the feathers. I got to use a propane torch to burn off the pinfeathers before Grandma cut the chickens up for frying.

I sipped my coffee and wondered if Carlos would be up for it. I wasn't sure I could do the intestinal surgery that needed to be done. I could try....but it might be a mess. However, I wasn't too worried. Carlos grew up on a farm with chickens, and he used to hunt large rodents. I definitely felt that Carlos was over-qualified for this endeavor. I walked over to Carlos's house. I sat down and drank another cup of coffee. I looked over at Carlos. It looked like Carlos's mind had floated away down the mountain.

"Carlos. Carlos!" He blinked his eyes and looked away from the television toward me.

"Yes?"

I smiled. He looked like he was still day-dreaming. I spoke a little bit louder.

"Do you want to kill a chicken?"

I don't know what word got his attention, "chicken" or "kill." I think it was probably the latter. He now looked at me, alert, but I could tell I needed to repeat the question.

"Do you want to kill a chicken?"

He smiled like I had just told him that Noah had his Ark parked outside and we had been invited to ride along with the Swedish Bikini Team.

"Yes, of course."

"I think killing one of those chickens right now is a good idea. I'm not saying this to you, Carlos, because I'm bored. I just think that now is a very humane time to do it. It will take at least one of them out of their misery."

Carlos laughed. "Yes, I'm pretty bored myself."

Carlos handed me a large piece of bamboo from underneath the coconut tree in the backyard. I guess since it was my idea I was going to get the glory of killing it. I stood under a branch and Carlos guided me into position. The rain was coming down hard enough that when I looked straight up, the rain impaired my vision. I lifted the bamboo into the air and Carlos inched me to where I needed to be. He had me move a little to the right and then a little to the left. He guided me so I would swing parallel with the branch and hopefully in line with a chicken's neck. Finally, he told me to swing. I swung with all of my might. I landed on my back as my feet slipped on the rotting Ackee pods under the tree. The piece of bamboo landed on my right side and the chicken fell to my left. There was no movement. I had broken its neck. Carlos was laughing and congratulating me at the same time. I boiled the water and then poured it into my wash basin. I plucked the feathers as Carlos sharpened his knife. I flicked my lighter and burned off the pinfeathers. Carlos, as I had expected, could dissect a chicken in his sleep. We cut him up and threw him in a pressure pot along with a ton of seasonings, yam, and green banana. As the pot began hissing, we tried to light up our Victory cigarettes. But first we had to dry them out.

Parque Calixto García

✦

Day 13
Wednesday, August 27, 2003

Mom picked the phone up on the third ring. "Hello, Valentines."

"Hi, Mom," I said. "How are you doing?"

"Brandon! Is it you?" I could tell from her voice that she had been worrying. The last time I had talked to my parents I was planning on heading for Cuba in about a week. That was three weeks before, and I'm sure they had imagined some pretty horrible things.

"It's me. I'm fine. Cuba is great. I'll start my Spanish class early in September. How's everything in Omaha?"

Mom talked about school starting in a couple of weeks and mentioned that the family would be going to the county fair in my dad's hometown.

"Well, this is expensive. I've been trying to get a hold of you every day," I lied, "but the connections between Cuba and the U.S. aren't very good. Tell everyone I love them." I'll call again when my class starts. Bye."

"Bye. I love you. I'm happy that you're okay."

Happy that I had finally talked to my family, I sat down on the same bench that Carlos and I used on my first visit to downtown. The plaza is named after Calixto Garcia, a hero of some war with Spain. On my first day in Holguin, when we were downtown looking at stores, Carlos had told me some of the history. "Did you know that Calixto Garcia shot himself in the head when he was captured while fighting the Spanish in the Ten Years War?"

I looked over at Carlos. Carlos was making conversation as we sat on the bench eating roasted pork and *marquitas*, plantain chips.

Carlos continued. "But he amazingly survived. The bullet went out through his forehead without killing him. He was sent to Spain. Then fifteen years later he escaped and came back to Cuba. He fought alongside the U.S troops to liberate Cuba from Spain in the War of Independence. I often wondered if he had known what the U.S. would do to us in the future, then he might have fought for the Spanish."

A week later, I was sitting in the same place feeling a little more at home than I had back then, but still definitely adjusting. I had not tried to call every day, but I had tried a few times and I was greatly relieved that I had finally let the family back home know I was still alive and not in jail. A boy in his school uniform struggled to master his new pair of roller skates. He circled around the monument of Calixto Garcia in the middle of the plaza. His mom would laugh with her child every time he would get wide-legged and fall down.

I walked around the park, exploring downtown. After grabbing a papaya batido, a milkshake, for a few pesos, I went to the *Parque Cespedes* two blocks away and sat down again. There were lines of people waiting to have their lighters refueled by the gentlemen who had stalls set up on the sidewalk. It was times like these that I just put my head into my hands and blocked out everything. I pressed my eyes into my palms and thought. I did this to put myself back into the United States. With every day that I was outside of the States it got harder and harder to go back. To go back and compare what I was going through to what I remembered back home. I shook my head and extended my curled fingers up through my bangs. We are so spoiled in the States. Here, people were waiting in line to refill their lighters, lines ten to fifteen people deep at times. If we have to stand in line at the local Wal-Mart we sigh deeply and shake our heads. We think that we are each the most important person at that moment. We are not patient in the land of microwavable food and self-checkouts. To us, "stopping and smelling the roses" is hitting every red light on the way home from work. They call life here "the struggle," "*la lucha*." Life is tough, life is slow, but life is real. From "*la lucha*" comes real friendships and real love. No one spends time pretending they don't have feelings.

I continued to walk around trying to get my bearings in a strange and unfamiliar landscape. A landscape I would hopefully be in for six months.

I walked back down to the main park and saw people looking in through the grilled windows of the Casa de Arte on the corner of the park. I paid a peso to enter into what I found out was an Artisans' display of woodworking from around the eastern part of Cuba. I couldn't believe how amazingly everything was crafted. There was a large wooden plant with carved leaves and flowers that you could detach and rearrange, creating a different shaped plant. About four feet tall, it had a price tag on it for twenty-five dollars. I knew how cheap that was for me and how unreasonable for a regular Cuban. There were gigantic birds made from shavings of cow horn. The entire display was incredible.

Before I went home I went into the Cuban shop to see if I could buy some toilet paper for the house. I knew Carlos would make a big deal about anything I bought, but on the other hand, wiping with the local newspaper wasn't my preferred option. In Jamaica, Carlos invited me over for supper every night and complained if I wanted to buy him anything. I'm the same way. I enjoy giving things to people, but hate the feeling that comes with receiving.

There wasn't any toilet paper in the shop so I went to the dollar store that was nearby and bought four rolls for two dollars. I smiled as I got onto the bike. I couldn't believe that if someone wanted to wipe with something other than the local newspaper they would have to spend over an eighth, or sometimes a fifth, of their monthly earnings just to avoid a paper cut. I came to realize that Cuba was full of victimless crimes and crimeless victims.

Where is the Water Drum?

✦

Day 14
Thursday, August 28, 2003

I grabbed another cracker out of the bag and gently spread some butter across it. I took a bite and crumbs fell into my lap. I washed the cracker down with a glass of milk, fresh that morning from the milkman, and coffee that Belicia had left for me on the table. She had gone downtown to check on how Galeno's pictures were coming along. The chubby lady from the wooden house across the street brought back over the pressure pot. Belicia had prepared congri for her the night before. Carlos had said that when he was in Jamaica, Belicia had cooked for the old woman and her husband, and now that he had returned, she continued. They weren't relatives, but Belicia had grown up in this place when it was just a wooden house. I'm sure that the old woman helped her family whenever she could, and now Belicia was able to return the favor. Belicia and Carlos had a slightly better life in terms of money, but not much. Most of the money was spent buying extra food or toilet paper and giving to those people who were unable to afford it.

I was outside washing my clothes when the old lady came back with a container full of milk. Apparently the milk had arrived when Carlos and Belicia had already left. She stood and watched me for about five minutes without saying a word. Finally she said, "Washing."

I turned to her and said, "Yes." She smiled and watched for a little bit longer and then turned away. I'm sure that she was amused that an American was hand-washing his clothes, but I was a master of the art. When first in-country, bicycling through the Jamaican countryside on a Sunday afternoon, I heard a wonderful, rhythmic "scrip, scrip, scrip," as I went by many houses. I discovered it was the sound of the proper hand washing of clothes. I spent the first year in Jamaica working on developing this "scrip, scrip" sound, developing the correct tone and rhythm. It has a lot to do with the way the hands are held when washing an article of clothing. Also, the water and air must intermix and be squeezed together against the clothing and the hands. This results in the perfect "scrip, scrip" sound that is required for cleaner, fresher clothing. After three years of practice I could do it in my sleep, with a Jamaican beat or with a slower, country rhythm. I knew in Cuba that I would develop a new Salsa tempo.

I hung my clothes on the clothesline that was tied to the roofless walls that would some day add more room to Juanita and Pedro's one-room brick house. The hot sun would quickly dry my clothes. I did miss throwing my clothes into the washer, pouring in some detergent, turning it on, and forgetting about it. But Cuba, just like Jamaica, wasn't a TV dinner type of country. Everything, from getting a glass of cold water to preparing a meal, required a lot of time and a lot of energy.

I was reminded of one of my most embarrassing moments in Jamaica. At my site in Jamaica I drank rainwater collected from my roof. One of the first things I did in Jamaica was to install a new bamboo gutter that caught the water from my roof and emptied it into a tank sitting in front of my apartment. When it rained, I would set out other containers and fill a fifteen-gallon drum, issued to all Peace Corps volunteers.

Ian trained with me when I came to Jamaica but was given a very different site for his Peace Corps experience. He was assigned a bungalow at Ocho Rios, a very popular tourist town on the North Coast. After a very good spaghetti lunch during a visit, I offered to clean up. He went into his room to get a book to lend to me and came back to find me searching his kitchen.

"Where is your drum?" I asked.

"I thought you were going to do the dishes? Now you are going to make music?"

"No. The Peace Corps issued you a blue drum for water. Where is it?"

Shaking his head, he went back into his room and returned with the drum. "Here. I still don't understand what you are doing."

I turned the drum over. "But the drum is empty. How can I do dishes?"

"How did you do dishes in Nebraska?" He walked to the sink and turned on the faucet, which looked like the useless faucet at my apartment. "There is this really cool thing called plumbing. It's like magic." He laughed about it every time he saw me for the next two years.

Around one, I decided not to wait any longer for Belicia. I decided to fix my own lunch, more crackers and butter. In the National Guard my last training had been as a cook. For two weeks at Camp Parks in California, outside of San Francisco, I learned to bake bread from scratch, julienne carrots, select a quality steak, and make a roué. But if I didn't have to cook I didn't. As I was preparing this gourmet meal I noticed that Carlos had a pretty nice kitchen. There was no cupboard. Everything from pots and pans to rice and Miguel's illegal rum was stored under the concrete counter. The counter and part of the wall had new tile on it, and the sink was new.

It was great compared to my kitchen in Jamaica. There, my old chipped sink was falling through the rotting particleboard. The countertops had holes in them, which I covered with cheap linoleum. The doors kept falling off the cupboards. I replaced the screws, but that didn't help. The doors continued to fall off, pulling the screws from the decaying wood. I tried driving nails at the base of the doors to keep them upright. I even taped them shut, and still they fell. It was like trying to nail Jell-O to the wall. On the other hand, the lady from across the road here would love to have my Jamaican kitchen.

La Universidad de Holguín

✦

Day 15
Friday, August 29, 2003

On Friday, Carlos had finished the things he needed to do at work so that he could go with me to the university. We headed out of town along *Avenida XX Aniversario*. The road started near the stadium and continued out of town. Carlos pointed out the *Plaza de Revolución* as we passed it. It looked like a large uncut football field. In the middle there was a large wall with a mural depicting important events in Cuba's history. We looked around the university. It was large, but most of it was comprised of unfinished buildings, victims of the Special Period. Carlos looked around for Tomas, but his daughter said that he had gone to Guardalavaca with some people from the school. Carlos showed me the university hotel where I might be staying. At this point I was getting excited to finally begin studying.

By January I would take long bike trips to Guardalavaca beach. My skin would be a little bit darker from lying on the beach. I would go to Carlos's house and really speak with Belicia. As Jamaica had opened up to me when I could fully understand what the people were saying, Cuba would become mine by opening up to me in the same way. I pictured myself cruising along *Avenida XX Aniversario* with the girl from the first float. Featherlike, I knew she wouldn't stress the springs in the front of the bike.

Then I started thinking about why I wasn't already assured the course. I knew that U.S. citizens were not the most popular people in the world. After the U.S. invaded Iraq, when a stranger in Jamaica started telling me what he thought, I claimed to be from Canada. Lately, *Tele Cristal*, the Holguín TV station, had been full of news about Cubans not being allowed to perform at the upcoming Latin Grammys in Miami. I didn't know any details but I knew that it was a big deal and would not help me get a class. Packing for Jamaica, I pictured beaches, palm trees, and cruise ships. Now remembering Jamaica, I saw the school in the mountains, goat farmers, and my students transplanting orchids from giant hard-wood trees. Cuba too would be full of surprises. Things both worse and better than I could imagine would become my reality.

Puppet House

✦

Day 16
Saturday, August 30, 2003

The five apartment buildings were ugly concrete blemishes built into an open area on the west side of Holguin between the community where Carlos lived and the hospital. The airport and cigar factory were further west. This was probably a rich plantation before the revolution. As Carlos's family and I approached the building where Belicia's mother lived I got the impression that I was watching one of those puppet shows where the puppets have strings attached to their arms and legs. Still too far away to see the ropes, I marveled as I saw a bicycle slowly rise up the side of the building.

In the open area we still had to cross, children were playing baseball with a stick and an orange. I first thought that the game might not last too long, but then I noticed a group of trees, orange with fruit, behind one of the apartment buildings. I decided they could play all day. Many shirtless men in sandals and shorts played dominoes and chess in front of the apartments.

Carlos stopped to talk to a friend and I was trying to figure out why these bags were rising and falling along the face of the building. A bag was dropping fast to a bicycle with a basketful of onions. The bag lowered to the cyclist's waist and stopped. He pulled some pesos out of the bag and put them in his pocket. Then he took the onions out of his basket and put them into the bag and gave it a slight tug, waved up to the woman, and rode off.

I was reminded of the many salesmen like this in Jamaica and wondered if the man selling onions from his bike was nicknamed *Cebolla* or Onion. Jamaicans gave people nicknames related to their work. My favorite person was Creamy, the ice cream man. The guy who did bodywork was named Chippy. I tried to remember a nickname for the man who regularly delivered fish to my house. I couldn't remember his nickname but I did remember that for $100 more he would scale an order of fish. This was not as bad as it sounded since $100 Jamaican was only about $1.80 American.

In amazement, I watched a rope lower to a bike. The rope was attached to the bike and a man on the fourth floor slowly raised it to his balcony where it would be safe. We climbed the steep, narrow stairs to Belicia's mother's apartment on the fourth floor. The first thing that grabbed my attention was a large display of saints. Glasses filled with rum, fresh flowers, and burning candles dominated the room. The apartment had two bedrooms, a kitchen, a living room, and a balcony. The apartment building was ugly and old but the apartments were much better to live in than most of the houses in the city.

Still the foreigner and guest, I had to sit at the table while eating Mariella's *congri* while the rest of the family sat in chairs around the TV. Mariella hovered, making sure that I had enough water and food. I smiled and nodded and smiled and nodded and smiled and nodded. I was frustrated with the attention and my lack of Spanish.

Later, on the balcony with Carlos, I smoked and complained about the attention and how I felt that I would never learn Spanish.

"Do you remember when you first came to Jamaica?" He asked in patois with his sneaky smile.

"Sure."

"Remember that you thought since English was the official language that you wouldn't get the opportunity to learn a language?"

"Yeah," I answered, switching to patois.

"Back then could you have understood anything I'm saying now?"

"No." I started to laugh.

"And did you smile and nod a lot?" Carlos continued talking patois.

"Yes. And since I left Jamaica talking patois with everyone about everything, you think that if I just take my time and relax I will learn Spanish."

His yellow eyes twinkled and his smile warmed me. *"Ever ting chris."*

Church with Carlos

✦

Day 17
Sunday, August 31, 2003

I don't worry much about religion. For one thing, it confuses me when I think about it, so I usually choose not to think about it. I just figure that if you live your life the best you can you will be alright. The whole thing about going to hell if you don't go to church and believe in Jesus doesn't make sense. I'm sure good people in China who believe in Confucius can't all be going to hell. So I think if you are kind, try to help people in need, and try to put the feelings and lives of others in front of yours, then you should be alright. I have spent a lot of time thinking about this, but now I just usually let it go. Today I was sitting in church and thinking about it again.

I knew that this day had some significance to the Catholics because this morning when I woke up, the dresser with saints on it in the living room/bedroom was covered with red and yellow roses. There were flowers outside the old colonial church which dated back to 1720 and vendors were selling candles in the street. Carlos's family and I filed into the old church and crowded into a rear pew. The service was a giant production with much smoke, chanting, and many people in robes and uniforms to welcome the bishop who led the service.

This was much different from the little Baptist churches I attended when I was growing up. I remembered sleeping through the sermons, waking up only for the hymns. I didn't go to church in Jamaica, although there seemed to be more churches per square mile than any other place on the face of the earth. I thought about the teacher of religious education at our school in Jamaica who was also a reverend at a local church.

One day while I was helping him wash his car he asked me a shocking question. "If you buy a girl a computer, should she be obligated to sleep with you?"

He was married so I thought he was joking. I responded, "It depends on what type of computer you buy her." We laughed and finished washing the car.

But one Sunday a few weeks later his wife came over to my house crying. When I asked her what was wrong, she told me that on Saturday a computer dealer called the house and wondered when they were going to receive the next payment on the computer. I knew that the couple didn't have a computer and I knew she wondered where the computer was that needed a payment.

That morning she had found a note sitting on the television. She read it while he was in the shower. It was to his girlfriend, with her name and everything. He came out of the shower, put the note in his back pocket and went off to preach. The topic of the day was probably about the terrible sin of adultery. The next day she confronted the woman at school and got into a fight. The end result was the principal telling her that she needed to go to counseling because she must be crazy. He knew that this fine upstanding citizen, who was an educator and reverend, would never be capable of such a thing. I realize that we are sexual creatures designed to procreate. Maybe that's why faith and true belief in the Bible are so difficult.

Lost in these thoughts, I was sitting with my elbows resting on my knees and my head resting in my hands. My eyes were closed and I could feel the sweat from my head trickle down through my fingers. "Brandon," Carlos whispered, "are you alright?"

I looked up at his concern. "Yes." I could feel the sweat from my forehead start to change direction and flow down my cheek. Carlos looked at me in puzzlement as I rested my head back into my hands.

Later, Carlos told me that he had never seen anyone listen to a service so attentively. I said that the songs and the sermon were interesting because I had to actually listen to try to figure out what they were saying. The whole ceremony was like a carefully rehearsed performance.

We walked up to the park so Carlos could buy Galeno some ice cream. The park was teeming with young people. We sat down on a bench and observed the crowd for a while. Carlos watched my eyes following young women as they walked by.

He leaned over and said, "You could pick a girl right now and take her home with you."

I glanced back and he could read the look on my face. "I know you don't want to disrespect any women, but we really do need to find you a girlfriend. You aren't going to be single here in Cuba; you would miss out on too much."

I frowned. "What would I miss out on?"

He turned to me and said, "The best way to learn about Cuba and its culture is having Cuba and its culture right by your side. A girl would talk to you in Spanish and you would learn not just Spanish, but Cuba itself."

He was right. I called myself a *pindejo*. I thought the word meant coward, although I knew it was also a favorite swear word that people in Cuba would use when we might use the word asshole. When I was back in the States, my dad explained it really meant "a pubic hair."

We caught a carriage home. Proving what a coward I was, I sat next to a beautiful woman and didn't say a word. I was pretty sure that the part of Cuban culture which I would have to learn from a girl would always be a mystery to me.

Bread in the Blender

✦

Day 18
Monday, September 1, 2003

Clip. Home alone in Cuba. Clip. Belicia went back to work today and I was by myself. I enjoy my own company and never really feel lonely. Clip. Carlos said that Belicia had gotten a note from a doctor friend saying that Belicia was sick so she could stay home with me last week. Clip. My foot was pulled in close to my body. I stopped trimming as I got to the big toe on my right foot. I smiled to myself and rubbed the bright red scar running up and down the front of this toe. My first scar in Jamaica was from a machete that nearly took out my eye. This was my second scar.

Struggling to fit into a new neighborhood or a new country probably leaves scars of one kind or another. Trying to be one of the guys in Jamaica meant playing cricket and football. Not football with a funny-shaped ball, but the real football played by the rest of the world. I looked silly as I shattered many a wicket attempting to learn the game of cricket.

I played soccer several years in New Mexico so I felt more comfortable on the pitch, but to fit in, I played barefoot like everyone else. On the day of my scar injury, the ball had gone out-of-bounds into some tall grass. Trying to show off my strong leg, I cocked back my leg and kicked with all my might. The ball trickled onto the field, but the swearing I did went much further. Still not practiced in patois, and only just starting to learn Spanish from Carlos, the swearing was pure American English. I raised my foot into the air and dangling from my big toe was a Lasco Corned Beef tin. The group laughed until I pulled the tin out of my toe and blood started to gush from the cut. Carlos laughed when I told him why my foot was bandaged.

Finished with my trimming, I was sweeping the floor when Miguel walked in. "¿*Agua*?" he asked.

Motioning to the fridge, I said, "*Hay polvo de refresco.*" I had been practicing that line so that I could offer people powder to make Kool-Aid.

"*Solo agua,*" he answered. "*¿Dónde está Belicia?*"

I told him that she was at work. At least I said the word for work and he nodded as though he understood.

Later, I watched TV, having done any chores I could find. Belicia joked about her house never being this clean before. But I am a cleaner, especially when I'm waiting to start something, and I was anxious to start my Spanish course. Tomas had told Carlos that we would arrange the course on the third, just two more days. The TV had nothing that caught my interest. I tried to listen to a program teaching chess, but it was too frustrating not understanding the words so I turned it off and started studying from a Spanish book I had brought with me from Jamaica.

I was soon interrupted by a knock on the door. "*Pase,*" I said.

Carlos's dad came in and greeted me. "*Buenos días. ¿Cómo estás?*"

"*Bien, gracias. ¿Y tú?*" I returned the traditional greeting.

"*Bien. Bien. Tengo pan para Galeno.*" He held out a small dinner roll. After asking about Belicia and then remembering that she had to go back to work, he said something about the bread and the kitchen. He came every day like this and put the bread into the blender and put the lid back on. "*Hasta luego,*" he said as he paused at the door on his way back onto the street.

Each day last week Belicia and I would be sorting rice when Carlos's father would come in, make small talk, and leave Galeno's bread in the blender. Each afternoon Carlos would ask why there was bread in the blender and Belicia would only tell him that she didn't put it there. Carlos told me in English that it must be the bread fairy. I wondered if his dad had wings under that baggy shirt he wore.

Pedals

✦

Day 19
Tuesday, September 2, 2003

We sat at the table in silence. We had just returned from a frustrating morning of bicycling around Holguin looking for new pedals for Carlos's bike. We had to stop frequently because the old pedals kept falling off. He would roll to a stop and wait while I then went back and picked up the pedal. He would screw it back on, knowing that it would soon fall off again. All the pedals that he thought were good enough for him were more than 200 pesos. He had argued with Belicia the past couple days about money. He said that he still had some dollars but he needed to start things like he had three years ago. He stopped drinking beers leisurely at bars, although I usually paid after arguing with Carlos about who was going to pick up the bill. I offered to buy meat but he said that if all the bodega had was eggs and rice then that is what we would eat. I told Carlos that I wanted to live like he did. I wasn't here to be a burden. I was here to live with my friend, how my friend lived. So it had been three straight days of eggs and rice.

Now we were sitting at his table in silence. He had taken the day off to buy pedals. First, at the *Candonga*, most of the pedals were the wrong kind or they wanted 300 pesos. We made five more stops at bike shops but none were the right kind or under 200 pesos. A friend had talked to a reliable person who thought he might have the right kind. If he did, he would bring them to Carlos's house. Finally, Carlos asked, "So what do you want for lunch? I'd like an egg sandwich." He slapped his hand down on mine with a smile.

"That sounds great," I said, returning the smile.

Walking our bikes back out toward the paved road, the pedal fell off again. Carlos bent over, picked it up, and shook his head. With a deep sigh, he replaced it again. Riding past just a few houses, he stopped and put his feet down on the ground. I stopped behind him, wondering what he was doing. He looked down the dirt road. Half-completed two-story houses lined the sides of the road. He then looked down the road that we were on that ran in front of his house in both directions. Children in their underwear were playing in the dirty rocky street. They were putting pieces of paper or whatever would float into the six-inch wide muddy stream that twisted back and forth down the road.

"What are you looking for?"

Carlos looked back at me. "I'm trying to see who is home and might have eggs or bread."

"But how would you know?"

"Well, I'm sure a lot of people are hungry right now and I'm looking for people carrying eggs or bread."

"Oh, I guess that makes sense."

"Let's go check this house down the road. I think that they might have bread."

I followed Carlos down the rocky road, away from his house. We stopped in front of a wooden house with its large, almost square, windows open and tied to the side of the house. I stayed on my bicycle while Carlos entered the dirt yard, calling the owner of the house. An old lady came out, shaking her head, when Carlos asked about bread. Carlos reached into his pocket and the woman vanished into her house. She came back and gave Carlos a handful of *Popular* cigarettes. He placed the pesos into her hand and said thank you.

Further down the road, past more wooden houses and two-story, half-finished brick houses, we stopped again in front of a completed brick house. Carlos called inside the house and a young woman with dark hair came to the door. Carlos asked if she had any bread. She shook her head with an "I'm sorry" look on her face.

"Where do these people get the bread that they sell?" I asked as we continued down the muddy street.

"Well, they steal it."

"But, from where?"

"They steal it from the places they work."

"The cheese you ate this morning with your crackers was illegal. Well, I mean, I bought it, but he stole it. He works at a factory that makes cheese to sell to restaurants to put on their pizza and other food. He steals some when he can. Sometimes he doesn't have any for months. Other times he sells some every week."

We stopped in front of Carlos's house and he took two cigarettes out of his pocket. He handed me one and I put it into my mouth. He pulled out a lighter and lit his cigarette and then tossed me the lighter. I lit my cigarette and watched Carlos stare at the houses around us. He took a long drag of his cigarette. The exhaled smoke drifted back over his head. I felt like a private investigator on a stake-out.

"You know, Brandon, ninety percent or more of the business you see and don't see is considered illegal. It's something I struggle with. If I raise a pig on my leftover rice from dinner, why can't I sell the pig? But the government wants to keep everybody the same even though it's not working. You know that hospital that is over by Belicia's mother's house that is still unfinished?"

"Yes."

"The government has spent enough money on that hospital to build three hospitals. In Cuba, when people are looking for a job, they don't think about how much they will get paid, they think about how much they can steal."

As Carlos finished those last few words he motioned with his head at a house about six houses down from where we were standing. Two people were heading out of the house carrying bags. "Those people have rolls in their bags."

I wrinkled my forehead, wondering if my friend had x-ray vision. I guess if you grow up with people carrying everything in plastic bags you begin to see how rice, eggs, garlic, plantain, and even rolls, sit in a bag. We peddled over to the house and called the owner. A little girl in a red dress came to the door.

"¿*Hay pan?*" Carlos asked if they had bread.

The little girl said yes and asked how many Carlos wanted.

"*Ocho,*" Carlos told her as he handed her a plastic bag.

The girl ran back into the house, returning in seconds with the bag full of bread. Carlos handed her thirty pesos. "*Gracias,*" he told her. Then he said to me, "Now we need eggs. I think I know a place. See those girls? I know where they got those eggs."

Two teenage girls nearly a block away were coming from a side street with a small sack. "Do you have telescopic and x-ray vision?" I asked.

"Yes, I do," he answered. "I just wish I could fly so I didn't need pedals for my bicycle." We went to a small brick house with a Lada parked in front of it. Carlos called inside and a man in his mid-thirties came out. Carlos asked him if he had eggs. He shook his head and said no. Carlos asked him another question and he got the same response. We turned our bikes around and headed out onto the main paved road about thirty yards away. Carlos passed a few men and greeted them. When we got out onto the main road, Carlos rode beside me.

"I think that guy had eggs but didn't want to sell any. I know those girls had eggs and he is the only one in this area who sells eggs. But sometimes people think that people who come up and ask for things are secretly telling the government who is selling things illegally. I asked him before we left if he usually had eggs available and he said no, which I know is a lie."

We went down the tree-lined road to a house about a quarter mile from the turn-off to Carlos's neighborhood. Carlos stopped in front of a man selling folded pizzas out of a cardboard box. Carlos asked the guy if he knew anyone who had eggs. The man motioned to a two-story brick house behind him. We went to the door and an old woman came to the door. Carlos asked if she had eggs and she did. She brought six eggs to the door and Carlos placed them gently in the bag with the bread. Carlos handed her forty-eight pesos, eight pesos apiece. As we rode back to the house I looked over at Carlos.

"Eight pesos apiece, that's kind of expensive, isn't it?"

"Yes, it is, but it's supply and demand. When the bodega doesn't have something, people can make pretty good money, illegally, of course.

We got back to the house and Carlos fried up the eggs and cut the buns in half. As he was shaking salt and pepper on the eggs, he looked up from what he was doing and looked at me sitting at the table.

"It took us over an hour to find ingredients to make an egg sandwich, but that's not the sad part. We spent over a day's wages on one meal. Yes, we have bread and a couple eggs left over, but it's still expensive. That is why people have to do some business on the side."

We finished the sandwiches and Carlos excused himself to take a shower. A few minutes later there was a knock at the front door.

"Is Carlos here?" asked the tall, skinny man through his black moustache.

"No, he is in the bathroom." I looked down at the pedals in his hand.

"How much?" I asked, looking at the pedals. He handed me one. The metal pedals were slightly worn but they looked better than any others I had seen that morning.

"*Doscientos veinte*." I knew that he said two hundred twenty. I had worked hard at learning and saying the numbers and was proud that I could count to one thousand. I didn't understand everything he was saying but I caught that these pedals were from Russia and were strong.

"*Un momentito*." I handed the pedal back to him and walked over to the dresser and grabbed my wallet. I pulled out eleven twenty-peso bills and walked back to the door and handed the money to him.

He handed the pedals and bolts to me. "*Gracias*."

He got back on his bike and rode down the street. I placed the pedals and bolts on the kitchen table. Carlos came in wearing shorts and still drying his back with a towel. I drank my water as he sat down at the table.

"Where did these come from?" he asked as he picked up a pedal.

"I forgot to tell you that I brought a pair from Jamaica as a gift for you."

He shook his head and gave me that "you're a bad liar" look. "How much did you pay for them?"

"One hundred pesos; they were on sale. Apparently they were getting in some new stock and needed to make room." I smiled and Carlos returned the smile. "Don't worry about paying me back; just buy me a bottle of rum for my birthday."

"Thanks, Brandon."

"So, Carlos?"

"Yes, Brandon."

"What are we going to have for supper?" We both laughed as Carlos pointed to the eggs and buns sitting on the counter.

Bad News

✦

Day 20
Wednesday, September 3, 2003

Tomas approached Carlos, wearing the face that people put on when they have to tell someone about a serious accident or other bad news. I've worn that face when I had to tell students in Jamaica that a trip we planned wasn't approved or some project we had been working on was ruined by the hurricane. Carlos was taking his lunchtime to escort me to the university to find out about my Spanish course. I could tell that Tomas had bad news. He told Carlos that U.S. citizens could only study at the University of Havana. There were people from Germany, Canada, and England beginning their courses at the University of Holguin, but I was from the U.S. and couldn't study in Holguin.

I couldn't understand the conversation but I understood the devastated look on Carlos's face. He approached me sadly and said, "If I would have known about this I would have told you not to come to Cuba. I would have told you to go study Spanish in Panama or Costa Rica. I wanted to share Cuba with you but I also know how much you want to learn Spanish. I don't want you to go through your time here wondering about whether or not you are going to get a course."

Carlos met with a couple of other people who worked with Spanish classes for businesses. Over pork *congri* and cold *Mayabe* beer in the *Candonga*, Carlos explained what he had learned. "The company is not part of the university but it is still owned by the government, and a lot of the rules that apply to the university apply to all of the other outside agencies. I'll go back tomorrow to talk to them. Don't worry. I'll get you a course."

Carlos was suffering. Still hopeful that he could find a way to get me a course he kept apologizing for not sending me to Central America. "No, my friend don't worry so much," I said. "Even if I never get a course I am glad I am here. In

Panama I would never have eaten beautiful Belicia's delicious *congri* or shared this *Mayabe* with you."

Illegal Rice

◆

Day 21
Thursday, September 4, 2003

I hate to have people go out of their way for me, so I hated that Carlos once again left work early to take me to the university. I also hated the bad news that awaited us. The people who teach private classes would have been happy for the paying customer, but said no when they found out I was a U.S. citizen. Carlos said that it wasn't anything against me or even the U.S. It was probably that they didn't want an American coming to their house because of the Committee in Defense of the Revolution (CDR).

Because my Spanish was still so limited I did not understand the importance of the Latin Grammys and how it very likely influenced their decision. I did not know at the time that the TV and newspapers were full of Latin Grammy news. The Latin Grammys in Miami were the night before this trip to the university. The Cuban superstar performers were still in Cuba, not allowed to participate. I know now how important that news was and how the Cuban government saw it as a direct attempt by the Bush administration to appease the anti-Fidel Cubans in Florida. Later, back in the States, I read an article in *The Miami News Times*. They reported that a change in status for these performers "was invoked by the one person with the legal authority to do so, President George W. Bush." Later that night I was numb. Carlos, Belicia, and I sat at the table eating our rice and plantain in silence, pondering what we would do. A beautiful, very serious girl in her mid-teens, calling to Carlos from the front door, interrupted the silence. He took the rice bucket out to her with some peso coins. Nothing else was said and we resumed eating in silence.

About ten minutes later the girl returned with the bucket filled to the top with rice. He scooped up some rice and put it into my hand. The grains of rice were about twice as large as the rice that I had helped pick through since I had gotten to Cuba.

"This rice is illegal. Not only does the U.S. have an embargo against the Cuban people, the Cuban government imposes one too." Carlos spoke angrily. "We are allowed to buy from our bodega cheap rice from the Dominican Republic or our own worst rice. All of the good rice goes to the tourist industry or private restaurants. We only get the little grains full of trash. I feel like a rat picking at the scraps. I work hard for my country and I love my country, but I need to get back more that second-rate rice."

Belicia was picking out some of what Carlos was talking about and said something to Carlos in Spanish. Carlos then told me in English. "Yeah, the bodega hasn't had salt for three months. I'll bet if you went to one of the hotels you would find salt. It just isn't fair after all the work I've done for this country. I went over to Jamaica and sent more than half my paycheck back to the Cuban government. When I come back, I can't get salt. I have to go buy it in the dollar shops. There needs to be a change."

El Valle de Mayabe

✦

Day 22
Friday, September 5, 2003

Going down the small hill, I finally built up enough speed to slide the chain on the back wheel up onto the biggest sprocket to reach the 24th gear. The warm Caribbean wind blowing in my face cleared my mind and I felt good in spite of all the ways I felt bad. The nagging worry about being in Cuba illegally had returned when I found out that I couldn't get a class at the University of Holguin. The stress of being a foreigner and not speaking the language was building. I worried about being a burden on Carlos and Belicia. My cowardice concerning women was bothering me more and more.

Earlier, sitting watching TV, it all started to suffocate me and I knew that I had to get out of the house. Carlos had talked about a park out past the hospital, so I rolled my bike out the door, locked everything, and gave the keys to the old woman across the street. The main road running west out of Holguin goes to a river valley which shares the name of one of the area's most common beers, *Mayabe*. A collective farm in the area is called the *Finca Mayabe*. Shortly after passing the hospital I passed five or six men with gigantic mounds of roses on the backs of their bikes. Pedaling, with the sweat starting to moisten my shirt, the warmth of the sun, and the red, purple, yellow, and white flowers bunched together on the bikes reminded me that life was good and worrying was a waste of time.

In Jamaica, the Peace Corps issued a bicycle to me so that I could work with farmers in the area around my school. I rode it continually. I used it to visit area farmers in order to work with them in marketing cassava and improving goat production, but I used it for other things too. For several months I rode it to the top of the mountain beyond our school every morning and watched the sun rise out of the ocean east of Kingston. I also used it to visit my Peace Corps friends, Garret and Mora, in the mountain town of Spaldings. I made the thirty-mile trip three times. It took about six hours because much of the terrain was steep and windy with very bad roads. However, there were also stretches of level riding along a river through an orange plantation. Women were always washing their clothes, with the perfect scrip, scrip sound. Then, while the clothes dried on the rocks, the women stood gossiping while their children played in the water. Back in the mountains, large black vultures would extend their wings to their full six-foot span and catch rays. Occasionally, as I struggled up a hill, a small child outside playing in front of his house would see me and start yelling. By the time I reached the top of the hill the entire extended family would be outside standing in a line, staring at this sweaty white man.

Reaching the main road to the *Mayabe* Valley, two trucks passed while I waited at the stop sign. One carried a large load of *fungo*, the small Cuban plantain, with about a dozen passengers lying on top of them. The other was loaded with oranges. This was my first chance to put miles on my bike outside of the city, and I played with the thumb toggles as I started to climb a hill. Pedaling like crazy, I tried every combination of gears.

Cruising on a level stretch, I had to stop suddenly for a horse harnessed to a flat metal trailer. No human seemed to be responsible for the horse or trailer. I took a breath, my lips parted, and the air built up in my throat. My lips came back together and I exhaled the air through my nose. I started to say something to the horse but changed my mind. As in Jamaica, animals in Cuba seemed to have the right of way. In Jamaica, the city of Spanish Town is full of goats along the roads, at the bus station, and around the city, chewing on whatever they can find. At times, security guards have to ensure they don't wander into the mall. I decided that speaking to this horse would be like trying to talk to those goats in Jamaica. It was his territory and I had to give him respect.

The *Mayabe* Valley was beautiful, with a large botanical garden full of amazing tropical flowers. I pulled into the José Martí Park and rode around a little bit. I stopped for a *cafecito* at a small café and noticed that there was a shooting range for teaching gun safety to young hunters.

The exercise, fresh air, and overwhelming beauty of Cuba had driven away most of my concerns, at least for awhile, as I headed back to Holguin.

Back at the house, a man waited by the front door. I asked him if he needed something. I couldn't understand his answer but one word sounded like mosquitoes. Carlos had shown me a piece of paper that the mosquito man comes and fills out once a month. He checked all the outside containers for mosquitoes and ensured that there weren't any containers lying around that mosquitoes could breed in. I put my bike inside and found the paper. The mosquito man checked the drums by the bathroom, lifting the ply board covers and peering inside. He was serious, no smiling and no friendliness. He wrote something on the paper and handed it back to me without a word. I'm glad he didn't ask me any questions because I doubt I would have been able to answer them. I needed to learn Spanish before he came back. I was afraid that next time he would quiz me about the length of time the mosquito stays in the larval stage.

El Coco

✦

Day 23
Saturday, September 6, 2003

The *panadero* was my alarm clock every morning around 5:30. "*Pan! Pan!*" he yelled as he pushed the cart through the rocky street. The squeaking and thumping of the wheels as they labored along always provided the beat to his melody. This alarm clock wasn't for sale, but a few pesos every morning guaranteed that it would come back every day.

As I rubbed my eyes and started to focus, Carlos grabbed three pesos for the bread. I relaxed, awake now, and studied the patterns on the ceiling; patterns from the wooden forms used to contain the concrete when the roof was first poured. This felt like home. It already felt more like home than Jamaica ever did. I had only physically been in Cuba for a few weeks but for the last three years I had lived in Cuba through Carlos's stories and photos. I was in Cuba. It was a beautiful day just like the day before and the day before that. Smiling, I rolled out of bed and headed for the bathroom. I had no idea how dramatically this day would change my time in Cuba.

As I opened the old wooden door to the outdoor bath, the cockroaches and mice scurried back into their hiding places. I was used to God's indispensable creatures. I remember one night in Jamaica that a giant rat was in my bathroom. I walked over to Carlos's house and asked if he wanted to take revenge for a childhood incident. A rat bit Carlos when he was a child, and he had to have ten painful shots, a precaution against rabies. Carlos grabbed a broomstick and ran to my apartment. Seconds later, Carlos came out of the bathroom with blood on the face of the rat and a smile on his.

This morning I waited for the creatures to grab their top hats and scuttle back into their dark corners before I removed the piece of plywood from the top of the stool. This was the beginning of my early morning video game. Standing over the single hole, I could wash the cockroaches back into the hole. It was better than the old games I played in the U.S. where the urinals usually had nothing more exciting to shoot at than cigarette butts. Yes, the action was great here in Cuba. I replaced the plywood and grabbed a bucket behind me. I stepped out of the bathroom and carried water into the kitchen to wash my hands.

Carlos started the coffee as Belicia was getting out of bed. We would enjoy the breakfast of champions, bread and coffee, again. This bread was like the French loaves we buy in the States when we want to make garlic bread to eat with spaghetti. At least it looked like that bread, but this bread was so hard on the outside that you almost needed a hatchet, and so soft, like cotton candy, on the inside that it was impossible to butter. Putting butter on this bread is like ironing a silk dress with a warm sheet of 400-grit sandpaper. If you try to butter your bread from top to bottom, the end result is a crusty, empty frame with a glob of butter and cotton-like bread mashed together at the base of this breakfast masterpiece. Most of the time, I didn't bother buttering my bread.

Carlos and I drank our *cafecitos* and ate our bread as Belicia floated around the kitchen, the old but pretty nightgown flowing with every step. This was one of those times I missed having a woman of my own.

They let Galeno sleep later than usual because they knew this would be a late night. Carlos's cousin, Lucia, flew in from Miami the Tuesday before and was hosting a party in El Coco. Lucia grew up in El Coco, as did much of Carlos's extended family. She left Cuba illegally sixteen years ago and this was her first trip back.

Belicia had to work a half-day so she took her shower while Carlos got Galeno up and fed him his coffee, milk, and bread. I made the beds and put the stuffed animals and a yellow doll back along the top of the cover. These are precious to Belicia because they were gifts from her father who died just after she was married. I grabbed the fan at the foot of Carlos's bed and positioned it by the TV. Belicia kissed Carlos, hugged Galeno, but only gave me an "*hasta luego.*"

"We'll drop Galeno off at my parents' house while we go buy some rum and razors," he informed me.

"Razors?"

"Yes, we have to shave the pig before we roast it. Today we'll have real *chicharones*. Not ones made from flour." He sounded excited so I nodded.

When Galeno came back into the house from the shower, I started putting clothes on him. "No," he told me, "I want to wear the blue shirt."

"*Bueno,*" I agreed. In Jamaica, Carlos was always showing me new clothes that he had bought for Galeno. He explained that when he was growing up, he had no option of what clothing to wear and that when he was in college during the Spe cial Period; he alternated between two pairs of pants for two years. His first time out with Belicia he had to borrow an old T-shirt from a friend. It was old but at least it was different. He wanted to give Galeno the opportunity to choose among clothing, but he said jokingly that sometimes he regretted it.

Galeno finally had clothes on and Carlos locked up the grills over the windows and the doors. After dropping Galeno off, Carlos and I headed for the dollar shop downtown. We stopped at the *guarapero* for a morning shot of sugarcane juice. We drank it slowly and let the froth coat our upper lip. There was already lots of activity on the streets. Horse carts were stopping and picking up trash. Horse carriages were carrying people to work. The pizza men were already beside the road selling personal-sized pizzas out of a box, already folded for your carrying convenience.

Downtown, we parked our bikes in a bici-park and headed for the dollar shops to buy Ron Guayabito. This sweet Cuban rum has a small guava in the bottom of the bottle.

Back home with the rum and razors, we sat down to relax in front of the television. *The University for Everyone* was the only show on. It was teaching chess again so we decided to clean and fine-tune our bicycles.

We left the house at about eleven o'clock to wait at the road for Carlos's parents and Galeno. A sister who lives with them, and her daughter, came with them. Carlos made sure we were all on a horse carriage and went back to the house to wait for Belicia. We squeezed onto the already full metal benches and rode downtown to wait for a bus to take us to El Coco.

Riding the *guagua* was always interesting. When the bus arrived, everyone guessed where it was going to actually come to a complete stop. Based on their best guess, they took offensive positions to improve their prospect of getting on the bus. It probably resembled the line at the Pearly Gates, with St. Peter as the conductor. The problem we would have was getting all six of us on the same bus without being separated. When the bus arrived, Carlos's dad pushed to the front. I followed him. The rest followed me. Trying to get on the bus, and trying not to get separated, gave me the sensation of trying to rescue a drowning person without becoming a victim yourself. We pushed and maneuvered our way onto the bus. The driver had difficulty closing the doors. We were packed tighter than sardines because in a can of sardines there's room to put tomato sauce. On this bus there was no room for sauce.

As we made our way out of town fewer people got on and more got off so that eventually we got to sit down. I was tired and sweat dripped off the end of my nose. I smiled at Carlos's mom as she smiled back. I noticed how cool and fresh she looked. I knew I was a rookie and she was a pro. Finally, we stopped and everyone still on the bus got off. This was El Coco.

Walking west on a snaking dirt road, most of the houses we passed were made of board with thatched palm roofs. I felt like I was in a new world, but looking back from a small rise, I could still see the tall telecommunications building in downtown Holguin. Merengue music poured from a simple unpainted board house with a board roof. Inside, large pots were cooking over wood in the kitchen and small *cafecitos* were being served.

Until Carlos and Belicia arrived I sat quietly and tried to be invisible. When Carlos arrived, it took him a few minutes to find me. Finally, he grabbed me and pulled me around, proudly introducing me to all of his relatives.

Carlos's Cousin

✦

Day 23
Saturday, September 6, 2003

For three weeks I had been perfecting Cuban greetings, so everything was going smoothly as I was introduced, one by one, to Carlos's cousins, uncles, aunts, nieces, and nephews. Then, as I was admiring the rear-end of a young woman in an old faded jean dress, she turned around, she smiled, and I forgot how to talk. Her shoulder-length hair was tied back and she was sweaty from working to help prepare the feast. She spoke, but I didn't. Two of the buttons were missing from the front of the dress and I caught a glimpse of her firm, slim stomach. I finally muttered the same greeting as I had for the older cousins, uncles, and aunts, but it took awhile for my heart to start going again. Later, alone with Carlos, I asked, "How did some relative of yours get that beautiful?"

He laughed, filled my glass with more rum and walked me past two domino games to a tree in the back, where a large pig was tied. Several men were preparing to kill the pig and prepare it for roasting, but they had been waiting for Carlos and his razors. Everyone had on shorts and sandals. About half wore shirts. Lucia's father stabbed the pig. It shuddered for a second and then lay still. With the same knife, he cut the length of the stomach to remove the guts. I was fascinated, but Carlos told me that my job was to carry water from the well so I only watched a little of the shaving process. They shaved every hair from every possible part and then ran a pole into the mouth and out between the back legs. Wires were wrapped around the pig until the pig would twist along with the pole, and the roasting began.

Then Carlos introduced me to Lucia, the hostess from Miami. In her early thirties, I started to talk to her in English, but she stopped me. "I don't speak English."

Through Carlos I asked how she could live in Miami for sixteen years and not learn English. She told him that since no one spoke English in her house or where she worked there was never the opportunity. I remembered back in Nebraska how people who only spoke English would say, "If they're going to live in America they should learn our language." I wondered how fast they would learn Spanish if it wasn't necessary to live.

Listening to the music, drinking rum, and helping turn the pig, I didn't notice that Carlos had gone until he came back almost an hour later. It's amazing how much Spanish you know, or think you know, when you have half a bottle of rum inside of you. I wondered where Carlos had gone. When he came over to me, he said the most amazing thing, "Carmen likes you."

"What did you say?" I asked. "I must be drunker than I thought." For some reason, the idea that Mariah Carey, my favorite country singer, was announcing to the world that she had a crush on Urckel, came to mind. Carlos said that Belicia had a girl-talk with Carmen. Carmen had gone to change and would be back.

This conversation had faded away with the turning of the pig and the drinking of rum when suddenly everyone stopped talking to watch a beautiful woman walk into the yard. The woman was wearing tight red pants and a sheer black blouse with a low neckline. Her hair caressed her soft, brown shoulders. My mouth dropped open. She looked straight at me and smiled as though she knew me. Already weak from the heat and rum, I almost collapsed. Everyone was looking at me and laughing, but I didn't get the joke. Then seeing Belicia for the first time in two hours, I realized that this was Carmen.

I was shy and stayed near the pig in the back of the yard. Everyone was dancing, so when Carlos came towards me, I knew what he was going to say before he said it. "Go dance with Carmen." Even aided by the bottle and a half of liquid courage pumping through my body, I was not that brave, so Carlos decided that the four of us needed to go for a walk. We walked back down the twisty trail to a park with swings, a merry-go-round, and many trees. I noticed all this because Carlos, Carmen, and Belicia were talking but I wasn't.

Next to the bus stop we ordered a pizza and waited in silence. Carlos finally pulled me aside and said, "Talk to her. Carmen thinks that you don't like her."

"How could I not like her? She's beautiful. I can't talk. I will sound stupid."

"Don't be nervous. Just talk. You know enough."

Carlos and Belicia held hands and walked very slowly behind Carmen and me on the way back to the pig roast. "*¿Cuántos años tienes tú?*" I asked.

"*Veintidos,*" she answered with a great smile that made me forget how old I was.

Struggling, I finally remembered and told her I was twenty-five. I said something that I meant for "three years older than you." She laughed, happily, not mean. I was encouraged.

She started talking and I gathered that she worked at a pharmacy. Back at the party we danced. Well, she danced. I probably looked like someone having a seizure. When we weren't dancing, we tried to talk but soon gave up and just sat listening to the music. I never thought communication could be so difficult. As the sun went down and the pig was removed from the fire, slow songs played on the tape player. I sat with Carmen, Belicia, and Carlos by my side.

About midnight, Lucia and her mother came to say goodbye. They said they would see me again. I finished my food and took in one more slow dance with Carmen before we had to leave. I snuck in a kiss and, pretending to be Arnold Swartzenegger in *Terminator 2*, said, "*Hasta luego*, baby." I knew I wanted to see Carmen again and I hoped she wanted to see me again too.

The Special Period

✦

Day 24
Sunday, September 7, 2003

When the Berlin Wall was dismantled, Cuba's Soviet lifeline was cut off. Cuba's economy changed dramatically, sliding into a wartime economy without a war. Cuba entered "*El Periodo Especial en un Tiempo de Paz*" or "The Special Period in a Time of Peace."

Carlos had decided to take me back down to the *Candonga* for some beer to help wash away yesterday's rum. I wasn't sure my state that morning was from drinking rum or from meeting Carmen, but the cold beer sounded good. Belicia laughed when Carlos told her what he was doing. I'm not sure exactly what he said but I caught the words rum, fresh air, and Carmen.

It seemed hotter than usual and the cold *Cristal* felt good in my hand and even better as it flowed through my system. We drank two beers slowly and then Carlos said he needed to go downtown for some toilet paper. Six people use a lot of paper and it hadn't been available in the peso stores for over a week, but before we could leave we heard Carlos's name called. Carlos answered with excitement in his voice, ran to a table, and hugged a man his age, but maybe four inches taller.

"Brandon. This is my best friend and roommate from college, Racho. Racho meet my friend Brandon. We taught together in Jamaica." Carlos introduced us and we exchanged greetings. Racho worked in the tourist industry and spoke English nearly as well as Carlos. I sat in astonishment as they swapped stories for over an hour. They started talking about the good old days, but the good old days weren't good at all. There were eighteen-hour black-outs with no air conditioning and no refrigeration. They talked about the Special Period and how they struggled together to survive it. The conversation was filled with, "Do you remember the time when…?"

One weekend, when Racho and Carlos were running low on everything except the passion for adventure, they biked four miles out to a nearby dam under the cover of darkness. Using inner tubes for boats, they floated out and netted some African food fish being raised in Latin America called Tilapia. They laughed that it reminded them of Jesus and his disciples. The nets were so full they could hardly lift them. They filled two sugar bags with the best fish and threw back the rest.

This was very illegal but their stomachs and pockets were empty. Many people did have money during this time but there was nothing to buy. When they sold the fish to the people, they felt like they were giving them something the government was unable to give them, food.

During the Special Period there were no cigarettes. Racho explained that during the time before the revolution the U.S. had turned the island into a U.S. sugar plantation so that all the good land was used for sugar. Russia also used Cuba to supply sugar, so there was little production of other crops. During the Special Period, there was no fuel from anywhere so nothing could be harvested or processed. Cigarettes were restricted to three packs a month for each adult. Carlos and Racho remembered picking through ashtrays to get whatever tobacco was left in the butts and rolling it in onion skins to make cigarettes. Carlos said they looked sorry and tasted strange.

Carlos talked a lot about riding out to area farms and gathering up as much produce as he could carry on his bike and bringing it back into town. He would either trade for the produce or pay the farmers a little for what he took. Most of the vegetables just rotted in the field because there was no gasoline for the trucks to come out and harvest them. Carlos and Racho said that they were skinny during the Special Period because they spent more than ten hours a day riding their bikes looking for food.

The Bucket and Bamboo

✦

Day 25
Monday, September 8, 2003

I had just established a rhythm; not as smooth as Carlos's, but I was feeling good about my technique. The bucket hit the water, the heavy knot tipped the bucket sideways, the bucket sank, I pulled on the rope, relaxed a little so that the bucket was full to the top, and then pulled the bucket up to me to empty into the second bucket. However, when the drum was about half full, the bucket plunked like it was supposed to, the bucket tipped sideways like it was supposed to, but when I pulled to straighten the bucket, I got a lot of rope with no bucket. Looking down into the well I could see the bucket sinking slowly out of sight. I swore and thought how much the bucket and I had in common; sinking to the bottom with no way to get out. The heavy knot had untied itself. Like everything else right now, this sucked.

Carlos and Belicia were at work and I was home alone again. Since I couldn't fill the drums I just sat on the couch and felt sorry for myself.

Hating to feel sorry for myself, I thought about my water system in Jamaica. When I moved into my apartment at St. Faiths, the gutter to catch water from my roof was broken, so one of the first things I did was build a new one.

I saw a large stand of bamboo along the road when I arrived there. It was about two miles down the winding dirt road. I took my cutlass and walked, with purpose, down the road. I passed children playing in the road with juice box cars. Cars the children make by using sticks as the axles, bottle caps for the wheels, and an empty juice box as the body. They stopped what they were doing, smiled, and watched me walk by.

I reached the stand of bamboo that rose like thin fingers eager to touch the clouds. I was amazed to think that this plant is classified as a grass. The piece I chose to chop down was about forty feet tall and about eight inches in diameter. Believe me, I looked for a smaller piece but this was it. As I took my first swing and hit the bamboo, two things occurred to me. One, this was going to take longer than I had anticipated, and two, I needed to learn how to sharpen my cutlass. After about fifteen minutes and the formation of numerous blisters, I had the bamboo lying on the ground. It took another 15 minutes and more blisters to chop off my eight-foot piece.

With my hands now numb and starting to bleed and my clothes soaked with sweat, I labored to balance the bamboo on my shoulder. I took some dry banana leaves from a nearby plant and wrapped them up to provide padding on my shoulder. I started down the road. After about a mile my body ached and the sweat was making my eyes burn but I had to keep going. I had four children following me. They never said anything. They just followed. As I turned to go down the road to my house the children stopped. I threw the bamboo down by my house and turned back to look at the children. I smiled and waved to them. They waved and then ran off, pulling their cars behind them.

When I left Jamaica, my bamboo gutter was black and mold-covered, but it still worked. At the thought of the mold I went back to feeling sorry for myself.

My plan to study Spanish in Cuba looked hopeless. It had been great meeting Carmen, but I couldn't imagine that she had any interest in seeing me again. Disgusted with myself, I left the house key with Miguel and went downtown to try again to call my parents. Astonishingly, my call went through and Mom picked up on the first ring.

"Hi, Mom."

"Brandon, how is everything? We've been hoping you would call."

"Everything is great," I lied. "I haven't started my Spanish lessons yet but I will next week. Things seem to go slow down here, but you know that from your time in Honduras. I'm having a great time with Carlos and his family."

"Are the women beautiful?" Dad asked from the second phone.

"Even more beautiful than Carlos had described." I laughed. "But I'm just enjoying them from a distance. It's expensive to call so I'd better go. I'm alive and well. Cuba is fantastic."

"We love you. Take care of yourself," Mom instructed.

"I will, and I love you too. Bye." I hung up.

Later, back at the house, I turned on the TV and watched a program about making cigars. The narrator talked slowly and I could catch most of what he was saying. The leaves are moistened and stripped when they come in from the fields, and then they are graded by color and strength. When the leaves are ready, the cigar makers sit in wooden desks that look like they are from old one-room schoolhouses in Western Nebraska, beside large piles of leaves. A person in front of the room reads stories or newspapers to the cigar makers.

When Carlos got home, he called Miguel's little brother over to climb down into the well and get the bucket. Then Carlos opened a bottle of Miguel's rum and asked me if I had been thinking about Carmen. I threw down a shot of rum feeling the burn go down my throat and the fumes float back out my nostrils.

"Well," I finally answered, "I've been thinking more about not having a Spanish course, but yes, I've also been thinking about Carmen. I think that after you made us take the walk that things went smoothly."

"Smoothly?" Carlos laughed. "It might have gone okay, but I sure wouldn't describe it as smooth."

I sat up and demanded, "What do you mean, it didn't go smoothly?"

"You didn't have to watch yourself dance," he said, laughing and sipping more rum.

"Do you think she enjoyed herself? That's a much more important question."

"Yes, she enjoyed herself and I can guarantee that she will call you."

"I hope so, but I still won't be able to talk."

"Sure you can talk. Just keep the bottle of rum close to the phone and everything will be fine."

Carmen Comes to Town

✦

Day 26
Tuesday, September 9, 2003

It felt as though my hair was crying as drop by drop the sweat rolled down my forehead. The miniature tributaries merged under my bottom lip, causing a Niagara Falls-like confluence from my chin. She probably felt like she was sitting next to a snowman that was melting in the tropical heat. I was melting but not entirely due to the heat. Carmen came in, sat down beside me, kissed me on the cheek, and put her hand on my leg. These things are not supposed to be a big deal but I could not help but sweat.

When she walked in, I felt as though I was reunited with an old friend after a long separation instead of seeing a near stranger after only three days. Carlos's mom had been sick so Carmen had moved in to help her around the house. Some of her friends working with her in the disposal of biohazardous material had gotten ill, so she was very happy for the excuse to quit her job. Carlos had told me that she was coming over and that I should ask her to go downtown for a drink.

It was already nine o'clock but I did what Carlos told me to do. "*¿Quieres salir conmigo?*" I hoped that was "Do you want to go out with me?"

She hesitated and said, "*Demasiado tarde.*" I was sure that meant it was too late.

"Carlos, she said it was too late." I didn't tell him I was relieved. I didn't know what I would say to her if we were alone. I needed Carlos, my security blanket.

Carlos began rapid-fire Spanish with Carmen. Talking back and forth, I thought they were both asking questions because every sentence started with "*por qué.*" I found out later that it means both "why" and "because."

"Is it because I'm white and can't dance?" I asked. It was great being able to speak in English so that Carmen couldn't understand me.

Carlos looked at me and shook his head. "All the women are the same. If you don't want to go out they want to go out and if you want to go out they're too tired." Glancing at Carmen on his way to the kitchen, he quickly returned with a bottle of rum.

"If you guys are going to stay here you are going to drink and watch a movie. You're not going to sit there like two statues." I assume he said the same thing to Carmen in Spanish.

Carlos started *The Count of Monte Cristo* on the VCR and headed to his parent's house to get Belicia and Galeno.

Passing the bottle back and forth, Carmen took very tiny sips. "You don't like rum?" I asked in my best Spanish.

"*Poquito*," she answered, and I knew that meant "not too much."

Sticking to Spanish, I was hoping I asked, "What do you like? Do you like beer?"

"*A veces.*" And again I knew what she meant.

There was a pause. Five seconds went by, then ten. I wanted to get up and dance. I had a conversation in Spanish. Okay, it was only four sentences and it was about alcohol, not philosophy, but I would take it. I put my hand on top of her hand and folded my fingers between hers. She looked at me and smiled.

"Do you want to go out tomorrow night?"

She looked at me and smiled, "Yes."

"I have a bicycle. Carlos's mom's house, seven o'clock?"

I didn't know how to say, "I'll swing by at...," or "I'll pick you up at...," but she did say, "*Sí.*"

Carlos and Belicia came back with Galeno. Galeno sat on my lap, smiling, and pointing at my hand interlocked with Carmen's hand. I couldn't understand what he was saying but Carlos and Belicia laughed. Carmen darkened a shade which made her even more beautiful. After the movie was over I walked Carmen back to Carlos's mom's house and gave her a kiss good night. That night I didn't worry about whether or not I would ever get a Spanish course. All I could think about was what I would talk about the next night. If nothing else, I could ask her if she liked rum. I pictured the night passing where we kept repeating our sixteen words over and over. I needed to talk with Carlos.

Counting to 1000

✦

Day 27
Wednesday, September 10, 2003

Rolling my bike through the living area, Carlos was laughing at my nervousness. "*Vaya con Díos*," he said.

"I don't need God," I answered. "I need a Spanish dictionary."

"You'll be fine. Just don't be home before eleven."

"*Gracias. Hasta la vista.*" I rolled the bike out the door and headed to pick up Carmen.

Earlier, when Carlos first told me that I couldn't come home before eleven, I almost choked on my rice. "Eleven o'clock, that's four hours! What the hell am I going to talk about for four hours?"

"It doesn't matter what you talk about. Just be with her for four hours. Have her teach you the numbers up to one thousand."

"But I already know the numbers to one thousand."

"Good, she will be impressed." He went outdoors to pay the man for the two-pound block of white, squeaky cheese he had gotten earlier that evening. When he came back, he repeated, "Seriously, Brandon, I don't want you home before eleven o'clock."

To calm my nerves I practiced counting in Spanish. The road to Carlos's mother's house was full of muck and large rocks so I had to pedal slowly and concentrate just to stay on my bike. Arriving a few minutes before seven, Carmen was standing outside waiting. She signaled that I needed to come inside with her.

"*Buenas noches,*" I greeted Carlos's father as he stood up and shook my hand. He had been watching a novella on TV. I thought about the bread fairy as he returned my greeting with the smile which seemed to be a family trademark. Shorter and thinner than Carlos, he had an "I've worked hard my whole life" look about him. His face was friendly, but badly scarred. Carlos had told me that they lived in Banes, about forty miles east of Holguin and close to the ocean, when Carlos was young. His dad had stacked a large load of wood about six feet high onto the back of the bike. Coming down a hill, his brake cable broke and he lost control. He crashed into the ditch. He walked three miles home, bleeding and dragging his mangled bike.

Apparently the reason Carmen wanted to come back inside was that she wasn't done freshening up. She sprayed on some of her cousin's perfume and told me she was ready. I stood up and shook hands with Carlos's father again and gave Carlos's mother a kiss on the cheek.

With Carmen on the frame between my arms, I went slowly through the puddles and around the rocks, out to the main road that goes into downtown. Picking up speed on the good pavement, the breeze picked up Carmen's scent. She leaned her head back onto my shoulder.

"You smell good," I tried in Spanish.

She laughed lightly and I hoped that I had said it correctly. I had heard Carlos say, "*La comida huele bien*," as Belicia was cooking. He told me that it means "the food smells good." I had replaced "*comida*" with "*tú*." As we neared the town center I noticed that it was nearly vacant. It was a Wednesday night and there were only a few bikes and no cars in the streets.

I got out of the bike lane, signified by a white line along the street, to make a right turn at a stop sign. "Where are you going?" Carmen asked in Spanish.

I thought to myself, I have heard this sentence numerous times but what does it mean? I then remembered that every time Galeno runs out of the house into the street, Belicia asks this same question. As I responded, I probably felt like Galeno feels, hoping for approval. "There." I pointed to the house with the door open. "*Bici*-park."

She looked back at me and smiled. "No, primero vamos a la casa de mi tía."

I nodded as though I understood, and asked, "Where?"

"*En linea recta.*"

I didn't understand. I knew she had said "*tía*" and I knew that meant "aunt." I knew she was pointing to go straight ahead instead of turning. I decided to play because I was sweating like a pig and needed to loosen up a little.

"*¿Dónde?*" I asked again as we slowed down at the next intersection.

"Straight," her hand and then finger pointing straight ahead.

I started turning right.

"No, Brandon, Straight."

"What, left, right, straight?"

I pedaled my bike in a circle in the middle of the intersection. I went around several times, repeating, "*Estamos perdidos.*"

"No," she laughed. "We're not lost, but you are loco."

I stopped turning in the empty intersection and went down the street she had indicated the first time. After a few turns and a few straights I was completely lost, but apparently she was not. Finally, she indicated that I should stop at a white, corner house with an open door, covered by a locked metal grill. A short, stout old lady with bright red hair and thick-framed glasses came to the door. I had been introduced to Damita at the party in El Coco and remembered her name and face. I also remembered that she was wearing bright red lipstick, carried an umbrella, smoked like a chimney, and drank more rum than most of the men.

Damita opened the grill with a smile that said how happy she was to see us. Like Carlos said a long time ago, "In Cuba, the bike is the first thing into the house." Carmen reached back, grabbed the frame, and handed the bike up to Damita. I went in after Carmen. Damita gave me a kiss on the cheek and a big hug. Lucia was sitting watching television, smoking a Salem. I thought to myself, she must have brought a suitcase of those with her from Miami because I don't think they sell them here. Carmen and Damita went back into the kitchen and Lucia started complaining about the television.

"Only three channels." She said "three" in English and held up three fingers.

I was still amazed that she hardly spoke any English. My dad tells me that many Mexicans in Omaha, Nebraska, are too busy with their lives to learn English, so I guess it shouldn't be too surprising that in Miami, a melting pot of Latin America, learning to speak English is optional.

"In Miami I have 234 channels."

"Do you have a dish?" I said "dish" in English, but she understood.

"I am ready to go back to Miami."

"Why?"

"I'm tired of wiping my ass with newspaper."

There had been a shortage of toilet paper in Holguin. Carlos was bringing home pieces of typing paper from work so we didn't have to use newspaper. Most of the time, when there wasn't toilet paper in the Cuban shops, there was some in the dollar shops, but the last few days there hadn't been any available anywhere.

We left the bike at Damita's house and walked to a small restaurant nearby, *La Begonia*. We had walked silently almost five blocks together, hand-in-hand, and I still didn't know what I was going to talk about. The night was cool, but a small kiss on the cheek as we sat down had me sweating again. Begonias, red and white, dangled like tentacles from the arbor above.

"What do you want to drink?" I finally asked nervously in my best Spanish.

"A soda."

I ordered a beer and a *TuKola*. She started asking about whether or not I had a girlfriend back in Jamaica. I hadn't had a girlfriend but I knew she didn't believe me. Romances are much more casual in Latin America than I am comfortable with.

"Do you like me?" she asked.

"Why are you asking?"

I thought that maybe Carlos told you to go out with me."

I was stuck. I didn't know what to say. I lit a cigarette. I mean, I knew what to say, but not in Spanish. I just said, "No, not Carlos."

"Then who was it? Belicia?"

I decided to say, "Un voz de mi corazón." I had learned "*voz*," "voice," just yesterday. I had been working on body parts, so I knew heart, "*corazón*." Plus, it's a word I hear regularly when I listen to novellas on TV.

She laughed and blew smoke at me.

We tried to communicate through charades. I talked about my family a little and about my life. It was limited, but I knew enough words that she could kind of understand what I was saying. It was amazing how you can still be a cheesy romantic with a few words.

After a few more beers, I became more fluent and came up with a joke. I am good at coming up with situational jokes in English, but when you don't dominate a language, it's difficult, so I was proud of myself. Carmen was drinking Cuba's most popular soda, *TuKola*. The name is made up of two Spanish words, "*tu*" and "*cola*." "*Tu*" is the familiar form of "you" or "your." "*Kola*" is like the "Cola" in CocaCola but can also mean "tail" or "butt." "*Quiero*" is used constantly for "I want," but it is also used for the romantic "I love."

Preparing to order again, Carmen said that she wanted another *TuKola*. I said slowly, "*No, yo quiero tu cola.*" She gave me a quizzical, shocked smile so repeated, "*No, yo quiero tu cola.*"

She slapped my hand, laughed, and told me that I might be learning Spanish too fast.

We walked back to Damita's house at about eleven-thirty. After some small talk, Damita locked the grill behind us and told us to be careful in the street. Carmen kissed me on the cheek a couple of times as I pedaled back to Carlos' mother's house.

Straddling the bike, I told her she was brave.

"I had a great time. Why do you think I have courage?" She asked.

"Because I don't speak Spanish very well it's difficult to talk."

She gave me another kiss on the cheek. She said that she was going to her mother's house but that she would be back on Friday. I pulled her close and gave her a long kiss on the lips. I felt like I was melting. We pulled away and I looked into her eyes. She kissed me. "*Adios, Zorro.*"

Zorro. What the hell did that mean? Did it mean "fox"? I wasn't sure, but I was brave too, so I changed the gender and gave it back to her. "*Adios, Zorra,*" I said as she was opening the door.

She laughed and went inside.

I walked the bike slowly back to Carlos's house, holding on tight so I wouldn't float away. It had been a good time. No, a great time. She didn't even have to teach me the numbers to 1000. If she was willing to go out with me again I still had material.

Carlos's Work

♦

Day 28
Thursday, September 11, 2003

"I don't know if this school has a home economics class, but they wouldn't need ovens to bake their cakes, they could just set them on the desks."

"Yeah, the fibrous cement roofing works exactly like an oven. We need cooler classrooms," Carlos answered me, as we entered a classroom in one of the three schools that Carlos supervises. Carlos had pedaled home on his lunch break to eat with me. He said that he didn't want me to be sitting home alone dreaming about Carmen, and he wanted to show me the school.

"Carmen who?" I asked.

The children were outside playing when we looked in at the classrooms. The school had five rooms, all full of old desks and very clean. Each had a blackboard and a television set.

"So, Carlos," I asked, "What are you doing today at the school?

"I'm writing the guidelines for the teachers, among other things."

"Why are you writing everything out? Can't you use the computer?"

"The schools have computers but no printer."

Carlos was copying a document in pen. It looked like he had finished about twenty pages and had about thirty more to go.

"It would be nice to have a printer, huh?"

"Yeah, every year we have to recopy these things. We make a few changes, but it's basically the same."

The children came in for their afternoon classes so Carlos and I went outside to have a cigarette. He showed me the school garden. "Every school has a garden. Here we just grow herbs and flowers because we have to have a garden. The country schools grow vegetables to feed the children for their lunch.

Cuban Cooking

◆

Day 29
Friday, September 12, 2003

Carlos adjusted the burning logs under the large black metal pot. The liquid was bubbling around the large pieces of pork. He took some broth in a large spoon, dumped it into his left hand, blew on it, and then sipped it up.

"More salt and pepper," he said as he grabbed the chopped green peppers sitting on a plate and threw them into the pot. The salt was in an open bowl. He tossed two pinches into the pot.

The party was for Lucia, who would be flying back to Miami in a few days. The lady next door was getting water out of a tank beside her house and Carlos offered her a piece of pork that he wasn't going to use in the stew.

Always smiling, Carlos's mom came out of her house and glanced into the pot. "*Más agua. Un poquito.*" Put in more water.

Carlos added a touch of water.

"Smells good," I said from behind Carlos. "I've always told you that you should open up a restaurant."

Carlos laughed. "Yeah, but I'm still learning things from my mom."

"I thought you already knew how to cook well enough."

"Everyone in Cuba is trying to relearn how to cook and other things."

"What do you mean, relearn?"

"Well, during the Special Period we lost a lot of our culture. We ate to survive. We didn't think about whether or not something needed more spice or more salt. If we had something to eat we ate it. Most spices were simply not available. Now I'm trying to learn from my mom and figure out the way the Cuban food should taste."

In Jamaica, Carlos always complained about cooking, but he cooked really well. He prepared many Cuban dishes for me and I loved them. In Jamaica spices were cheap and he used a lot of cumin. Cumin is still expensive in Cuba. For many meals, I would bake something simple in my toaster oven to take to his house and he would prepare *congri* or soup. I'll never forget the first time I ate his coconut drops. He just cooked freshly shredded coconut and sugar together until it started to get stiff, and then dropped spoonfuls onto a banana leaf. Simple to make, but wonderful to eat.

Carlos tasted the broth one more time. "Perfect, I think. Mom!"

Carlos's mom came out and Carlos placed a drop of liquid into her hand.

"Perfecto," she said with a smile on her face.

Still floating from my Wednesday evening date, food wasn't really the first thing on my mind. "Carlos, do you know where Carmen is?"

"Yeah, her mother is sick so she is staying there. You never told me, how did the other night go?"

"It went well, I think. I dropped Carmen off at nine. Then I pedaled around until midnight so you would think I stayed out late enough."

"Liar." He laughed and stirred his soup. "No you didn't. My mom called me at eleven o'clock wondering what time Carmen was coming home, so I know you didn't drop her off at nine."

"What did you tell your mom?"

"I told her that you would be home when you ran out of words to say."

"But, Carlos, that wouldn't take very long. You know that."

"There are a lot of numbers between one and one thousand."

The pork was perfect. We ate it with rice, cassava, and a small salad. We passed some rum around. Santiago talked to me about his work as a security guard. "Boring, but the pay is okay, two hundred and fifty pesos per month."

As Santiago was leaving for work, Galeno came in with some guinups. I had grown fond of these rose apples in Jamaica and was excited to find them in Cuba. About the size of a cherry, each green pod grows on the end of a stem. When a person bites into the green skin and sucks out the single seed, their mouth is filled with a tingly tart strawberry taste. The light yellow flesh comes off the seed, which is then spit onto the ground. Both in Cuba and Jamaica children pick guinups and sell them in bunches when they are in season.

A Dollar Restaurant

◆

Day 30
Saturday, September 13, 2003

"It's jail, Brandon. Even if we're only a peso short, they can put us in jail."

I had just made a remark about washing dishes, but quit smiling when I heard the seriousness, near panic, in Carlos's voice. This was not a great way to end such a great day. Since I had been one month with Carlos's family, he wanted to celebrate in a special place, just his family and me.

A 24-hour dollar restaurant, *El Tocororo*, is on the east side of Plaza Calixto Garcia and he insisted it would be a great place to relax and celebrate. From air-conditioned comfort and comfortable chairs one could see the Plaza and the traffic. We ate spaghetti and pizza while Galeno rode a mechanical dolphin and tried to talk Carlos into getting him a stuffed animal from the coin machine with the claw on the end of a crane. He quit bothering his parents about the stuffed animals when Belicia took him to the ice cream cooler.

Carlos's eyes are so clear that I tried to read the reflection of the bill in their gray yellowness. This was the first time since I'd gotten past the airline people in Kingston that I'd thought about jail. I couldn't make out anything from the reflection. I think his intensity was sucking the numbers into his mind so fast it made them blurry. What went wrong?

"Carlos, how much is it?"

Instead of answering me, he asked, "How much money do you have?"

I pulled out my wallet and counted my money. I had told him while walking the two blocks from the bicycle garage before we entered the restaurant that I had five dollars.

"Five dollars."

Carlos, still clutching the bill, refusing to let Belicia see it, reached for his wallet. He counted his money.

"Seven dollars."

He put his wallet back into his pocket. He continued scrutinizing the bill. "This can't be right."

He finally showed the bill to Belicia. Belicia started to add the bill in her head.

"Brandon, the bill is for thirteen-fifty. That means we are a dollar-fifty short. That means jail. It doesn't matter if it's a peso short."

He took back the bill and once again said, "This can't be right." He rested the bill on the table.

"Carlos, do you have money back at the house? I do."

"All right, look, I have some money back at the house. I'll go back and get it."

He looked at Belicia. Our conversation had mostly been in English but Carlos talked fast and often said things first in English, then in Spanish. Belicia understood and the "*carcel*" didn't sound good to her.

Carlos grabbed Galeno, who had ice cream on his cheeks and chin, from under the glass-topped table. He had been sucking the remnants of an ice cream bar from his fingers, oblivious to what was going on. I figured they would be gone thirty minutes. He would have to walk three blocks down to get his bicycle, pedal two miles home, get the money, wash Galeno's face, pedal two miles back, return his bike to the bici-park, get his number for the bike, and walk back to the restaurant. Belicia, an accountant, was still studying the bill as Carlos left.

"Can I see it?" Belicia handed me the bill. I looked it over. Four pizzas, then three beers, then two more beers, then spaghetti for Belicia and an ice cream for Galeno. I looked up from the bill. Belicia was looking at me.

"It's you," I said jokingly. "A pizza, and spaghetti."

She smiled.

"I know. I don't know what's wrong with me. I eat, and then fifteen minutes later I look in the fridge, nada. I go back to the fridge ten minutes later, nada. I don't know."

She did eat a lot and I knew why. The list of work she does at the house, washing, cleaning, cooking, carrying water from the water truck, chasing after Galeno goes on and on. She was thirty-one and still Cameron Diaz slim. Women in Cuba worked hard and few had extra food. I poured the rest of the beer into the glass cup in front of me. As I raised the cup to my mouth, Belicia extended her hands that were folded on the table and discretely moved them up and down, like she was helping to land a helicopter.

"*Dispacio*," she whispered.

I smiled and took a teensy weensy sip and put the cup back down. The amount I took into my mouth, if dropped by a syringe, at shoulder height, would have evaporated before it hit the ground.

Belicia laughed. She reached over and lifted Carlos's beer can. "*Tome un poco más. La cervesa de Carlos es medio llena.*"

I continued sipping as slowly as possible, not exactly understanding the words, but getting the idea that I could slowly sip what Carlos had left after I slowly sipped mine.

To ease the silence Belicia started a conversation that we had before. "How many brothers and sisters do you have?"

"I have three brothers, one is older and two are younger. I have a sister. She is younger. And you?" I responded in Spanish.

"I have three brothers, two older, one younger."

"Do you want to have more children?"

"Yes, I want a girl. However, the house is too small. If we are able to finish the house then hopefully we can have more children."

"Your house. In the past. Like the one." "*Cono.* Shit. *Clot.*" I could cuss in three languages but I couldn't ask a simple question in Spanish. Why couldn't I say, "You know the house you lived in before you tore it down and built the brick one? Was it like the one across the street?" If it worked with Carmen it could work with Belicia, hand motions, pantomime, charades. Belicia smiled patiently, waiting for me to gather my thoughts.

"Okay." I felt that I was ready. "Your house." I placed a beer can down on the table. She nodded her head. I made a motion with my hand, "the road." Again she nodded her head. "A house." I placed another beer can across from the other. I went over everything. "*Tu casa, la calle, una casa.*" I think she understood everything, but I needed more. I thought of the woman Belicia has probably known for her entire life. I looked back at Belicia. "*La mujer vieja, con pelo aquí.*" I grabbed my chin. Belicia laughed. She understood. The old lady could probably grow a fuller goatee than I could.

"Your house, the same before?" I asked her in English.

"Yes, it was difficult. We needed more, with Galeno." Her English was getting better than my Spanish.

As I was about ready to get up and dance, and start saying, "Send me into the deepest part of the Amazon. I can communicate with anyone," Carlos walked in. He was sweating, but he was also smiling. He picked up the bill again. "Yeah, I was right, they did overcharge."

I was thinking to myself, "How did he know this," but he read my mind.

"I was thinking about everything and adding it up in my mind. Look."

He showed me where they had overcharged a few cents here and a few cents there. In total, it was exactly fifty cents. He called the waiter over and they fixed it.

"Brandon, you have to be careful. They will do that. Yes, it was only fifty cents, but think if they do that to enough customers, they've made more money in one day than I make in a month." Carlos was whispering angrily in English. "Plus, they're getting paid two hundred and fifty pesos per month. It doesn't matter how much the bill is. If the bill is large, they think they can sneak in an extra fifty cents. If it's a beer, five cents. Tourists won't notice, but they also do it to Cubans. They do it in peso shops. They shouldn't do it to anybody, tourists or Cubans. That's one thing I don't agree with. I know that stealing rice from my company and selling it to the Cuban people is wrong, but stealing money from people is worse."

Belicia couldn't understand the torrent of English and it was making her nervous. She nodded toward the police lounging in front of the restaurant, but Carlos went on. "I know it sounds stupid, but you do have to think about whom you are hurting. Yes, we take stuff from the government, cheese, rice, eggs, bread, meat, cement, steel, beans, everything. We resell it to people who need it. But the government puts us into these situations. We are not stealing so we can buy a television or a new car. We are stealing so we can eat meat during the week, so I can buy my son a new pair of shoes. All we want are the basics."

I think that the threat of jail and the waiter trying to steal fifty cents released a lot of things that had been bothering him since he had returned home from Jamaica. I smiled, although I was a little uncomfortable and worried about him. He smiled back and relaxed. "Do you want another beer?"

"Do you have enough money?"

"We could drink all night and still have change."

I was thinking about saying "Unless we get overcharged," but I decided it wasn't a good idea. Belicia had started smiling again. On his way back with the beers, their eyes met and held for a moment. They both smiled a smile that left out the rest of the world. Putting the beers on the table, he walked to the freezer and took out some ice cream. "This is for you, my love." He placed the ice cream in front of her and gave her a big kiss.

Watching Carlos and Belicia the rest of the night was beautiful. I realized that Carlos and Belicia didn't get married because Carlos had a nice car, nice clothes, jewelry, or lots of money. They got married in the Special Period when the times were the toughest. What they had wasn't for sale, at any price.

A Shirt for a Friend

✦

Day 31
Sunday, September 14, 2003

I was at the age where I hated my parents because they didn't understand me. I was fifteen and had been caught shoplifting three pairs of pants. I don't know if it was the discussion about jail the night before that got me thinking about my youth. It took me two days to finally rid my fingertips of the black ink. However, I was never able to rid my stomach of the sick feeling that resulted from seeing the sad and disappointed looks on my parents' faces. I felt that same disappointment and sadness in myself. I didn't need what I had taken. I hoped that being here in Cuba and trying to fulfill a dream would make my parents proud.

I remembered this shoplifting incident when Carlos described Rose's family. "He and his wife come from good families. When I say good families, I mean that if they found a yellow peso in *la calle* or a José Martí blowing around *la casa* they would try to find the owner."

Yesterday's worry about jail and being arrested had me thinking. In Jamaica, Carlos and I had spent many long nights working through many bottles of rum. We had talked about everything. He talked about Castro and seemed to respect him. He hated the frustrating poverty of Cuba, but Cuba was his home and he loved it. The intense poverty and hunger of the Special Period was hard for him to talk about, but he talked about it. When he talked about the way Cuba was in the early '80s, he made me think of heaven, maybe better. Fear about saying the wrong thing? Jail? He never talked about friends being put in jail unfairly. He didn't complain about the lack of freedom when talking to me about Cuba.

Since last night I had been thinking a lot about jail and the fact that as an American in Cuba, if I went to jail I might stay for a long time. I didn't know then that the following day I would be thinking about jail even more.

Carlos's parents lived a few blocks from Carlos. We visited often and I was especially anxious to visit them since Carmen had come to stay with them. Carmen was sitting on my lap when Rose, a neighbor from across the street, came in and sat down next to us. Like every woman in Holguin, she was beautiful, with a great trim body, a little taller than Carmen, maybe a volleyball player when she was younger, maybe a volleyball player now. She certainly looked like she could jump and hit. She was probably about the same age as Belicia and Carlos. Every time I saw her she had on one of two dresses. Their house was in pretty bad shape even for this neighborhood. Instead of some brick walls, the house was constructed entirely of mismatched boards put together with wire and string. Her husband rarely wore a shirt.

I remembered the first time I came to this house she had been outside sweeping barren dirt with a broom made from twigs tied together. I smiled and was taken back to Jamaica and the first time I had seen this sweeping of dirt. Leaves and loose dirt are swept away, the stiff broom leaving streaks in the clay.

I put out my cigarette and passed the ashtray to Carlos's mom. Carlos worked on his parents to quit smoking and drinking coffee. They just told him that they were going to die of something and they felt that not having a smoke or a *cafecito* might kill them. I whispered sweet nothings into Carmen's ear. She smiled when I told her she smelled nice. She elbowed me hard when I practiced a new word and told her I wanted her butt.

Rose hadn't said anything after "*Buenas tardes.*" Galeno jumped on my unoccupied leg when he came in with Carlos and Belicia. He smiled at me and told his dad, "*Brandon besó mi prima.*"

Carlos smiled, agreed with Galeno that I was indeed kissing his cousin and invited me outside for a smoke. He handed me a *Popular*, the same filterless, strong, occasionally spit the tobacco off your tongue, *Popular*, that I had in my pocket. I knew he wanted to talk.

We walked outside and leaned against the big avocado tree beside the house. In Jamaica, my Environmental Club had rescued orchids from lumbered trees, potted them artistically in old bark and sold them. I had learned about orchids and recognized the ones growing in this tree. Unfortunately, they weren't blooming and wouldn't bloom until after Christmas. "Have you seen Rose's husband?" Carlos asked.

"I haven't seen him today, but I've seen him across the street sometimes, by his house."

"Well, I promised him some clothes and I forgot. I gave some of my clothes to my cousin in El Coco. Then my friend in San José needed..."

"Carlos, I am your friend, Brandon. I am the Darth Vader of the black market. I am the dark side." Playfully I cut Carlos off because I knew that he would go on until the orchids bloomed. The orchids would be a beautiful sight but I just wanted Carlos to tell me what he wanted. Every time Carlos came home, Christmas or summer, he made a list of things to take back to Cuba. A bookbag for his niece, a baseball cap for his friend, clothes for everybody, electronics for cousins, and the list was usually longer than Santa's.

Carlos laughed again. "Rose's husband needs a dress shirt for an interview. Now he works as a crop harvester, but he is trying to get a job driving a truck. Obviously, in Cuba it doesn't matter what you wear. You've seen me go to work in a pair of blue jeans and a shirt, but he is a little nervous and it never hurts to look good. Plus, he can wear it for church or fiesta. I just gave my mom a pair of pants and some shoes, but right now I just don't have an extra shirt.

"Carlos, I have two he can have. No problem."

Carlos relaxed a little, even though he never relaxed much. Then he told me how Rose and her husband came from good families, the kind of family that would look for the owner of a lost peso. "I'm not saying that is a bad thing, but…"

"Da people dem jus wicked nice." I cut off Carlos.

"Ya dun kno," he responded in patois and laughed.

"Mom helps when she can," he went on with a smile. "They won't even raise a pig because it's illegal. They wouldn't do like I did and just start building a new house, even if they had a million dollars. They would wait to get a building permit because the house is owned by the government. Do you think I could have built my brick walls if I would have done paperwork and waited for permission? I was tired of rain coming in through the wooden walls. I was tired of cooking outside. I'm not proud that I bought the cement illegally, the bricks illegally. I did get some paperwork done so it looked legal, but I did the paperwork illegally. They won't do anything that is against the law, so that means having nothing but a very poor house and enough food to survive. Invention is how we survive. We have to trade to make money. We're not doing anything bad, but it is illegal. We just sell meat for dollars or trade rice for something nice."

My dad has warned me that the worst culture shock I would experience would be when I returned to the States after three years immersed in Jamaican poverty. I thought, "Carlos is experiencing culture shock now, after returning to his country." I knew Carlos's work at his schools was stressful and getting to him. I started getting ready for another long night.

"When does he need the shirts?"

"I just want him to get this job. His family needs the money. They are such good people."

"When does he need the shirts?"

"Tomorrow. The interview is on Monday."

"No problem. Is there any rum left over from Lucia's party? I think we need to play dominos."

Immigration's Machete

✦

Day 32
Monday, September 15, 2003

"Carlos will be fined one thousand, five hundred dollars."

I heard a machete chopping off large branches. I blinked. I didn't understand. "What?"

The immigration officer, congenial when I first came in, was now cold and distant. The machete whipped through the air. "Carlos will have to pay one thousand five hundred dollars, United States dollars. Also his house could be taken away because you have stayed with him."

I blinked again, perhaps trying to draw myself out of this nightmare I was having. The words I heard chopped off my future. *Swish.* I couldn't say anything. *Thwack.* I couldn't navigate my mind around what I was hearing. *Swish.* I put my mind in reverse. *Thwack.* Dazed, I went back to how the day had started.

I have breakfast planned out and I'm still lying in bed. Life is pretty good. I know that there is coffee and warm milk in the kitchen. There are crackers in the fridge. Everyone is already gone. Galeno is at school. Carlos and Belicia are at work. I'm in Cuba, a little headachy from another long night, but okay. The back door by the kitchen is open and the sunlight is creeping along the bed up towards my face.

I think it's about seven-thirty. I need to go pick up Carmen at nine o'clock because I will renew my visa today. I'll need her to watch my bike when I go to the immigration office. Also, the more time I spend with her the more time I want to spend with her. Juanita comes in through the kitchen door carrying rice from the bodega. She tells me to get up and I do. I drag myself to the kitchen and hear her climbing the metal stairs to the roof. I mix my coffee and milk and grab the crackers out of the fridge. As I nibble at a cracker I am thinking about the day ahead. I hope renewing my visa goes smoothly. I finish my crackers and down the rest of my coffee and milk.

I grab my towel off the back of the chair and head for the bathroom. I grab the small piece of mirror Belicia has on the dresser. I take off my shorts and hang them on a nail. I splash water onto my face and lather up some soap in my hands. I spread the soap on my face. I catch a ray of light, coming through the boards of the bathroom, onto my face and begin to shave. I pick out a light blue, short sleeve dress shirt and a pair of nice blue jeans. I get dressed and find my passport and my visa. It's eight thirty.

I take my bike out of the kitchen and lock the back door. I give the keys to Juanita and she wishes me luck. I twist down the dirt road, avoiding the trash tractor with its flat-bed. I turn right and pass two narrow roads with houses jetting upward. I turn left down the next road and go down the block to Carlos's mom's house.

Carmen is waiting outside. "*Pase adelante. ¿Quieres un cafecito?*"

"*Sí, mi amor*," I respond, trying to sound charming.

She smiles, puts her arm around me, and gives me a kiss on the cheek as we walk into the house. After the *cafecito*, Carmen and I walk the bike to the road and she climbs onto the frame. I keep the bike in low gear so that Carmen's ride between me and the handlebars won't be too rough. She smiles and chatters happily. I nod and pretend to understand. Even though I don't always understand everything she is saying, her speaking is like a beautiful song. It is something I want to hear when I open my eyes in the morning, and it is a timeless lullaby that can put me to sleep at night. I never want it to stop.

I love having Carmen with me, but I don't like having people wait on me, so I promise to be right back. "*Volveré pronto*," I say as I hand her my pack of cigarettes.

I climb the stairs to the office for foreigners to renew their visas. There are four people ahead of me. One by one they go into the office and minutes later come out. I think to myself that this is going to be a breeze. I enter the office and the immigration officer is sitting behind the desk. He has neatly trimmed hair and mustache and he is in his mid thirties. I sit down, say good morning in Spanish and politely ask if he speaks English. With a smile, he says that he does. I say that I'm here to renew my visa. He asks what am I doing here in Cuba and I say that I'm trying to get a course in Spanish. He then asks me where I am staying. I say with a friend. He takes down his name and address and then leaves the office and goes in the back. After waiting twenty minutes, he comes back and swings the "machete" that has me in this daze.

When he returned, he was not friendly. He still had neatly trimmed hair and mustache but he looked different. "We have a problem. First, you are staying a an unauthorized location. Visitors to Cuba must stay in a private authorized house or a hotel. For someone to stay with a Cuban friend, that would have to be approved before that person came into the country. Second, you can't study at the University of Holguin without permission from Havana. If you were from some other country maybe you could get a private tutor, but it is very difficult since you are from the U.S."

I listened carefully, my heart breaking. "So what can I do?"

"We are going to extend the visa for a month. If you don't have a course by that time you will have to leave the country."

"I understand." I was thinking that this wasn't that bad. I knew already that I couldn't study at the university, and I was pretty sure I could secure a course within a month. Then he took the giant machete and chopped off every good thought. Carlos would be charged one thousand, five hundred United States dollars and they could confiscate his house because I had been staying there. He swung the machete and I couldn't think.

"Señor Valentine, Señor Valentine. Are you okay?"

Struggling, I asked what he had said.

"Carlos will be fined one thousand, five hundred dollars. Also, his house could be taken away because you have stayed with him. Did you pay any money for staying in his house?"

"No. Carlos is my friend. He invited me to stay with him. I know that Carlos would have done the paperwork if he would have known that he needed to ask permission."

The officer wrote for a long time while I sat in shock. "Here is a copy of our conversation," he said finally. "Can you sign it?"

I signed it and he signed it.

He wrote again, less time this time. "Here are the charges against Carlos. Please sign here."

I signed it, and he signed it.

"Now, to stay in the country one month your visa must have stamps. Go buy them and I will sign your visa. Maybe you can get a course at the teachers' college. Why don't you want to study in Havana?"

"I don't know anyone in Havana. I have a friend here."

"Yes, I understand. I talked to Carlos's sister-in-law. Remember you must not stay in his house another night."

Silence Means Yes

✦

Day 32
Monday, September 15, 2003

I went into shock when the immigration guy said they were going to take Carlos's house. The afternoon of drinking beer in order to get dollars to buy stamps for my visa had dulled the shock a little, but now something more shocking was happening. I thought it was happening, but I couldn't believe it. Carlos, Carmen, and I were standing on the paved road a football field distance from Carlos's house. We were looking for a good *bici*-taxi to take us, Carmen and me...us, Carmen and me...us, Carmen and me...no. This couldn't be real.

A taxi stopped. It was an old red Chinese bicycle from the beginning of the Special Period when there was no fuel in Cuba. A padded metal office chair with a footrest was welded to the frame of the bicycle. A third wheel was welded to the outside of the chair. I put my bags on the rack sticking out the back from beneath the chair. Carmen sat in the chair, put one bag on the footrest, and held the rest of her things. Carlos gave us each a hug and we were off to my new apartment with my new roommate. I was really in shock. How did this happen?

In shock after almost two hours with the immigration officer, I had walked down the inside steps, wondering if Carmen would be waiting. I was still amazed that any girl that beautiful would be interested in spending any time with me. It seemed every young woman in Holguin was beautiful, and because of the diet and the bicycles, even those who weren't beautiful had great bodies. Carmen was more beautiful than most. At the fiesta, both men and women often stopped in the middle of a sentence or the middle of a beer to watch her. Why would a girl like this be waiting for me?

Carmen was sitting on the curb next to the bike. "*Hola.*" She looked up with her great smile as though I had only been gone a minute.

"*Lo siento. Yo need to comprar stamps.*" She laughed and took me to the post office. She laughed more when she found out I needed stamps for my visa. We went to the bank and there was a gigantic line.

"*Que rápido.*" She smiled when I returned in less than a minute. Rather than make Carmen wait longer, I decided to come back later for the stamps. We grabbed a pizza and coke and for the first time since I met her Carmen was quiet and serious. She knew I couldn't enjoy silliness so she just quietly held my hand. After dropping her off at Carlos's mom's house I went back to Carlos's house and talked with Juanita. She said she told Belicia the situation. Carlos was working at a school in the countryside so he couldn't be reached by phone. I went back downtown and, after an hour in line, started to buy the stamps. I had them in my hand, but when the cashier saw my *Peso Convertable* dollars, she took them back and scolded me for not knowing that I needed U.S. dollars.

Carlos's house was empty and now Belicia had the keys so I couldn't get in. It was two o'clock. I had plenty of *peso convertable* dollars because whenever I needed pesos I bought some and they gave me the rest in "*convertables*," pronounced "cone—bear—TAH—blace." I knew that the *cambio* banks wouldn't change them. I thought maybe if I went into a dollar cafeteria and bought a beer, then maybe the change would have some U.S. dollars. The U.S. dollars and the "*convertables*" were randomly mixed. In seventeen dollars change I might get four U.S. and the rest "convertables." I was fairly lucky and it only took five different cafeterias and five beers to get my twenty-five U.S. dollars.

I went back to the bank and pulled on the door but it wouldn't open. The door said the bank closes at three o'clock. I looked at my watch and it said two, fifty-five. This was obviously not my finest hour. I took a few steps away from the door and leaned against the peeling paint of the wall. I looked up at the intense sun. I felt it turning my already sunburned face to a deeper red. Perhaps it would hide my anger, guilt, and shame. There was only one thing I could think to do, so drink another beer before I go find my friend whose life I had just ruined.

I walked down the crowded street to *La Begonia*, where Carmen and I had spent our first night out. It was an open-air bar with begonias hanging from wires above the tables. I sat down, ordered a beer, and lit a cigarette. I took a long drag from my cigarette and plopped my hand back on the table. I wished I was the smoke lifting away from the hot, frenzied end of the cigarette. I wish I could spiral upwards, dance among the hanging begonias, and then vanish out into space. I wish I didn't have to go see my friend.

I slowly walked back to the *bici*-park, got my bike, and went back to Carlos's. I was half drunk and sweat had turned my light blue shirt dark soggy blue. Carlos, sitting at the table, looked up with his wonderful eyes and told me it would be okay as soon as I walked in through the back door. All I could say was "Sorry."

After hearing my story, Carlos sent me back to the immigration office to explain. The officer saw by my fatigue, sadness, and defeat that I was telling the truth. "Come back tomorrow," he said in English.

Carlos always took immediate action when there was a job to be done, so as soon as I showered, we went to see Aunt Damita. Tiny and full of energy, she had lived in downtown Holquin most of her life and knew everything that was happening. Finding a room for the American would not be a problem. The first four houses she led us to were full. Then we went to see Victoria, who had a three-story apartment building one block from the main central park. Victoria's son said that he had a room available, but Victoria was at work. We were told to come back at seven o'clock.

Carmen went with us when we returned to look at the apartment. Victoria took us up to the third floor and showed us the room. I was still in shock from the news about the money and Carlos's house so I paid no attention. It had two beds, hot and cold running water, a balcony, and a closet. She said that the room was usually twenty-five dollars a day, but because Damita was her friend, she would give it to me for twenty.

Riding back to Carlos's house, the most unexpected thing in my young life happened. The beer and Carlos's chatter had me almost relaxed. Carmen and Carlos were talking and laughing, but I wasn't listening. I couldn't have understood much if I had tried. Then Carlos asked in English, "Are you going to ask her?"

"Ask her what?"

"Oh, you know. Remember what you were saying about Carmen last night?"

"Oh no. I was just joking. She wouldn't."

"Ask her. Ask her."

I didn't ask her bravely. I just asked because the shock and the beer had dulled my brain. If I had been conscious, I would never have asked. "*Carmen, ¿quier quedar conmigo?*"

Carmen was silent. I figured she was trying to think of a good way to say "Maybe, if you were the last man on earth, but probably not even then."

"See," I told Carlos, "she doesn't want to. Or maybe my Spanish was so bad she didn't understand."

"No," Carlos laughed, "you asked perfectly. In Cuba silence always means yes."

"Is that true?" I asked.

Silence...silence...silence..., and then she started laughing and nodding her head. Now I was really in shock.

And that's how we ended up going together to my new apartment on the plaza in downtown Holguin. We arrived at the apartment house and took everything up to the room. We did the paperwork and Carmen had to give Victoria her national I.D. card so she could write down the number. Carmen and I were smiling the whole time. After that was finished, we both took showers. It had been a long day. Life does have its ups and downs. As I turned out the light, I thought to myself, "At least I can end this day in the arms of a beautiful, smart, amazing woman. This can't be real."

Carlosito

◆

Day 33
Tuesday, September 16, 2003

Carmen squeezed into the large metal box, off-white and fading, made in Russia a generation ago. I watched her hand two pesos to the bus driver, and then lost sight of her as she was swallowed by the crowd of standing passengers. She was going to go to her mother's house to get a few more clothes and make sure that her mother was feeling all right. It was Tuesday morning, and she would be back on Thursday. Missing her already, I was thankful that she was with me the night before. I appreciated many things from the night before, but what I kept thinking about was the captivating glow of her deep green eyes. That glow could make a man walking across the Sahara forget about thirst. Last night that same glow made me forget about what the day had been like.

Normally the immigration office wouldn't be open on Tuesdays, but Carlo said that if the officer said to come back on Tuesday, it would be open. It was almost nine o'clock and I took my bike to a *bici*-park near the church downtown. I walked across Calixto's park, headed for the bank. Since the bank was just opening, there were no long lines, so I bought my two stamps without incident and went to the immigration office. The stamps were small, with "$5" and "$20" printed black in the middle of some bright colors. I was glad that I had gotten there just as the bank had opened because I didn't want to keep the officer waiting. He knew what time the bank opened and he knew that I probably wouldn't get to the office before ten. He would be waiting for two hours. I quickly got my bike and went to the office. There wasn't anyone outside the office. I carried my bike up the steps to the top office, for foreigners. I sat outside the glass door where he could see me from his desk. I sat there for about five minutes when he came back to his desk from a side room and sat down. As he sat down he looked up. He motioned for me to come into his office. He was still neatly trimmed, but today, apparently being his day off, he was wearing a polo shirt and a pair of jeans.

I smiled as I entered the room.

He replied with the same greeting.

Now he spoke in English. "Did you buy the stamps?"

"Yes." I slid the passport, stamps, and visa to him.

He put the stamps on the visa and marked the top with a seal. After signing and putting the visa into the passport, he slid it back across his desk to me. As I picked it up he said, "Remember. You have one month to find a course."

"Thank you." I was thinking of asking about Carlos's situation, but decided that I would just leave it alone for now. "Um, thank you." I also didn't want to hear something that would make me feel worse again.

I biked back to my new home, opened the front grill, and parked my bike in the main bottom room. I climbed the three flights of stairs to my third-floor room. As I entered the room, I took off my clothes and put on a pair of shorts. I opened the balcony door and sat down on the bench outside. I put a cigarette in my mouth and lit it. I sat there, breathing. The sun penetrated the begonias in some areas and a ray of light was warming my thigh. I thought to myself and laughed so I wouldn't cry. Fifteen hundred dollars and confiscate the house. How could Carlos not have known about the law? Maybe it was passed within the past three years while Carlos was working in Jamaica. I don't think there is much television coverage or any debate about changes in the law. Also, Carlos had never accommodated foreign visitors. Maybe that's why he didn't know the policies of private houses, public houses, or hotels.

I put on the clothes that I wore the day before. The light blue shirt was full of sweat and salt stains. The pants were dirty from the bike chain and everything else. I stepped into the largest shower I'd seen in more than three years. The bottom of the curtain brushed against the tiled lip as I pulled it closed. There was only one tap for water, so I opened it to see what would happen. The water was immediately warm. Then I saw that the shower head warmed the water. There was a blue dot on the right side and a red dot on the left. Near "*tibia*," in the middle, I found my temperature, grabbed the bar of soap, and started scrubbing the clothes I had on. The last time I had taken a warm shower was one of those rare days in Jamaica when the barrels beside Carlos's kitchen had been warmed by the sun.

Ever since I began hand-washing my clothes I had wanted to try this, and it worked well. I finished scrubbing down every inch of the pants and the shirt. I took them off and cleaned my skin. I rinsed off my skin, and then the clothing. I wrung out the clothing and then dried off myself. I put back on the pair of shorts and went to the closet and took a new blue robe out of my bag. Carlos had told me I would need this at the university. I thought it would be okay to try it out here, outside on the balcony of my "*casa privada*." I hung up my clothes where tourists who stayed in hotels could see them and sat back down on the balcony bench.

Trying to decide between a Super Hamburger and a pizza for lunch, I passed a stand selling "*bocaditos*." The vendor took my five-peso bill and handed me back a one-peso bill of José Martí. The sandwich wasn't that bad. It was soft bread with pork meat and three pickles. The *helado* of the day was chocolate. The last few days it had been pineapple. I handed the ice cream guy the change from the sandwich and got twenty centavos back. The little glob of ice cream on the brown swirl shaped cone only took about three licks. It was gone quick, but it was satisfying. I knew my parents in Omaha would appreciate a call, but especially now, what could I say? Maybe the *Populares* would kill me before I had to talk to them. The pack of *Populares* cost seven pesos.

Carlos stopped by the house around four o'clock on his way to pick up Galeno from school. We both avoided talking about our problem. He asked how I was doing and laughed about my laundry operation. As he was leaving, I called down to him on the street.

"Hey, Carlos." He looked up to the ledge of the balcony.

"Did Rose's husband get the job?"

"Yeah, he got the job. Thank you," he said, smiling as he rode away.

Later, a knock woke me up. "Come in," I managed.

A skinny, bald head with a smile wrapped around it, stuck itself in and asked, "Do you want to drink some rum?"

"What time is it?"

Cuba looked at his watch. "Nine-thirty."

"Yeah." I stood up as I answered.

"I will be downstairs."

I put on my khaki pants and an old blue dress shirt and kicked my feet into some slippers by the door. Cuba was waiting on the street. We entered a small workshop attached to my new home and sat down in old folding chairs by a table cluttered with tools and wood. Immediately Cuba handed me a small glass of *Corsario*. A thin, short man, old enough to be Cuba's father, came through the door. "*Buenas tardes*." I stood and shook his hand.

"*Soy Pedro. Bien venidos a mi studio.*" The words came from a smiling face with warm brown eyes and dark black hair cut off straight just above his bushy eyebrows.

We sat down in silence, enjoying the rum, until Cuba asked if I would help buy another bottle of rum. I laid two dollars on top of the two-fifty in his extended hand. He gave one back to me, closed his hand, and left.

Pedro asked the usual questions. Why was I in Cuba? How long was I going to stay? Did I like Cuba and did I like the rum? My Spanish was getting good enough to understand these questions and have answers in Spanish. Then he said, "*Mi hijo habla inglés.*"

Pedro spoke slowly and clearly. I understood that he had a son that spoke English.

He continued. I didn't understand everything, but I could pick out words and piece the sentences together. Pedro said, "I told him that there was an American that was going to come over and drink rum with us. He jumped right into the shower as I was still talking to him. His name is Carlos."

Another Carlos, I thought. Pedro showed me the artwork hanging on the walls. Most of it was by his father, who had just recently died. Pedro said that he painted like his father but he was also a sculptor and a woodworker. One piece, a rooster, was so detailed and perfect that I could almost hear the "cock-a-doodle-doo." Then Carlos came in, his hair still wet. In his early twenties, he was a little taller than his father, but he had the same hairstyle and same build. He introduced himself in perfect English and told me that he had been studying English for a year. Pedro got up and left the room, letting us talk. In English, he asked me a lot of the same questions that Pedro had asked. Cuba brought back some *Guayabito*, slightly sweet rum with a small guava at the bottom of the bottle, placed it on the table with his giant, wrap-a-round smile and a "*Buenas noches.*"

Carlosito (I called him little Carlos so I wouldn't confuse myself) and I talked until the wee hours of the morning about everything. He asked a lot about the States. We agreed to help each other with our languages.

When we were finally talked out, he said, "Come to the CDR party tomorrow." Looking at the small plastic electric clock, he smiled. "I guess it will be today." He laughed. "We are celebrating because we have the best Committee in Defense of the Revolution. The CDR takes groups on vacations, makes sure that all of the children go to school, and makes sure everyone is watching out for everybody else. You can come and dance and drink more rum."

"Sounds great," I answered as I slipped from the shop back up to my apartment.

The Philosophy of Don Pedro

✦

Day 34
Wednesday, September 17, 2003

"Sorry about my father. He doesn't drink that often so when he does, he talks on and on." Carlosito offered me a cigarette. It was late, the end of a long day without Carmen. A day spent wondering if my night with her had been real or some sort of delirious dream.

I smiled and showed him the one I had just pulled out to light. We sat there filling the street with smoke, thinking about what Pedro had said. "I remember when the streets were filled with smoke from the vehicles, before the revolution. Now that's the only smoke that fills the street."

I stayed in my apartment all day, happier now because Carlos had called. Around six, I was still trying to sleep when Victoria knocked on the door and handed me the white cordless phone from her bedroom. I smiled when I heard Carlos's voice, but my smile faded when he told me how things were working out. The news about his house was good. "An empty threat," he called it, but he was mad at himself. He had invited me to Cuba and instead of having fun I was feeling guilty and depressed. He felt bad that I was going to have to spend so much money to keep him out of jail. "You should have gone to Costa Rica to study, Brandon. Then you wouldn't have had this problem."

"The money doesn't matter, and I'm still glad I'm in Cuba. I'm just glad they didn't take the house you've been spending all your money on for the last three years," I told him before hanging up.

Anyway, I felt better and worked on the Spanish Carlosito had given me. At lunchtime I ate crackers, and then went to Damita's house for a *cafecito*. Watching an Argentine *telenovela*, I laughed when the father told his teenage daughter "*Nunca. Nunca. Toda su vida. Nunca va a salir de la casa.*" Grounding for life and other empty threats, seems to be universal.

I went back to my room to study and sleep some. When I went down to the street, it was almost sundown. The eating part of the CDR party was over. The street was roped off and Carlosito sat on the doorstep to his house. There were still a few plates and glasses on the tables but they had been pushed to the side of the table so domino games could be played under the light of the street lamp overhead. I sat down next to my new friend.

"You came."

"I don't have anything else to do," I said, as he handed me a glass of rum poured from last night's *Guayabito* bottle. "So what do you do during the day? Do you work, or are you going to school?" I asked.

"Well, right now I am studying French. I love it."

That's when Pedro came over and sat down on the curb. I could tell that he had been drinking for awhile. Nelly started singing *"It's Getting Hot in Here"* from the stereo that was set up on a chair a few houses down. Pedro told a little about the party and then asked, *"¿Entiendes?"*

"Do you understand?" Carlosito asked in English. Even if I said, "Yes," he would repeat what his father said. I think he enjoyed translating for me.

"I was born outside of Holguin about seven miles," Pedro said. "We moved to town when I was two years old. We moved to this house right here." He would pause and wait for Carlosito.

"This whole street was filled with cars." He motioned up and down the now vehicleless street. "And then, when the Revolution happened, the streets became emptier and emptier. People sold their cars and left the country, or went somewhere else. Not us. This is home. We stayed."

He paused. We passed the bottle of *Guayabito* around.

That's when Pedro said, "I remember when the streets were filled with smoke from the vehicles, before the revolution. Now that's the only smoke that fills the street." He pointed to a domino player smoking a cigarette. The smoker exhaled and you could see the smoke rise from his mouth up towards the street light, and then disappear. "In the '80s, the streets were getting busy again and the shops were full. Then the Russians left and the Special Period started. No gasoline. You walked or fixed a bike..., don't want to talk about that. That was not good."

"Now...Now we are happy. We are poor, but we are happy. We don't have a TV, but a lot of people don't have televisions. Some people in the world are never happy. They want and want and want..."

He would have probably continued saying "want," but he took a drink of rum.

He continued. "So they are never happy. This person has a television. This person has a computer. This person has a new car. This person has...." Another drink.

"So there is always pressure. Pressures from friends and family to buy this, buy that. They struggle to buy all of these things, but there is always more stuff to buy. That is why there is so much crime, because of money. Everyone wants a better life, more things, material items. They think those things will make them happy, but they never are happy. They just want and want and want."

The streets were dead. It was probably three o'clock in the morning and Pedro's cheery-faced wife was standing just behind Carlosito. She told Pedro that it was time to come to bed. He got up and shook my hand, patted his son on the back, and went inside.

Gracioso

✦

Day 35
Thursday, September 18, 2003

Struggling in oil, in a panic I turned around and around. Someone was knocking. Someone was calling my name. I could walk toward the sound but all was black. I was drowning, but I was running. I kept looking for the knocking. Then I was drowning again. I snapped to a seated position, sweat pouring from my face. I discovered I was in bed and my floral motif blanket was soaked with sweat. I blinked a few times, remembering the dream, but still hearing the knocking. The clock told me that it was 7 a.m. I opened the door.

"*Buenos días, Brandon.*" A nice gray business suit told me that Victoria was on her way to work at *Tele Cristal*, the Holguin television station. Victoria is a production manager. "*¿Estabas durmiendo?*" she asked.

I rubbed the sleep from my eyes and yawned. "No, I wasn't sleeping," I lied in my best Spanish.

I don't know if she laughed at my attempt to be funny or at my Spanish. She started to talk in English but ended up in Spanish. "There is man. He live here, in *barrio*. You go college. Nine, morning, *el veinte y tres. Hables con Solana. Ella es directora de relaciones internacionales. ¿Me entiendes?*"

"*Sí,*" I answered. I understood that someone at the teachers' college wanted to talk to me at nine in the morning on the twenty-third. "*Gracias.*"

Victoria headed for work and I lay back on the bed. Excited about the news, I wanted to tell Carlos. Relaxing, I started to sink back into the big vat of oil and blackness when the knocking started again. This time I went quickly to the door and opened it to a beautiful woman with two bags and a great smile. "*Hola, mi amor,*" Carmen said.

I grabbed her bags and gave her a small kiss on the cheek. I placed her bags by the closet and then pulled her close and just felt her next to me for awhile. She proudly showed me her fingernails. A neighbor had painted an intricate design on each nail. After I showered we walked downtown for pizza.

"After handing an attractive older woman her pizza, the pizza man turned to me with a warm smile and an extended hand. "Hi, brother. How's it going?" I'm sure he doesn't have many regular red-headed customers so he remembered me from earlier in the week.

"*Bién, ¿ y tú?*" I answered.

"I'm well. Would you like two pizzas?"

"*Por favor,*" I answered.

He pulled out the cookie sheets that had the pizzas stacked on them. The pizzas were just a little smaller than a Pizza Hut personal pan pizza. We each took our cardboard for holding the pizza and then the pizzas.

Eating on a park bench, Carmen told me as well as she could about her family and I told her as well as I could about my appointment at the teachers' college.

Walking back from our great breakfast, which we washed down with some *granizado*, Carmen said she needed to sleep for awhile, so I stopped to sit on the step with Carlosito. The Peace Corps had taught me to take advantage of any opportunity to delve deeper into a culture. Opportunities to talk should not be passed up. Heck, this was one of the reasons I decided to come to Cuba. My two years in Jamaica turned my American vision of the world upside down. I had visited Central America and some Caribbean islands. My goal was to become more than an American citizen; I wanted to be a citizen of the world.

A part of my personality interferes with this process because I really enjoy being alone and I hate to inconvenience anyone. Peace Corps taught me how important it is to take whatever is offered. At the Carnival I could see what joy people got from giving, but it was still hard for me. When Carlosito's mother asked if I wanted water, I said yes, but then I almost protested when they sent Anita, his eager little sister, for ice. She had to run two blocks with a plastic container for the ice. I was relieved when she handed both Carlosito and me a glass of water, but I still felt uncomfortable taking ice from them.

Later, in his workshop, Carlosito said sentences in Spanish for me to repeat. "*Esta sillita se hace de la madera de Angola.*"

"Angola?" I asked in English. "Why is the wood from Angola?"

"Well, in the '70s we sent soldiers to Angola to fight against the South African forces. They sent what they could to say thank you. A lot of this kind of wood. Someone gave some to my father to carve, but it isn't good for carving. It makes a good stool."

"Do you carve too?" I asked.

He showed me a sketchpad with landscapes, people, and plants. "I mostly draw. I like to do abstract stuff. Right now I'm studying French. He demonstrated some French and it sounded cool. I told him that I might get a course at the teachers' college. Then remembering who was in my apartment, I was anxious, eager, to go upstairs. I excused myself and hurried up the steps.

Carmen lay on her stomach, half covered by the pink bedspread covered with red and blue flowers. She had only kicked off her shoes before collapsing. Careful not to wake her, I eased myself next to her, held her tight, and drifted off to sleep, a dreamless sleep. Waking around two, we walked back to the park, hand-in-hand, looking for the ice cream man.

"*Hola*," I greeted him. "What is the flavor of the day?"

"*Fresa. ¿Quieres dos?*"

"*Sí.*" I did indeed want two strawberry cones.

The skinny gentleman, sitting on the wooden crate, cranked out two cones and handed them to us. Carmen's ice cream was slightly off kilter. We watched a mini-landslide of ice cream start down the side of her cone. She quickly gulped down most of the ice cream from the top of her cone. As quickly as I noticed the wave-like motion in her neck, she placed her hand over her mouth. A large smile peeked from behind her hand and I laughed.

"*¡Qué frío!*"

I smiled and agreed, "*Sí, frío, como yo en la cama las dos noches pasadas.*"

"But, Brandon, it hasn't been cold in bed. It has been very hot."

"Yes, you are right, but without you in my bed my heart is cold."

She slapped my arm and said her favorite word when she is with me, "*Gracioso.*" That word brought back memories of my first night out with Carmen under the fragrant begonias. That night she had repeated "*gracioso*" many times. I thought, "I'm not trying for gracious, kind, considerate. I was trying to be funny, enjoyable." When I got back to Carlos's house that night, I pulled out the dictionary and looked up *gracioso* and found out that she did think I was funny.

Now, though, I was serious. I didn't mean to be funny. "It's the truth." Our eyes locked and I didn't notice the river of *fresa* running down my hand. She leaned over and kissed me on the lips and then licked the ice cream off the side of my cone.

I thought to myself, "I am the luckiest man in the world." Whether I thought it in patois, "*Mi ah eh di luckiest man inna di worl,*" or Spanish, "*Tengo más suerte que cualquier hombre,*" I knew it had to be true.

El Cauto

✦

Day 36
Friday, September 19, 2003

Dimly lit, with the furniture made of wood and stretched leather, I thought of bar for Fred Flintstone. *El Cauto* is a peso restaurant named after the largest rive in Cuba. Peso restaurants do not have fancy pictures or air conditioning, but thi one had atmosphere. Just two blocks from Calixto Garcia Park, it had been short walk for Carlos, Belicia, Carmen and me from my new apartment. W decided to celebrate the possibility that I would finally get a Spanish cours because there wasn't much else worth celebrating.

We had three beers. Carlos and I had one each and the women were sharing They were talking like they hadn't seen each other for years, with special excite ment over the new design on Carmen's nails. Carlos toasted us and I returned toast to him and Belicia.

Carlos turned to me. "You can bring Carmen here once in a while. You ca probably get chicken *asado, tostones, and congri* for about thirty pesos. Plus, th beer isn't bad."

Carlos lifted his beer. It was Polar. It tasted a lot like Cristal but was cheap and was only sold in pesos. Belicia ordered a plate of *tostones*. *Tostones* are refrie plantain. Plantain which is fried, smashed, and then fried again. I had enjoye them many times in Jamaica at Carlos's house.

"Carlos, do you have enough money this time?" Belicia asked.

We both looked in our wallets. We looked back at each other, and said at th same time, "Yes," and began laughing.

"So, how do you like the room?" Carlos asked me.

"It's nice. It's not free, but twenty dollars isn't bad. Victoria said she mig lower the price to ten or fifteen dollars once I get the course. So, how is wo going?"

"Well, I'm working like a donkey, as usual. This school out in the country is killing me. It's five miles outside of town and they're fixing the road, so it's tough biking out there. I got approved for the passport and now I'm talking to my boss to see if I will be able to leave."

"I hope you get through. That way I can fly directly from the States to come see you in Jamaica."

"I don't have the permission to leave yet so let's not drink to it yet. How is it going with Carmen?"

"I think it's going great. There will be some tough times but I think she has the patience to help me through them."

"She is a good woman. Her family is kind of in a mess and she tries to help her mom. You could get a lot of women in Cuba, but all of them are *banditas*. They won't steal your money (well, some might), but most of them will want clothes, jewelry, and to go out to dollar restaurants all the time, three meals a day. But Carmen, if you take her out every once in a while, even here, she will be happy. As long as you are treating her well she will be happy."

"Yeah, I know. I forgot to thank you for introducing us."

"I thought that it would take you six months to kiss her, but you were quick. Just like learning Spanish, you have to be confident. You can't be afraid to make some mistakes. That's how we learn. And that's why I'm not very smart myself. I never make mistakes."

Carlos and I laughed and clanked our bottles together. Belicia had finished the *tostones*, with a little help from Carmen. We ordered three more beers. Belicia told us that she was getting a new accountant job just down the road from this restaurant. She was happy. The pay would be the same but the new office had air conditioning. We walked back to the room where Carlos had left his bike. I gave Belicia a kiss on the cheek and shook Carlos's hand.

"*Likkle more.*" I gave Carlos a traditional Jamaican parting.

"*Likkle more*, Brandon."

Shopping with Carlosito

✦

Day 37
Saturday, September 20, 2003

I stood with my arm around Carmen when the taxi slowly pulled away, taking Lucia back to Miami, with its hundreds of TV channels and soft Charmin toilet tissue. Damita was sobbing and tears filled Carmen's eyes. Damita told Carmen that she'd like some coffee, so Carmen and I went into her kitchen to start coffee. A green rubber hose connected a coffee can hanging on the wall to two large burners. Carmen rotated the metal knob on the side of the metal burners until a kerosene mist began to rise and she lit one burner. Carmen adjusted the flame and put a metal pot filled with water on the burner. She put three large scoops of sugar into the water. When the water started to boil, she took the pot off the burner and turned off the fuel. Then she put three large scoops of coffee into a cheesecloth funnel. She let me pour the hot sugared water through the cloth funnel. She caught the coffee in another metal pot.

It was close to noon, so I asked if a pizza and ice cream would be alright. Damita smiled and nodded. Walking back toward Parque Calixto, I saw Carlosito coming out of his house carrying three empty nail polish bottles.

"Where are you going? Did you get a job painting nails?"

"No, I'm going to get some cigarettes."

"Cigarettes?"

"Yeah, I'm going to go sell these and then buy some cigarettes. Where are you going?"

"I'm going to go buy pizzas for Carmen and Damita, and some ice cream. Do you want to come?"

"Yeah, the person I'm selling these to lives down by the pizza man."

We walked down the street, both on a mission.

"I did get a job," Carlosito said about half-way to the pizza man.

"What are you doing?" I asked.

"I'm carving ostrich eggs."

"You're doing what?"

"Carving ostrich eggs. Wait here." Carlosito went inside an open door. About five seconds later he came out.

"Money for four cigarettes. Look, I'm going by my work later this afternoon. If you want, you can come by anytime today or tomorrow."

He explained which corner building had his new ostrich egg-carving job. I knew where it was and I told him that I would come by tomorrow. We stopped and I bought four pizzas. I placed three in my bag and gave one to Carlosito. I never asked him because it was as if I had passed him a bottle of rum. He just took it and bit into it. That's what I wanted him to do. We then went and I bought some ice cream from a lady standing behind a white freezer outside of a dollar store. I bought four, put three in my other bag and gave one to Carlosito. He had finished the pizza and bit into the chocolate-covered ice cream bar without a word to me.

We stopped by a corner coffee shop. It had three blue concrete walls while the fourth wall, which would have been along the sidewalk facing the street, was a large grill instead. It had two doors. Boxes of *Popular* and *Criollo* were stacked against the wall and bottles of rum ran alongside the cash register. Everything was in pesos. There were about twenty people sitting at the bar either drinking coffee or rum. Carlosito and I were waiting to buy cigarettes when an old man wearing dirty clothing walked up and told Carlosito that he was hungry. Carlosito looked at the change in his hand. He placed the change into the old man's hand and looked up at me. "I'll be outside waiting for you."

When I made it to the front of the line, I bought two packs of *Popular*. I handed fifteen pesos to the short plump girl in a blue dress and she gave me one peso back. I tossed one pack to Carlosito, waiting outside the coffee shop. He tried to give them back. I told him that I was buying them for a friend, from one smoker to another. He laughed and said thanks.

Back at Damita's house, I put the ice cream bars in the freezer and locked down the handle. Carmen and Damita were watching *Marimar*, a popular *novella*. When they finished their pizzas, I gave them the ice cream bars.

A clank—clank on the grill brought Damita to her feet. She unlocked the front grill and let two young guys come into the house. As she was unlocking the grill that secured the door to the roof, she said, "*El puerquito está arriba.*"

They climbed quickly up the stairs. After much squealing and some cursing, they returned down the stairs, holding a small pig by its hind legs. They stuffed the pig into a plastic crate wired to the back of one of their bikes and rode away.

Ostrich Eggs

◆

Day 38
Sunday, September 21, 2003

Abstract geometric designs formed slowly under his steady hand. Beside Carlosito another carver was covering his softball-size ostrich egg with graceful palm trees. After I watched for a few minutes, Carlosito suggested we go outside for a cigarette.

"Man," I said. "I can't believe how steady you are. I know I'd be nervous and break the egg."

"They had us practice on plastic first. We use real dentist tools." Carlosito slowly exhaled smoke from his cigarette and continued. "Those shells are really thick. They aren't as easy to break as I thought they would be. I've been lucky so far."

"I'm sure I would break one. Just watching you made me nervous." I leaned against a blue part of the building where Carlosito worked. The building had many colors, depending on which of several layers of paint had chipped off. "Do you get paid for each egg?"

"I get paid two hundred and fifty pesos per month. This company sells these eggs to places in Europe for four dollars apiece. I have to do one egg every day."

"But today is Sunday. Do you have to work on Sunday too?"

"We can if we want."

"Well, I'll let you get back to work," I said, anxious not to get him in trouble.

"Sure. If you come down to our place tonight I could help you with some more Spanish and I can keep practicing my English."

Carlosito went back into the multi-colored building to finish his egg and I headed to the park to buy flowers for Carmen and Damita. For ten pesos I bought a large bunch of red and yellow roses. The ladies showered me with praise and kisses when I put the flowers in water.

Later, Carmen and I joined several housewives holding their plastic bags in front of the neighborhood bodega, waiting to collect Damita's food ration. Carlos told me that in Cuba a bag is a man's best friend. They are not discarded like the grocery store bags in the U.S. Whenever we would return from buying meat or vegetables, I would wash the inside of the bag, turn it inside out, and hang it on the clothesline to dry. Most houses had bags of many colors hanging around them.

Tele Cristal Party Invitation

◆

Day 39
Monday, September 22, 2003

Carmen and I were returning from a lunch of fried eggs at Damita's house when we met Victoria coming home from work. She invited us to a *Tele Cristal* party on Friday. The television station sponsored the best parties in town and Carmen was excited about taking me to the party.

We went upstairs and washed some clothes and watched some TV on the new black and white TV in our room. At least it was new to us. It had been new when it came from Russia in the '60s. It was fun to watch the TV shows I watched when I was a kid, but with Spanish dubbed over the English. The more Spanish I learned, the more I laughed at the translations.

I could tell by the look on Carmen's face whether or not the sentence I was writing was correct or not. I had filled up about two pages worth of sentences. These weren't complex sentences about philosophy or medical problems found in mice. They were simple, like "The fox is big," or "The fox is over there." I was focusing on two verbs, *"estar"* and *"ser."* Both are translated as "to be," but *"estar"* is used in situations that can change and *"ser"* is used with permanent conditions.

I wrote, *"La zorra es bonita."* I looked at Carmen and she nodded. *"La zorra está enferma."* Carmen nodded again, indicating that I was right. "The fox is beautiful" is a permanent condition, barring the fact that later on she may run into the three little pigs. The second sentence indicates that "the fox is sick," but not permanently.

Next I tried it orally. "Carmen *es.s.s.s.s...bonita.*" I drew out the s sound and her eyebrows raised, afraid I might turn *"es"* into *"está,"* so that she would not be permanently beautiful.

"Y tú," Carmen said, gesturing to me.

"*Bueno. Ahora estoy hablando contigo.*" I said, "Good. Right now I am talking with you." I used the right form of "*estar*" and she gave me a long kiss. It was nice getting answers correct when she was teaching me.

"*¿Y qué más?*" She asked, trying to get me to make more sentences about myself.

"*Yo soy un hombre de los Estados Unidos.*" I said that I was "permanently" a man from the U.S. and she kissed me.

"*Yo estoy visitando Cuba.*" I said I was "temporarily" visiting Cuba and she kissed me.

I thought maybe I didn't need a class at the university. I didn't believe that their grading system could match Carmen's wonderful system and I was sure that no teacher at the university would have her glorious eyes or smile.

Colegio de Maestros

✦

Day 40
Tuesday, September 23, 2003

"On your way out to the Teachers' College stay on the Avenue of Liberators after you pass the stadium. After the stadium you'll pass by three statues." Carlosito patiently gave me instructions to get to the Teachers' College for my important meeting. "The first statue is Federico Maceo. Like many of our famous leaders, he was born out here in the East. The second statue is Máximo Gómez. He was not from Cuba. He was born in the Dominican Republic. They were leaders during the Ten-Year War against Spain from 1868–1878. Cuba lost that war. They were leaders again during the War of Independence in the 1890s. That time Spain lost. The third statue is of Che Gueverra. Like Gómez, Che was not born in Cuba either. He was born in Argentina.

"I mentioned that Maceo was born here in the East. Other leaders born in the East were Calixto Garcia and, of course, Fidel. He was born near Banes." Carlosito was stroking his chin as he ended his history lesson. When complaining about the government, a Cuban never mentioned Castro by name. Instead, the speaker would stroke his chin two times, Cuban sign language for the Supreme Leader.

Rolling past the second statue the morning after Carlosito's history lesson, realized he had given me the order of the first two statues backwards. The firs statue I passed after the stadium was Gómez. The statue of Maceo was further ou along *La Avenida de Libertadores*. When I came to the statue in honor of Che Guevarra, I knew that I was still headed in the right direction. I stopped at a rec light while a city bus, called a *guagua*, and a horse carriage crossed the avenue The white bus with blue trim was already completely full of passengers and left heavy black cloud of exhaust as it strained away from the intersection. Starting up the hill going out of town, on my right there was a large open field and on my lef were large blocks of apartment buildings just like the ones where Belicia's mom lived.

Carlosito had told me that just before the Teachers' College was the Sports School. The Sports School was a large complex of gymnasiums, soccer fields, baseball fields, tennis courts, and swimming pools. The swimming pools were empty. At the Teachers' College I paid the man at the bicycle building one peso and he gave me a ticket. He tried to give me change, sixty centavos, but I waved it aside. Carlos told me, "If it's centavos, let them keep it. They will take better care of your bike.

The beautiful receptionist, with a great smile and hair neatly piled on her head, pointed down a hallway when I asked to speak with Solana. Knocking on the half-open door that said "*Relaciones Internacionales*," I was told by another beautiful young woman to wait in the hallway. I was ten minutes early and Solana was teaching.

"You are Brandon?" A plump and perky lady in her forties came to my chair, extended her hand, and spoke with a smile.

"Yes. Solana?"

She nodded. She was dressed in a light blue suit top with a skirt. A golden peacock pin glittered on the right lapel. She wore thick glasses with a chain tied to the ends.

"Come. My office," she directed me in English.

Then, seated at her desk, she asked in Spanish, "Do you speak a lot of Spanish?"

"No," I answered, as I thought to myself, "If I spoke a lot of Spanish I wouldn't need to be here."

"Well, I don't speak much English," she said, "but I will speak slowly. If you don't understand something, tell me and I will repeat it, okay?"

"Fine."

"What type of course do you want?"

"I want to be able to speak and write Spanish."

Apparently that was a good enough answer and she wrote it down on the small yellow pad she had in front of her.

"How many hours do you want to take per week?" I didn't answer so she continued, "It's five dollars per hour."

"*Uno día, dos horas. Uno semana, cinco días.*" I knew I didn't have the articles right but I hoped she understood that I would like to have the class for two hours each day from Monday to Friday."

She wrote something down. "How long do you want to study here?"

Hoping that I understood right, I answered, "Six months."

She wrote again and then told me that she would ask at a meeting tomorrow if any teacher would be available. She said that she isn't supposed to be teaching but they are having a teacher shortage right now because so many teachers and nurses were going to Venezuela. Those last words weren't encouraging.

With an appointment for Thursday, I headed back to get my bike. I passed a small group of students and my first thought was that these girls who want to be teachers were more beautiful than the girls back in Jamaica who wanted to be flight attendants. Then I realized that something had changed. I used to pick the most attractive girl out of a group and fantasize about talking to her. Now I compared them to Carmen and realized again how crazy life was. Plain, not so handsome, Brandon was living with a woman more beautiful than any of these outrageously attractive women. Unbelievable.

Back at the apartment, I scared Carmen a little by how eagerly I grabbed her. "*Jueves.*" I answered her "tell me something" look.

I held her tight until she wriggled free and said, "Carlosito is downstairs. He said he wanted you to help him with something."

Carlosito was sitting in front of the apartment with an older man with a full beard. They were looking at a magazine with ads for professional-grade walkie-talkies. They ranged in price from $300 to $800 U.S. Carlosito was trying to translate the ads for the man, an ex-police officer. The man showed me a Motorola radio pictured in the magazine priced at $500. Then he pulled one exactly like it out of his pocket. Carlosito said the man wanted a better one. The technical words they wanted help with were a mystery to me too, so I couldn't help any.

Cuddling later with Carmen on the balcony, I felt like I was lost at sea. They probably wouldn't let me study in Cuba because I was from *Los Estados Unidos* and the U.S. had not let the Cubans perform at the first Latin Grammys on network television. Carlos still might lose his house. I was lost at sea, but Carmen was my lighthouse. Her head was lying in my lap. I picked a begonia off of a vine and put it upside down on her nose.

Carmen's Shoes

◆

Day 41
Wednesday, September 24, 2003

The picture on the TV screen looked like it was torn apart and then pasted back together. "*¿Qué pasa?*" I asked Carmen.

"*Nada*," she answered, without looking at me.

As we watched *Marimar*, a popular Mexican soap opera, I kept adjusting the tracking on the old VCR but it usually only helped for a few minutes. Damita had borrowed the video set of the entire season and invited us to eat lunch with her and watch the *telenovella*. I also kept asking Carmen what was wrong, or more literally, "What's happening?" She kept telling me, "nothing," but I knew something was wrong. As we were walking over to Damita's, she started to say something several times but then stopped and said, "Nada" or "Es nada," which means "it doesn't matter."

I had been wondering how long my little paradise would last. I thought how difficult it must be to be with me, a plain looking, silly-acting foreigner if you are beautiful and could clearly attract any man, Cuban or "*extranjero*." I figured that she had finally decided that our little time together was over, and just hadn't decided how to tell me. She was a nice person and didn't want to see my heart lying on the pavement. That was what I was figuring, but I wasn't sure, and I couldn't get her to say whatever was obviously bothering her.

Coming from the kitchen, Damita waddled into the living room. After carefully preparing her end of the couch, she sat down beside me. The furniture in the living room made me think of Jenga, the game where small rectangular logs are pulled from a stack until the whole stack collapses. Before sitting down on a chair or the couch, a person needed to push the joints together and have everything aligned so it didn't collapse.

"I have *congri* and plaintain almost ready," she said with her wonderful smile which created canyons of wrinkles around her mouth and eyes. Her large red glasses sat precariously at the end of her tiny nose.

Her warm smile was infectious and I smiled back and said, "*Bueno*," or "Good." I wish I knew more Spanish so I could tell her how I really felt. I wanted to tell her that she was one of the sweetest women I have ever met and I wished could repay her wonderful hospitality and generosity.

Carmen looked over at me from just in front of the television. The TV picture was completely unwatchable again so I ran the head cleaner for the third time.

She was sitting about four feet from the screen because she needed glasses but didn't want to wear any. When I sat back down, she stared at me, wanting to say something, but silent.

"Tell me," I said. I figured if I was going to have my heart ripped out that might as well get it over with. She looked at me, shook her head, and then started watching again without saying a word. She took one last drag off her cigarette, got up from the chair, and flicked the butt through the locked grill out onto the road. She went back to the chair, aligned everything, took the pack of cigarette off the top of the television, took out another, lit it, and sat back down. This was at least her fifth cigarette this morning. Cigarettes are expensive and I had never seen her smoke this much.

"What's wrong, Carmen?"

"Nothing," she said with a quick glance to me and then back to the television.

I looked at Damita. "Women," I said. She laughed, got up, and went back to the kitchen. I looked out through the locked grill to the activity on the street. Water vendors were pushing carts with large barrels of water. Bicycles went by with pigs trotting alongside, out for their exercise, maybe. Across the street, the barber sat on the steps of his shop, smoking a cigarette and waiting for the next three pesos to walk in for a haircut.

"The food is on the table," Damita called from the kitchen. Carmen stopped the video but wouldn't look at me as we went in to eat.

The *congri* was already on our plates. In the middle of the table were two serving dishes, one with *fufu*, smashed plaintain drizzled with pork fat, and the other with sliced avocado drenched in lime juice and sprinkled with salt. A glass of water was placed in front of each plate.

"I'm sorry there is no meat and...."

"*Es perfecto!*" I interrupted Damita. I mixed a scoop of *fufu* and three slices of avocado into my Congri. It was a simple meal but the ingredients that made the food so delicious and smile-inducing were the generosity and love included with the cooking. We ate in silence. Damita finished first and went out onto the street for a smoke.

I kept glancing at Carmen, wondering about what she was thinking and when she was going to tell me that she just wanted to be friends, but she just stared at her food, nibbling some but not really eating. My knowledge of Spanish and women are about the same, enough to get me into trouble. "Let's go buy some ice cream," I said to break the silence. I pushed my chair back from the table.

Carmen looked up. "Okay," a slight smile forming on her face. I wished I could get the same answer to "Let's talk." We put the plates by the large cement sink. I had eaten every morsel but Carmen had just rearranged the food on her plate. I took her hand and we walked hand-in-hand to the living room.

"We'll be right back. I don't want your ice cream to melt," I said to Damita as we stepped out onto the street beside her.

She smiled. "Thank you." She went back inside and locked the grill.

I was wishing that I could unlock Carmen's mind and see what she was thinking about. Then I thought of another reason why Carmen was probably through with me. I think too much.

We bought three chocolate-covered ice cream bars on a stick. Eating her ice cream bar, Carmen seemed to forget whatever was bothering her and concentrated on the ice cream. A drop of melting ice cream dribbled down the side of her mouth to her chin. She tried to reach it with her tongue, but missed. I kissed the drop away.

Back at Damita's, I put her ice cream in the freezer. The old green, white, yellow and rust-colored refrigerator had an extra freezer unit welded to the outside since the original freezer unit must have died.

We sat all afternoon, watching the *Marimar* tape and drinking *cafecitos* from Damita's old red thermos. Finally, late afternoon, the sky over Holguin darkened and I could smell rain. "Damita, I need to go back to Victoria's. I have clothes outside." She nodded with a smile, not breaking eye contact with the television.

Running the two blocks to Victoria's house, we didn't get wet until I was unlocking the front door. We climbed the two flights of stairs and then back out the door on the second floor to climb the metal stairs on the outside of the building to the third floor. Rain dripped from the begonias hanging over the outside door to the room. I rescued my clothes and lay down on the bed. Carmen lay down beside me. "*¿Qué pasa?*" I asked.

"*Es nada,*" she answered.

"*Yo quiero más helado,*" I said.

"*¿Por qué?*"

"*Pongalo en tu cuerpo.*" Carmen laughed and kissed me on my cheek.

"Are you hungry?" I said.

"No, we have crackers and mayonnaise from yesterday." I loved how frugal she was but I needed to take her out for some more pizza or something very soon. My struggle with Spanish made it easy to just stay in the room instead of going out and sounding ignorant.

Later, sitting on the balcony, I watched the busy streets as people strolled, enjoying the cool evening air after the rain. Near the park, just a block away, the reflection of the corner streetlight on the wet street was cut numerous times by bicycle tires and deformed by shuffling feet. Carmen stepped out onto the balcony with a towel on her head. "The bathroom is free," she said with a small kiss on the cheek, acting as though she hadn't been acting strange all day.

In the shower I started to think about why I think so much while I'm in the shower. Maybe it's because I can't open my eyes and think about what I see. I have to think about what I can't see. I have to think about what's in my confused and wandering mind. I thought about coming to Cuba to learn Spanish as the U.S. screwed the Cuban musicians, so I couldn't get a course. I thought about coming to Cuba to be with my friend, and all the trouble that caused Carlos. I worried about his house and the money. I thought about living with a beautiful woman and why the thought bothered me. I wondered if Carmen was about to say goodbye. I still couldn't understand why she had agreed to stay with me. If she told me it was over I wouldn't be surprised. I realized then why I take such short showers. Thinking hurts.

I dried off, put on my shorts and T-shirt, and walked back into the living room, now dark. Carmen had closed the balcony door and lay facedown on the bed under the covers. Lying beside her on my back, hands laced together behind my head, staring up toward the ceiling, I said, "*Mi amor, por favor.* Tell me what's happening."

There was only silence.

"*Por favor,*" I said softly. She threw off the covers, turned on the light, grabbed her cigarettes, unlocked the balcony door, and went outside. I took a deep breath and rotated my head from the balcony door toward the ceiling, hoping what to do next was written on it. I blinked my eyes and threw off the covers. I walked out to the balcony and sat down beside her, watching her nervous smoking.

This situation would be difficult if we both spoke English. If I talk in English she'll understand nothing. If I talk in Spanish I won't be sure what I said. When she talks, I only catch a word now and then. I kissed her on the cheek and I could taste the salt from the tears that she had been crying.

If she understood English I would tell her I would understand if she wanted to leave. I wanted to say that we were friends and always would be and nothing she said would change that. It must be hard being with someone twenty-four hours a day that you can't really talk to. I know I am from a different culture and maybe I am doing many things wrong.

"It's difficult," she said, bringing back my wandering mind.

"It's okay. You have time." I took one of her cigarettes, now thinking that it was going to be a long night.

After a few seconds, she said through her tears, "I'm independent. I'm not used to relying on someone."

I thought, "Here it comes, game over, thanks for playing."

"I've never been able to ask anybody for anything," she continued.

"What is it, what do you need?" I asked. "You can ask me." I wasn't sure that I used the right verb for ask, but I knew that a run for the dictionary would definitely be a mood-breaker.

"Do you remember on Monday, Victoria invited us to go to the *Tele Cristal* party on Friday?" Carmen spoke slowly and clearly, even saying her *s*'s.

"Yes, do you need something for the party? No problem. Tell me."

"I only have one pair of shoes and they don't go with…"

"If you need shoes…." BAM, I slapped my hands together. "*Como Cinderella, tu tienes zapatos.*"

I smiled at her and she gave me a kiss on the cheek and said, "*Gracioso.*"

Pulling her close, feeling the warm tears on her cheek mingle with mine, I asked, "The whole day you were worried about asking me to buy you a pair of shoes?"

"Yes."

"If you ever need something ask me, okay.?"

Later, in bed, just before I drifted off to sleep, I thought to myself, "Maybe I should try showering with my eyes open."

Movies

✦

Day 42
Thursday, September 25, 2003

I counted out thirty fifty-dollar bills, folded them, and put them into a small white envelope. I recounted the remaining U.S. currency, also about $1500, and put it back into the manila envelope. The white envelope with the 50s went into my left front pants pocket. The manila envelope with the rest of the cash I had saved from Jamaica went into a plastic envelope with my passport, visa, plane ticket back to Jamaica, and some more small white envelopes. I kept this plastic envelope in the bottom of a small black nylon bag that was always in the bottom of my luggage. Handling the money, wishing for a safer way to keep this cash, but never thinking of one, I felt like I was in a bad spy movie.

Today, I had two errands to run before eleven. I promised "Cinderella" I would be back by then so we could go out and buy her shoes for the ball.

"¿Quieres cafecito?" Belicia greeted me with a hug, a kiss on the cheek, and the usual offer of the small cup of strong coffee.

I handed her the white envelope and declined the coffee. Using my appointment at the teacher's college as an excuse, I told her to tell Carlos, "Good luck," and hurried on my way. I felt too guilty to stay and chat. Because I was in Cuba, Carlos's reputation was hurt, we still weren't sure what would happen to his house, and we hoped this money would keep him out of jail. He argued that I shouldn't have to pay and even told me that he could go to jail. He hated to take anything from me. I just hoped this wouldn't come between us or hurt our friendship.

I knew it hurt Belicia that I didn't take time for the cafecito. Hearing her yell, "¡Buena suerte!" as I pedaled away, I wanted to go back and tell her how sorry I was for messing with their lives.

The teacher's college was even worse. With a sad face, Solana said, "We have to get permission from Havana before we start the course. I am going to Havana

150

tomorrow. Come back to the college on October 3 and I can tell you if the course is possible or not." "Good luck," she said.

I left feeling like I had the wind knocked out of me. Why did it take so long? To me it was simple. Call Havana. Tell them that you have someone who wants to learn Spanish. Find out if it is possible. If not, tell me. But maybe it wasn't that simple. I wished it were. I wished I had a course.

In the afternoon I discovered that shopping for shoes could also be complicated. Through five stores we repeated and repeated the same scenario. Carmen looked until a shoe caught her eye. She picked up the shoe, found her size, and tried it on. She took it off and looked at it some more. She looked at the price and then put it back. She did this through five stores and then suggested that we try one of the peso shops to see if they had anything.

"Which shoe did you like best?" I asked. She looked away and wouldn't answer.

I gently took her upper arm and led her back to store number two where she had spent five minutes admiring herself in a pair of black heels. I handed her the shoes and a fifty-dollar bill. Grinning, speechless, she made the purchase, and gave me the forty dollars in change.

"We can afford spaghetti." I laughed and kissed her. Eating spaghetti, I was trapped in another movie. Like Lady and the Tramp in the old Disney movie, sucking on the same noodle, we ended up kissing. Everyone in the restaurant laughed and cheered.

Tele Cristal Awards Party

✦

Day 43
Friday, September 26, 2003

The yellow paperback dictionary hit me in the side of the head and fell to the floor. Purchased new in Kingston before I came to Cuba, now it was worn and falling apart. It was falling apart for two reasons. First, it was worn, written on and torn because I was constantly looking for the way to say something or trying to figure out what Carmen said. Second, it was falling apart because, like now, whenever the words "*No entiendo*" came out of my mouth because I didn't understand, she threw the dictionary at me. Before I could respond or throw something back at Carmen, Cuba knocked on our door and said he was leaving for the *Tele Cristal* party in about an hour.

I thumbed through the dictionary. I found "*mentiroso*" and it gave me another word "*embustero*." Both had to do with lying. "*¡No es mentira!*," I yelled at the bathroom. "*¡Tú es muy hermosa!*" Oh, God, she was beautiful. How could I be with someone this beautiful. Beautiful, no matter what. Beautiful in the morning, in an old T-shirt, or beautiful in her midriff blouses and blue jeans. I wandered out onto the balcony and looked back at the long white dress she had laid out for the party. Tonight she will dress to be even more beautiful and I wondered if my heart could take it. But then I remembered last night, when she was naked and her glorious breasts stopped my heart. No clothes or make-up could make her more beautiful than that.

I focused on how important it was to enjoy Carmen and the party tonight and worked at pushing my worries away for awhile. I would try not to think about how I should be in a dorm room at the University of Holguin studying Spanish. I would try to forget the lies I told my parents last night. I would not think about spending $1500 to keep Carlos out of jail. My crazy attempts to expand my horizons seemed to have run into a ditch at the bottom of the hill, but tonight would drink and dance and enjoy the fact that plain homely Brandon was with the most beautiful woman in Cuba.

Carmen came out of the shower and I told her again that I wasn't a liar and that she was beautiful. She smiled her little half-smile which I was trying to understand with no luck at all. We kissed softly, and I grabbed a dirty shirt and a pair of shorts I would wash while I was in the shower.

After the shower, I hung the shorts and shirt on the blue nylon string that was tied from a pole at one end of the balcony to the concrete ornamentation at the other end. I went back into the room and Carmen turned toward me, worried how she looked in the white dress and new shoes. I tried to talk but I couldn't. She laughed and brushed her hair out of her face. I suddenly didn't want to go to the party. I wanted to keep my treasure here and not share her with the others. I don't understand how some people are blessed with so much beauty and others have to work so hard to achieve it; whether it be through plastic surgery or crash diets. I knew one thing. Carmen did not have to work at it. For her it was as natural as a mountain lake reflecting a full moon. Absolutely captivating, with no fillers or additives or preservatives.

Of course, I didn't seriously entertain the idea of not going to the party. Carmen had never been to a party put on by the media and her excitement reminded me of a city girl's first chance to ride a pony.

I had washed the sweat out of the blue shirt I had worn to the immigration office and my pants covered up my worn shoes. Carmen smiled that smile and said, "*Muy bien.*" That rating seemed a little high, but I didn't argue.

When we stepped out the front door, Carmen said hi to Inez, a Peruvian student who lived in the apartment building. Inez screamed and started babbling about how great Carmen looked. Inez was plump, and when she laughed, her whole body jiggled. Whenever I saw her, she reminded me of my Navajo classmates from when my parents were teaching in New Mexico. Her exclamations and laughter caused her boyfriend to turn. He actually dropped his beer when he saw Carmen, which made Inez laugh even louder. I thought of many great lines about beautiful women and ugly men, but my Spanish couldn't handle them, so I just stood off to the side and smiled.

Walking to the party, Carmen was struggling to be cool and control her excitement but several times she stopped and hugged me for no reason. When we reached the museum, Victoria greeted us with kisses on the cheeks and walked in with us. The museum was unbelievable. There were great oil paintings hanging on the wall and sculptures scattered around. In the center of the museum where there was no roof the natural sunlight maintained a small garden. Chairs were set up in front of the stage where the musicians and artists would be performing. This was definitely a museum that had a lot of tourists, but I hadn't visited because I wasn't a tourist. The walls looked freshly painted and everything looked new. We sat down at a bar in the corner of the main area. I liked the bar-in-the-museum idea. Surely abstract painting would make more sense after a few shots of rum.

"What do you want to drink?" I asked.

"A *Cristal*." She laughed at the look of disbelief on my face. For her rare drinking, I knew she would prefer the light *Cristal* beer rather than the dark, stronger-tasting *Bucanero*.

"*¿Quieres cigarillo, también?*" I asked. Again, there were so many ways to tease her about drinking and smoking if I knew the language, but in Spanish I probably didn't even ask correctly if she was going to start smoking too.

"Please, but *Hollywood*, not your ugly *Popular*." I smiled and bought one pack of each. We lit our cigarettes, sipped beer, and watched the other gorgeous women arrive. None could compare with Carmen.

The party started with an hour of comedians and musicians. I didn't understand much but I did understand the smile on Carmen's face and could laugh at the slapstick part of the comedy. Cuba joined us about halfway through the entertainment and Victoria joined us afterward, apparently done with her duties. They were selling *Cristal* from a keg now, and when I looked at Carmen, she smiled her smile and nodded. I knew that the four of us would dance late into the night. I thought briefly about my struggle to get a class and the difficulties I had caused Carlos. I did not know how horrible tomorrow would be and foolishly thought that maybe everything would be okay.

A Celebration

✦

Day 44
Saturday, September 27, 2003

As I walked into Carlos's house through the open kitchen door, my friend smiled, "*Buenos días.*" It wasn't his normal smile and his normally twinkling eyes were full of pain. He put his head in his hands and stared down at the table.

Carlos had called Victoria around midday and said that he needed to talk to me. Victoria told me that Carlos sounded different. "It was like he had something important to say but he didn't know how to say it. You'd better go see him right away." I rushed over, eager to find out what was happening.

"What's wrong?" I asked. Belicia was silent and her eye contact pleaded for help. She was standing beside Carlos, a hand on his shoulder.

"Carlos, what's wrong?"

He slowly turned to me. I had never seen him look like this. It was as if someone had stabbed him and he couldn't remove the knife or he would bleed to death.

He said softly, turning toward Belicia, "I'm going to jail Monday."

"What? But I gave Belicia the money on Thursday, two days ago." I wanted to scream this, but I knew about the CDR and that when you talked about money, or anything else for that matter, you talked softly.

"I know you did, Brandon, and I am extremely grateful."

"So what happened?"

"Some immigration officers came by the house and said that the paperwork wouldn't be complete until Wednesday. Then I can get out."

"But that's bullshit, Carlos."

"I know. The fine that you paid was bullshit too." He paused after saying this. "I think that they are upset that I was able to pay and they want to make an example out of me. Brandon, remember what I told you in Jamaica. There will be a lot of things that don't make sense to you, and there are a lot of things that I

155

don't understand, but I am Cuban and I have to do what they say. It's only for three days and I will be out. Don't worry." Carlos, as always, was more concerned about my worry than he was about himself.

"Can we drink some rum to celebrate?" since I couldn't scream, I decided to entertain.

Carlos slightly smiled and said, "What are you talking about?"

"Well, Carlos, life is about experiences and you are getting the chance to experience something new. Something most people don't get the chance to experience. Let's have a drink to celebrate."

He laughed and told Belicia in Spanish. She laughed, looked at me, and shook her head as she grabbed a bottle of rum from under the sink. Carlos took it from her, opened it, and splashed a little on the kitchen floor. We drank and hugged and I went back to my empty apartment.

Before Carlos had called that morning, Carmen had gone out to her mother's house to help with some sewing. She would spend the night so I had the evening to myself, with myself and the horror that my best friend was going to jail. He would be going to jail because I had decided to be crazy and break the law of my country and travel illegally to a country that didn't want me.

I started laughing at a new absurdity. Cuba did want me here, but Cuba the man, not Cuba the country. Cuba and I had enjoyed talking and joking the night before. He was a leader in the CDR in the area around my apartment. He had invited me several times the night before, at the *Tele Cristal* party, to a celebration they were having today. Pedro and Carlosito had continually urged me to go during the past week. Now alone, and feeling too guilty to be alone, I arrived about 7 and immediately joined the drinking.

The doorsteps were full of people watching the commotion in the middle of the street. I had been pushing down the feeling of horror since the immigration officer first told me that Carlos was breaking the law because I was living with him. Now, with Carlos going to jail, the knot in my stomach was nearly the size of the mountain north of Holguin that all the tourists climb.

Cuba was dancing with an older woman and motioned me to join them. I stepped over the rope that was tied from one corner building to the other corner building, blocking off the street. Cuba grabbed my hand and placed it in the hand of the woman. She danced gracefully and wondrously to the salsa. I was young and did neither my partner nor the music justice, but enough beer and rum had been taken that nobody cared. The woman was probably about sixty-five but her body swayed to the music like she was twenty.

Focused on moving my feet the right direction and not stepping on her feet, I was startled and looked up when everyone started yelling. The noise was in celebration of the food being placed on a line of tables. Cuba made a speech before anyone ate. I couldn't understand much but I'm sure he spoke of Cuban freedom and the 40th anniversary of the CDR. Then they sang the national anthem and waved Cuban flags.

Then we ate *caldosa* and bread. They served me beer poured from a white bucket into a plastic cup and I drank quickly each time the cup was refilled. They kept throwing more bread on my plate. I was thankful for being here and sharing in this celebration. By the time the food was finished it was time to play dominoes. I was horrible so at first I merely watched and made sure that their cups remained full of beer. It got late and soon I was playing dominoes with three guys I had never met. Since there was only one cup left for the beer we passed it around the table. At four o'clock the game broke up and I helped put up the tables and chairs before going back to my room. I had consumed enough beer that I had forgotten my pain and went quickly to sleep, still wearing my clothes, even my shoes.

Americans at Restaurant

✦

Day 45
Sunday, September 28, 2003

Carmen returned a little after noon and found me still asleep with my clothes on
When she woke me up, I told her that Carlos would be going to jail. We cried
together while she held me. Finally, feeling a little better, I said, "Let me shower
and then let's go out for a walk and some food."

Victoria had told Carmen and me about this restaurant just a few blocks away
that had fried chicken and French fries, plus three beers, for only three dollar
and twenty-five cents. The small restaurant, with only six tables, was empty when
we walked in and ordered.

While we were waiting two guys and a girl came in. I didn't really look a
them at first, but the two men were teasing the girl and it got loud enough w
couldn't help but look at them. The men may have been forty, but both were
athletic-looking, trim and muscular. The woman was younger and, like mos
women in Holguin, beautiful.

I smiled at the noise and started to talk to Carmen again when I heard one o
the men start a joke in English. I shushed Carmen and listened. At the punc
line, all three laughed loudly.

The man with his back to the table turned around and started to apologize i
English for being loud.

"Don't worry about it," I responded in English.

The other man asked, "Where are you from?"

I considered my Canada line, but said simply, "The United States."

"No shit, so are we!" the first man exclaimed. "Where from in the States?"

"Nebraska."

"Oh my God, we're sitting at a restaurant in Cuba with a guy from
Nebraska." He spun back around to talk to the other guy.

"*Son Americanos*," I whispered to Carmen.

158

She laughed and told me that all Americans were noisy and funny.

They invited us to join them. It felt good to talk in English. They asked me how I came to Cuba, and all of the other questions that naturally follow.

Then I asked them the same set of questions. They were from the Chicago area and flew to Cuba from Toronto. They loved Cuba so much that this was their sixth trip. I could tell that they truly loved the country and the people.

Carlos Goes to Jail

✦

Day 46
Monday, September 29, 2003

I imagined his view obscured by a thick metal wall. He would be wishing he wasn't there. He should be at home with his family. I was the one who put him there and it was me that was keeping him from the people he loved. Carlos would smile and say, "No, no, no, it was me. I invited you to my home. I should have asked about the rules. It was my fault that things turned out the way they did."

However, Carlos was in jail and I found it hard to concentrate on anything. It was my fault that he was in there, despite what he thought. I wanted to go home to Nebraska. I didn't want to cause any more pain. I was sitting with my head between my hands and my elbows on my knees. Damita put her hand on my shoulder. "*Vamos, Brandon. Vamos a comprar algo para comer.*"

Looking up, I smiled slightly and forced a weak, "*Sí.*" I was getting hungry and food would hopefully take my mind off of the situation for a little while. Damita and I walked down to the nearest *tienda* to buy some frozen chicken and *refrescos.* I noticed that the blue brick dollar shop on the same block, which was usually near empty this time of day, had a long line. I also noticed several people each carrying a blue box, long and skinny.

The food store had a small line and I looked over the choices while we waited. Cookies and snacks, all in dollars, were along one wall and different types of drinks on the other. Setting next to the cash register were large freezers with ice cream and frozen meats. Damita slid back one of the glass doors and reached inside. She grabbed a few pieces of chicken and twisted them around in her hand, poked at them, and then put them back into the freezer. She kept looking, twisting, and poking until she had three pieces that suited her needs. I smiled the whole time and started to think that this must be a Cuban thing. In Jamaica, thought Carlos was just extremely picky, but now I think it is all Cubans.

As we neared the cash register Damita started to look at the refrescos. I was glad when she asked for three *Tukolas* without doing a taste-test. Luckily, just like what type of cigarettes she smokes, she knows exactly what she wants. As we exited the store she motioned toward the long line at the blue brick dollar shop. I asked, "*¿Qué pasa?*" and her look told me she didn't know.

She led me to the shop, handed me the bag full of chicken and soda, and said, "*Espérate aquí,*" so I stood and waited.

She was doing her rapid-fire Spanish as she entered and I could see that the line was still quite long inside. In just a minute, she returned with two of the long blue boxes and said, "bombilla." For a second, I was thinking that Damita, and many others, had just purchased some sort of bomb. However, when she traded me a "bombilla" for a bag so that each of us carried a bag and a "bombilla," I looked at the box. It was a florescent light bulb. I imagined that the store was selling them extremely cheap or they hadn't had any "bombillas" for quite some time.

I remembered one of my first days in Cuba, when I thought that having a rubber inner tube draped over your shoulder was a fashion statement. But the real reason for so many people having an inner tube at the same time was that one of the peso shops had gotten a large order of bicycle inner tubes which had been in very short supply for some time.

I guess that is one big difference between the street scene of Jamaica and Cuba. In Jamaica, a free-market society, you would see bras, shoes, sunglasses, kids' T-shirts, purses, and just about everything being sold along the road. It often looked like a Wal-Mart had exploded and everything landed along the road. The items were displayed in little wooden make-shift display cases or laid out on blue tarps. Very little was sold this way in Cuba.

I could tell that all this walking and the excitement about the bombillas had Damita a little exhausted. She told me that we needed to go have a guarapo. The neat shop on the corner had wooden doors and a wooden bar. While enjoying the sweet drink, Damita talked to the guarapero and, of course, the conversation involved the bombillas. The bulb was removed from the box, inspected, and returned to the box. The guarapo was excellent so Damita bought a second round before we headed back to the house. It took awhile because we stopped numerous times to talk with people sitting on their doorsteps. Each time the bombilla was inspected.

When we got back to the house, Carmen asked what took us so long and, once again, the conversation turned to the bombillas and, once again, it was removed from the box and given a good looking-over. Carmen took the chicken and sodas and went into the kitchen to cook. I watched as Carmen prepared the chicken and the congri.

Carmen had been washing. Damita placed the laundry into buckets and took them onto the roof to hang up. I tagged along. When she pulled out the stool to stand on, I had to ask, "*¿Puedo ayudarte?*"

She smiled, happy to let me help. She handed me the items one at a time, and distributed the plastic yellow clothes pins as I needed them.

Later, as Carmen and I sat down to eat in the livingroom, Damita came in and offered us avocado. We smiled and she handed us a plate with thin slices of salted avocado drenched in lime juice. Again, we were watching the telenovela, *Marimar*. Thalia is extremely cute, but I was getting a little sick of her.

Jail and Karaoke

◆

Day 47
Tuesday, September 30, 2003

The light started to crawl in through the cracks in the shut windows. I watched it creep up her leg and then across her face. I had been awake for quite some time, just sitting there, watching her sleep. I knew how much it hurt for Carlos to be away for only a few days. I feared that in just a few days it would be me that would have to leave. Carlos would only have one more day in jail. Time was something I couldn't control, but maybe I could form images that would last. I wanted to remember Carmen forever. Today I would try to capture everything about her. I wanted to be able to close my eyes fifty years from now and remember the way she looked, the way she smelled, and the sound of her laugh. That way, no matter what happened in the next few days, I would have her.

I crawled back into bed and pulled her body close to mine. Her back was resting against my chest. I closed my eyes and once again drifted off to sleep. Later, when I woke up, I felt Carmen move. Since I was hungry, I asked, "*¿Tienes hambre?*"

She rolled over to face me, "*Sí, un poquito.*" Her smile made my heart hurt.

"What do you want to eat? Pizza?"

She nodded, her smile growing.

"How many? Six?" I blocked her attempt to slap my leg. "Oh, I'm sorry. You want more? Ten?"

She slapped my leg. "*Gracioso, quiero uno, solamente.*"

I got out of bed, put on my pants, and grabbed a white plastic bag from the clothes line on the balcony. I wondered what Carlos was eating as I walked down to the street. My pizza brother smiled when he saw me. "*¿Cuántos hoy?*" he asked as he pulled his cookie sheet full of pizzas out of its metal box.

"*Dos, por favor.*" I handed him the money and he grabbed two pizzas from the metal sheet and placed them into the bag.

"*Adiós, mi amigo.*"

"*Adiós,*" I said as I turned and walked away. I went into a dollar store at the opposite end of the park. I grabbed two refrescos and a pack of the green boxed menthol cigarettes and paid for them. Back at the apartment, Carmen was sitting out on the balcony where we ate our breakfast.

That night, still sad, still thinking about Carlos, Carmen decided we needed to go to the karaoke bar at the Pico Cristal. The Pico Cristal is listed on web sites as Holguin's brightest night spot. It is on the second level of an old building on a corner adjacent to the main plaza. We could hear Shakira singing inside as I paid the security guard ten dollars and Carmen presented her national ID card. Inside we found out that it wasn't actually Shakira, but someone doing a really good job singing one of her songs.

We sat ourselves in a corner and the waiter came over to us. I told him that wanted two Cristals. Two beers and a meal came with the cover charge. The waiter came back with the beer and the meal. The meal consisted of a piece of fried chicken, some potato salad, and a hot dog that was cut in half. Apparently, hot dog that is cut in half is more elegant sitting on a plate than one that is whole. We drank our beers and watched people perform. I asked Carmen if she was going to sing, and she laughed.

"*¿Y tú?*" She said with a smile on her face.

I laughed harder than she did. We also laughed about how hard it was to get our second beer. We drank it slowly, enjoying the show, continuing to try to get the other to go up and sing. Carmen saved her chicken for later. After the bar, we walked across the park, holding hands, still thinking about Carlos. Later, at Damita's house, Carmen heated up the chicken. As she was eating, I asked her if she had enjoyed the Pico Cristal.

"Yes, but it would have been better if you would have sung."

I did my best in Spanish to explain that I knew that singing is wonderful. It can help support, invigorate, and even heal. However, I was sure that with my voice I would have done more harm than good.

Back at our home, I held Carmen close to me as she slept. I lay awake wondering about Carlos.

Bike Repair

✦

Day 48
Wednesday, October 1, 2003

The first sudden jerk almost threw Carmen and me off of the bike. We were headed southeast towards Carlos's house. It was early morning and there was still very little traffic downtown. We had only made it a few blocks when the back tire started to seize up, acting as though I was squeezing on the brake. We got off and looked at the back tire. This reminded me of taking my black Nissan pickup back home to a mechanic. Of course, when he pops the hood, I am right by his side. Sometimes I think, "What am I doing standing here? Am I going to impart some type of useful knowledge upon him?" I started to laugh because I also know nothing about bicycles.

Carmen looked at me and shook her head when I laughed. It was too hard to explain with my Spanish, so I grabbed the bar just under the seat with my right hand, lifting the rear tire slightly off of the ground. With the other hand I grabbed the handlebars. "*Vamos,*" I said, and headed back to the apartment.

Anxious to find out if Carlos was out of jail, we decided to leave the bike at the apartment and catch a bici-taxi to Carlos's house. The two-wheel carts, pulled behind a bike, had a station at a church located on the eastern edge of another park just two blocks south from Parque Calixto. *Tele Cristal* was located on the south side of this park.

The bici-taxi dropped us off at the entrance to Hilda Torres Barrio. He probably would have taken us all the way to Carlos's house but the fee would have gone up quite a bit due to the conditions of the roads. It was easier to walk.

The back door was open, so we walked into the house where Carlos was sitting on the couch, wearing shorts and sandals, shirtless, and taking a long drag on a cigarette. "*Buenos días. Buenos días,*" he exclaimed with his great smile. He gave me a big hug and a pat on the back. He gave Carmen a kiss on the cheek. I was

165

glad to see him and apparently he was happy to see me too. I looked at him and said, "*¿Cómo estás?*"

"*Bien, bien,*" he said and that was it. I never asked any questions about his time in jail and he never talked about it. That was fine with me.

Carmen told Carlos about the problem with the bike and he said something about cones. I had no idea what this meant and Carlos wisely talked to Carmen because she understood much more about bikes than I did. He drew out a detailed map to help us find a garage. He said the owner was honest.

From the map, I realized that I knew the shop, on the edge of a tourist park. It was one block west of Calixto Park on Martí. In that area shops sold paintings, local art, and T-shirts. The shop has a swinging metal gate, painted green and large enough to drive a car through. Along that side of the street there were buildings side by side, and then, a ten-foot void where the gate was. The gate seemed out of place and maybe that's why I noticed it. Carmen seemed puzzled, but I assured Carlos I knew where the shop was.

We gave Carlos another hug. Belicia invited us back for dinner and we gladly accepted.

On the main road we waited nearly an hour before a bici-taxi stopped for us to take us back to the apartment downtown. I wheeled the bike on the front wheel again to the corner of the block with the bicycle shop. Then I gave Carmen the bike to take the rest of the way. I sat down on the corner, out of sight, per instructions from Carlos. Carmen came back in about ten minutes and said "tres horas."

"Great," I thought. We have three hours to go grab a bocadito and a refresco. I said, "Let's go to *La Begonia*." She smiled. She loved going to this place. I don' know if it was because it reminded her of our first date or because she liked the flowers.

Carlos said that the repair should cost less that 250 pesos, as long as I stayed out of sight. I sat down at the corner again, while Carmen went for the bike. It only took 165 pesos to get it fixed. I thought that was pretty good, but then again, Carmen is beautiful.

We celebrated our repairs with orange ice cream and a nap. When I woke up it was already around five. I bought a bottle of Guayabito Rum to take to Carlos's. This is the rum with the guava in the bottle. Pedaling, with Carmen on the front bar between my arms, I knew that once again, Carmen and Belicia would eat and talk in the kitchen while Carlos and I ate in the living room, talking about the good old days of falling bananas and killing chickens.

Carmen's Sister

✦

Day 49
Thursday, October 2, 2003

I sat up, stretching my arms toward the ceiling and trying to part my eyelids. I exhaled deeply and let my arms fall against the bed. The balcony door was already open and the morning light reflected off of the plastic face of Don Sabroso. Don Sabroso, mayonnaise in a pouch, sat on the table about four feet from the bed. Next to Don Sabroso was a large bag of galletas and a wad of dollars and change. These galletas were shaped like a Ritz cracker but with the texture and taste of a saltine. I could tell that Carmen had already gone shopping for breakfast. My breakfast was in a blue bag on the table, a cheese pizza. The galletas and mayonnaise were for her sister and her sister's friend. They were coming by later on this morning and Carmen asked for some money to buy them something to eat. I thought she would by some stuff to make sandwiches and maybe some cookies for dessert.

"Carmen, this is it?" I asked. "*Señor Don Sabroso* and *las galletas?*"

She poked her head through the door and smiled at me. "No, there are also *refrescos*, but I put them downstairs in the fridge. Victoria lets us use her refrigerator. *Es bastante.*"

Every morning, the first time I see her, I shiver with delight at her radiance and beauty. She said it was enough, so it was. I have learned that the best response when dealing with a woman is a nod in agreement. It's just easier that way.

She pointed near the picture of the three hundred pound chef on the mayonnaise package. "*Y tu cambio está allá, encima de la mesa,*" she said, letting me know that the change was on the table.

I looked over, even though I had already seen the wad of green. I spread apart some of the bills with my hand. I looked outside through the balcony door, shook my head, and then tossed the money back down on the table. I had given

Carmen ten dollars. The change was almost six dollars. I found it hard to believe that she hadn't spent more and didn't want to. She was beautiful, but what made me shake my head in disbelief was that on the inside she was beautiful too. She was so amazing it was hard to believe that it was real. I have always said I wanted to marry a girl that drove a Pinto and chewed her nails. I guess I thought that if I could find a girl like that I could make her happy. Even if I can't give her a diamond necklace, if I can pick her wild flowers or paint her a picture she will love not only the thing I am giving her but know the underlying love and admiration I feel towards her. I hope Carmen feels this when I hug and kiss her. I took a cold shower and then ate my pizza that was still warm.

Carmen's sister arrived at about eleven o'clock with a friend. I used my best Spanish to greet them. Carmen showed them the apartment, which takes about 25 seconds. Then she took them out on the balcony and they smoked cigarettes.

The sister and friend waited at the table while Carmen went downstairs for the drinks. When she came up and told them to eat, they looked at me and said something real fast to Carmen.

Carmen looked at me and said slowly, with a smile, "They can't eat with you in here." As I was getting up to disappear onto the balcony, I thought of a word I wanted to look up. Walking over to the table, I reached between the two girls. "*Permiso*," I said as politely as I could. I grabbed the dictionary, brought it to my chest, bowed, and said, "Enjoy your meal."

They giggled, and that night, as we were going to sleep, Carmen whispered to me, "*Mi hermana dijo que tú es cómico y amable.*"

"She didn't say I was handsome?"

"She didn't say, but you are." Carmen kissed me and took my breath away.

Later, just before I slept, I thought, "Her sister said I was funny, but nice. I hope that means she thinks I could be accepted into the family."

Calling Havana

✦

Day 50
Friday, October 3, 2003

Today was the day that I would find out from the Teacher's College if it was possible or not to study there. The ultimatum played over and over in my head, "Get a course or you will have to leave the country." I sat slumping in the chair by the small table in the apartment. Carmen was still lying there in the bed, sleeping. I exhaled deeply. I hated the anticipation of waiting, and I had already convinced myself that they were going to say that it wasn't possible. That seemed to be the most popular answer since I had arrived here. I knew how frustrating it was for Carlos.

At about eight o'clock I heard a whistle from the street. I went downstairs and grabbed my bicycle. Carlos went with me to the college, once again taking time away from his job as principal, to try to get me a course.

The glasses sat precariously on her nose, like an avalanche waiting to happen. A noise with just the right wavelength would cause them to cascade to the floor. My hopes of getting a course mirrored that of her glasses, a simple two-letter word would trigger the surge of pain. She had Carlos and me sit down at the long narrow table just outside her office. She spoke mainly to Carlos but I could pick out a few words, and the expressions playing out on Carlos's face formed complete, devastating sentences. I picked out of many sentences the news that she just didn't have the teachers available to teach me, she was short-handed as it was. Carlos got up mid-sentence and we left. He told me as we were walking back to the bikes that he didn't want to say something that he would regret. He said that she should have known when I first went there whether or not she was going to have enough teachers, and trying to get permission from Havana just postponed the inevitable.

"Carlos, I need you to call Havana for me."

He frowned, not wanting to hear what he had already been thinking. "I need to go back to work. I will call them from your apartment this afternoon, about two. Later, friend." We pedaled off in opposite directions.

Back at the apartment, I told Cuba that I would probably have to go to Havana. Facial language is universal, and the disbelief on Cuba's face was easy to understand. He told me that he would go get his bike and take me to someone who could fix things. Cuba did get me in to see Alexi, the Director of Foreign Relations. He listened sympathetically, smiled, and said that I could come back to the university on Tuesday to see if it was possible.

When I got back from the university with Cuba, Carmen was out on the balcony hanging up her laundry to dry. She turned around to look at me as I came through the door and onto the balcony.

"*No te preocupes*," she said and then went back to hanging clothes. I sat down on the bench. Had she seen the look of defeat so many times that she was able to tell me not to worry without even hearing a word? I've always been told that women are more perceptive than men. I guess they were right, at least about this woman.

A few minutes later Carlos came up to the apartment to make the phone call. He told the registrar in Havana that his name was Brandon Valentine and that he was from the United States. Whenever she had problems understanding his English, he explained in his perfect Cuban Spanish.

This must have made the lady in Havana suspicious because I heard Carlos explaining in English that his Spanish was so good because he had been practicing with his friends in Holguin.

Hanging up, after a long conversation about the level of Spanish, the dates of the course, and places to stay, he looked at me with a sad smile and said, "There is a course available, and I located a good place for you to stay if you decide to study in Havana."

"Thank you," I laughed. "But now they will expect someone who talks perfect Spanish. I'm sure you used words I'll never learn and used every tense of verb perfectly." I threw a pack of *Popular* at him. He opened it up, and we each smoked a couple of cigarettes, sitting there in silence, thinking about what might happen.

That night I didn't sleep very well, and I kept thinking about Havana. What would it be like living in Havana? Would it be a lot different than Holguin? The small town in western Nebraska where I graduated from high school is a different world from Omaha, the Nebraska city where my parents live. I'm sure New York City and Omaha are poles apart. Would Cuba still be wonderful if I left Holguin and went to Havana?

I don't know why, but when I thought of Havana, I thought of Ernest Hemingway and his book *The Old Man and the Sea*. I wondered, "Will the pain I feel when I have to leave this place be the price I have to pay for venturing out into a forbidden place in search of adventure, in search of a catch? I may end up just dragging a carcass onto the shores of Omaha when all this is over with. Will it be worth it?"

Selling My Clothes

✦

Day 51
Saturday, October 4, 2003

"No, Carlos," I said. "It's better for me to sell them here. In Havana, whom do I know who knows everybody? Do you think I could have gotten a decent bike in Havana?"

"Okay. Okay." He patted me on the back. "I see your point. They would have robbed you blind and left you with a broken tricycle. I just don't want you to sell your clothes. I don't want you to go to Havana."

We had been arguing about my clothes for some time. On the bed there were four pairs of pants, some polo shirts, and four pairs of shoes. These were the newer clothes that I had recently bought in downtown Kingston. I had hoped to wear them over the next six months, but now it was more important to me to leave some money with Carlos to help him get permission to return to Jamaica. I knew that he still had a lot of paperwork to do and it all took money.

"I wish I could stay here, but I can't. We've gone over it too many times. I'll still be in Cuba, hopefully, for at least four months. You can come visit me. I'll come out and stay over Christmas." I was tired mentally and physically. I hadn't slept much, and the mental anguish I went through yesterday was starting to take its toll on me. Then, to get away from the argument, I asked, "How much do you think you can get?"

Carlos was adding everything up in his mind. Numbers rolled out of his mouth, stringing together in Spanish. Finally, he said, "I think that we can get at least 150 dollars for everything. My friend David should be able to sell everything for about three hundred."

Carmen had left early this morning to go to her mom's house, returning tomorrow for a birthday party. I think that she knew that I needed some time alone to think, or maybe, she needed time to think. I tried to think about how she must be feeling. For me, my time had been a roller coaster, and I was tired of going up and down. I just wanted the ride to end.

There was a knock on the door, and the man that had come for the clothes shook my hand. A name was never exchanged, and Carlos did all of the talking. I could tell they were talking about how and where he could sell them and the price that he might be able to get for all of the things. After about five minutes, the man pulled a wad of dollars out of his pocket and paid Carlos. He put the clothes into a blue backpack and was out the door, leaving 150 dollars and a hand shake. I told Carlos that the money was for him. He argued with me for a while before taking it. I told him that he needed the money more than I did, and I wanted the money to be a gift and a hope that he would reach Jamaica. I believe that there is a common bond between two true friends and that bond is the deep feeling of happiness for the other. I think that Carlos could see that there was no way that he could refuse to take the money. He knew that it was something I truly wanted to do. I also saw that Carlos truly wanted to go to Jamaica. Between friends, you always hope for the best.

I ate lunch, crackers and mayonnaise, and then sat in a daze of sadness, defeat, and uncertainty while an old John Wayne movie, dubbed in Spanish, played on the TV. Carlos slapped me on the back, his eyes twinkling, and said, "Let's celebrate our friendship." The rest of the afternoon we drank Miguel's rum and remembered our good times. I felt okay. I had to live in Havana for awhile, but I'd be back. Pain is temporary, and memories last forever. I didn't know that afternoon that I wouldn't be back, and that the pain was only beginning.

The Red Pill

✦

Day 52
Sunday, October 5, 2003

You could see the reflection in his sunglasses. He had his hands outstretched, and in one hand he had a red pill, and in the other he had a green pill. When I watched the movie the first time, I knew that Neo was going to choose the red one. Morphius said that he would wake up, and it would be as if nothing had happened if he chose the green pill. Then there wouldn't have been a movie. However, it was Neo's destiny to choose the red one and go on to help save the world. Our tape of the movie was in English with Spanish subtitles. We were watching *The Matrix* in the apartment of some of Carlos's family. Carmen was sitting on my lap, and I was wishing for a pill I could take so that I would have a Spanish course when I woke up in the morning.

The small apartment was crowded for Federico's 7th birthday. Federico is the son of Carlos's cousin and Marco. Marco is mulatto, with a shaved head and a linebacker build. I had first met him out at the party in El Coco. Carlos had borrowed twenty dollars U.S. from me to give Marco about two weeks ago to pay for this party. Marco plays guitar in a band and said that he hadn't been paid for awhile. I told Carlos not to worry about paying me back, but he had returned the money when I walked into his house this morning. A bottle of rum was being passed around the apartment, and the kids were drinking punch. This was the same apartment building I had visited earlier to visit Belicia's mom. I had the opportunity to help raise a few bikes, by rope, to the fourth floor.

When it was time to bust the piñata, the parents were as excited as the children. Federico, the birthday boy, gave the brightly colored horse the fatal whack, and the candies spewed onto the floor. There were as many adults as children scrambling for the candy. There were drinking and dancing until about midnight. I was finally starting to dance well, Merengue style, and I didn't want to stop. I definitely didn't want to stop holding Carmen. I needed a red pill.

Damita's Rainbows

◆

Day 53
Monday, October 6, 2003

The coffee was black and sweet. I poured the last drops from the thermos into Damita's mug. Yesterday at the party she said that she knew a librarian at the university, and she wanted us to go talk to her.

We finished our coffee and headed down the street to catch a horse carriage. Damita talked to her friend in the library for a few minutes, and then we ended up at Alexi's office again. He was the same man that Cuba and I had spoken to on Friday afternoon. The secretary recognized me and smiled. He wasn't there but I already had an appointment for tomorrow.

In the carriage back to the house tears streamed down Damita's face, and she said that she didn't want me to leave. As the tears popped out of her eyes and ran down her face, they washed away some of her make-up. As the droplets stopped on her chin, they became little rainbows. However, neither she nor I were sitting on a pot of gold. We were just sitting on a hard wooden seat behind a skinny man driving a horse.

Last Try

♦

Day 54
Tuesday, October 7, 2003

Carlos, instead of Cuba, took me back out to the university to visit Alexi. The secretary smiled, and shook her head sadly. Alexi told us that they didn't have enough teachers. We all shook hands politely.

Carlos was upset that people from other countries were still coming in and getting teachers. I asked him if he could make arrangements for me to leave the next day.

Carlos came by in the afternoon and gave me all of the information about where I would live in Havana. We went to the *Cauto* and had some drinks. Carlos gave a toast that I would learn Spanish and come back to Holguin.

Carlos left Carmen and me alone for our last night together.

Good-bye, Holguin

✦

Day 55
Wednesday, October 8, 2003

I was on my back, lying in bed, my hands locked together behind my head. Carmen lay face down, her arm draped over my stomach. I caressed her arm with my hand. I could see the light of day struggling to push away the darkness of night. I didn't sleep much that night. I would drift off, and then wake up, probably in fifteen-minute intervals. When I was awake, I relived every painful memory in my life. I thought about basic training at Fort sill, Oklahoma.

Three o'clock in the morning, in the pouring rain, the drill sergeant screamed, "Push, Valentine! Raise your fuckin' stomach off the ground!"

I pushed, but nothing happened. It seemed like I had been doing pushups every second of every day for two weeks, and my arms wouldn't work.

"You fuckin' piece of shit! You have three fuckin' seconds to raise your fat worthless body off of my fuckin' ground." The brim of his drill sergeant hat was pressed against my temple. In the last two weeks I had probably averaged two hours of sleep a night. I couldn't tell what fluid was running down my face, tears, rain, or saliva coming from the drill sergeant's mouth. I pushed as hard as I could. My arms started to wobble. For the past two weeks this was a nightly ritual. Three inches, then four...after what seemed like an eternity, my arms were fully extended.

"Are you tired, Valentine? Do you want to go home to your mommy?"

"No, drill sergeant!" I answered as loud as I could.

"Good, you worthless piece of shit, do another push-up!"

One week later I tried calling my girlfriend. Basic training for the army tore at me mentally and physically. I needed to hear a soft and comforting voice, the voice of someone I loved. She was in Spain, visiting a friend. I called to Spain several times, but she was never at the house. I finally got a hold of her when she got back to Nebraska. I hadn't talked to her for weeks, and she told me immediately

177

that she had met a guy from France and had sex with him. We started dating when she was 16, and she told me that she wanted to wait until she was married. I was in the middle of basic training, and I just had the love of my life rip my fuckin' heart out. As I saturated my pillow with tears, I thought, "It doesn't matter because a heart's no use in basic training anyway."

When I was fifteen, I was living with my parents in New Mexico. I did some stupid things, including raising my hand when the principal asked who on the bus had drunk some alcohol that was being passed around. Almost everyone on the bus had drunk some, but only my best friend and I were dumb enough to raise our hands. We got kicked off the team. To avoid more of the same kind of trouble, my parents sent me to live with my grandpa in Nebraska. On the bus I remember I ran out of tears, and my eyes went dry.

I didn't cry that morning because I kept hoping I was just leaving Holguin for awhile. However, as I relived those wrenching times in my past, I thought I might not be back. I might not see Carlos again. Carlos, the best friend I have had in this life. I might not see Carmen again. I was starting to imagine a life with her, and I didn't want to hurt her. I wanted the night to end.

Finally, sunlight slowly started to fill the room, but I was too numb to move.

"Brandon!" I lifted my head and looked around the room.

"Brandon!" I heard my name again and looked at the clock.

"Oh shit!" I thought. "Is it already eight o'clock?" I raised Carmen's arm and kissed her hand. I threw the covers back, got up, and unlocked the door to the balcony. I went to the ledge that faced the street, stuck my head through the begonias, and looked down below.

"Me soon come," I yelled down at Carlos.

He smiled. "*Everting cris.*"

I went downstairs to open the door for Carlos. He picked up Carmen's foot as he walked by the bed. She just groaned, and Carlos dropped her foot. He followed me out onto the balcony, and we sat together on the bench. I handed Carlos a cigarette. He had his lighter ready and lit both cigarettes. Car horns, bicycle bells, and calls from salesmen filled the morning air. The shrillest sound came from the squeaky cart wheels. The carts, some pushed from behind like a grocery store cart and others pulled from in front with a pole in each hand of the salesman, were loaded with water, bread, oranges, bananas, or vegetables.

"I'll come back to Holguin when I finish in Havana," I said as I slowly looked towards Carlos, taking my eyes off of the withering begonia flowers lying on the tiled floor.

"I'm just glad you have a course." He smiled with the same smile and the same twinkling yellow eyes that had encouraged me so many times.

"Me too, but I still wish it was here. I wish I didn't have to leave."

"I called Viazul before I came over. They said they have a small mini-bus leaving at noon for Havana. You should pack your things, and then take Carmen out to eat. They said that they will come here to the house to pick you up, and then go back to the terminal to wait for some Italians that are coming in from Santiago." Carlos stood up and flicked his cigarette through the hanging begonias out into the street.

"I'm going to come back with Belicia at eleven o'clock to say goodbye."

As we walked back into the apartment, I heard Carmen turn on the shower. "Thanks for arranging everything, Carlos." I extended my hand.

"No problem, my brother." He shook my hand and then pulled me in for a hug.

"I'll see you at eleven o'clock," he said with a pat on my back as he was leaving.

I lay back, waiting for Carmen to come out of the bathroom.

I cut Carmen's pizza and slid it over in front of her. I started cutting mine. I cut and cut and cut. The pieces were small, then bite-size, and then smaller and smaller, and still I kept cutting. Carmen glanced over at me several times but never said a word. I must have had a pretty intense look on my face, and one doesn't bother an open-heart surgeon in the middle of a triple bypass. Finally, I slammed the knife into the middle of the pizza and looked up at Carmen. I reached over and squeezed her leg. She smiled and placed her hand on mine.

When the Viazul van pulled up to the apartment, the rain was pouring down, and Carlos was taping my departure.

"I will return quickly," I said as I gave Carmen a kiss and a hug. I gave Belicia a hug and a kiss on the cheek. I shook Cuba's hand and gave Victoria a kiss on the cheek.

"Carlos, thanks for everything." I gave him a hug and grabbed my bags.

I stepped out into the rain and then through the open side-door of the blue mini-van. I shut the door and looked back. As the van pulled away I waved. I had said four words to Carmen before I left. Only four words. I hated good-byes.

Hello, Havana

✦

Day 55
Wednesday, October 8, 2003

We arrived at the terminal and waited for the Italians to arrive. They arrived at about three o'clock, three hours late. I hadn't slept much for several nights, so I slept as much as I could on the trip to Havana. I tried to sleep and tried not to think about anything but sleeping. The road was modern, but poorly maintained, full of potholes and rough sections. This was not a road on which you wanted to attempt to drink a hot cup of coffee or even sleep soundly, for that matter. We picked up some people standing along the road, holding money in their hands, so we were fairly crowded. The driver stopped some for personal business, one stop lasting several hours. As it got dark, I finally got to sleep.

One of the other riders shook my shoulder, and the driver asked, "*Muchacho, ¿que es la dirección?*"

Waking up, I stuck my hand in my pocket and pulled out the piece of paper that Carlos had given me. "*Calle 19 de Mayo, Número 24, entre Ayestarán y Almendares.*"

He drove a few more blocks and parked in front of a brick apartment building with a large number 24 painted on the glass above the door. I paid him the forty-five dollars for the trip, grabbed my bags, and got out of the vehicle.

"*¿Está bien?*" the driver asked as he leaned forward to see me through the passenger-side window.

"*Sí, todo está bien,*" I answered. I was alone, heartbroken, and had no idea what I was supposed to do next, but, of course, I told him everything was fine. With my luggage sitting on the curb, the driver pulled away. The glass door was locked, and nothing happened when I knocked. Through the door I could see stairs going up to the second floor. Looking up, I could see the balconies of the apartments stick out over the sidewalk. When I woke up on the bus, someone had said it was almost four o'clock. The sun would come up in an hour or two.

The only thing I could do was to sit on my bags and wait until people woke up and unlocked the door.

Paloma and Neron

✦

Day 56
Thursday, October 9, 2003

As I watched a burly man push a broom along the street in front of me, I won
dered, "How did so many things go wrong?" The man had a great mustache and
wore a green cotton hat. It was five in the morning, still dark. Except for the
occasional vehicle, he was the only thing moving. I had no idea where I was.
knew that the school where I would study was within walking distance, but I had
no idea in which direction. I could tell that I was in a residential/business district
Across the street, two large apartment buildings, side-by-side, ran the width of
the block. A clinic stood on the next corner, and then there was another apart
ment building, four stories high.

The sweeper collected empty *cuchillo* wrappers, void of the once-warm pea
nuts, empty *Popular* packages, and dead mango leaves into a pile. When a pile
was large enough, he grabbed a shovel from his cart and put the trash into a barre
which also rode on the metal cart. I stretched, walked out into the street, and
looked up at the balconies, hoping to see some lights on. I didn't see any lights
but I did see that the mango trees were full of fruit. I also saw that on each side c
my small apartment building was a store. The one on the right sold power tools
and the one on the left sold safety equipment.

As the burly man worked his way down the street, sweeping and shoveling, the
glow of day started to show above the apartments in front of me. Finally, I hear
a key being inserted into a door. My head spun around as an old man with a plas
tic bag came out of the lower glass door and locked it behind him. Yellow taxi
slowly began to creep out into the early morning light. It was six o'clock.

After about fifteen minutes, the man came back with his bag full of bread
When he crossed the street and passed by me, I stood up and spoke. "*Permise
señor. Necesito hablar con Neron.*"

"*Sí, pase.*" I grabbed my bags and went in through the door which he locked behind us. I followed him up two flights of stairs. He motioned to the first door on the right and said, "*Aquí,*" before continuing up the next flight of stairs.

"*Gracias, señor.*" I thanked him as I knocked on the door. After about five seconds I heard footsteps, and the doorknob turned. A woman, probably in her mid-fifties, opened the door with a questioning smile.

"Hello, I'm Brandon," I said in English.

"*Soy Paloma,*" she answered with an extended hand. She had on a nice blue suitdress, very professional. I assumed she was ready to leave for work. She shook my hand and gave me a kiss on the cheek. The apartment was very nice, perfectly kept, with expensive furniture. She showed me two rooms from which I could choose. The first one was next to the living room. It had a fan, a closet, a dresser, and a single bed. The other room had the same items, but was closer to the bathroom and about a third larger than the first one. It was right across from Paloma's room.

I chose the larger room. I put my bags into the room and then used the bathroom. Paloma was putting a *cafecito* onto the table and looked up as I was coming out of the bathroom.

"Can you get your passport and visa for me to look at?" She spoke very slowly and clearly in Spanish, and I understood exactly what she was saying.

I nodded and went back into my new room. I dug into my little carrying bag and grabbed my passport. The visa was folded into the passport.

As I handed her the papers she said, "Here is a *cafecito* for you." She pointed to the small cup filled with coffee.

"Thank you," I answered. As I slowly sipped the hot syrupy drink, I watched Paloma's face as she thumbed through the passport. She slightly nodded her head and made a sound like everything looked good. She then picked up the visa. Her face changed immediately. She glanced across the table.

"You've renewed your visa?"

"Yes," I said with hesitation in my voice. Was "yes" a good or a bad answer?

"But you only have three days to change your visa to a student visa."

She could see the confusion in my face.

She spoke slowly, ensuring I would understand the situation. "To study at the university you have to have a student visa or your visa has to be in the process of being changed from a tourist visa to a student visa. Do you understand?" She looked at me, and she could tell I understood by the nodding of my head. She could also tell that she had told me something heart-crushing.

She continued. "Most of the time it takes three to four weeks for the process of changing the visa from a tourist visa to a student visa. I don't think it's possible for you to change the visa in three days because Friday is a holiday. You will have to leave the country if I can't change the visa. I can check today at work if it will be possible, but it is unlikely. If you can't change the visa in three days then you can leave the country and then return, getting a new visa."

"If you can change the visa, how long would I be able to stay?" I wanted to hear something encouraging, but I didn't.

"I don't know. You are from the United States, and I've never tried to change such a visa before. I need to go to work, and I will find out everything. I will be back at about four o'clock. Alright?"

"Okay. Thank you."

At that moment a man came out of the bathroom and extended his hand. "Hello. I'm Neron." He was older than Paloma, with thinning white hair and deep wrinkles. His handshake was firm. I trusted him instantly.

Paloma gave Neron a quick kiss and headed for the door. Just before closing it she turned back to me, smiled, and said, "*Adiós, Brandon. Todo estará bien.*"

"Goodbye, Paloma." I didn't believe that everything would be okay. Judging from my past two months it was difficult to be optimistic. Neron came back into the dining room with a buttered bun and a glass of coffee and milk. He asked if wanted more coffee.

"Yes, thank you," I answered, handing him my empty cup.

He returned with a full cup and placed it down in front of me. We made small talk for about half an hour, talking about what I had been doing in Holguin and things I had done before coming to Cuba. There was a break in the conversation and I said that I wanted to go take a shower and then lie down for a little bit.

After the shower, I went into my room, turned on the fan, and closed the door. I lay down on the bed and tried to imagine a white piece of paper. Almost immediately I woke up to a knock on the door. I opened the door, and Neron was standing there.

"Dinner is on the table," Neron said with a smile.

"Dinner? What happened to lunch?" I thought. I glanced back to the window in my room and saw that it was almost dark outside. In the bathroom, I splashed water on my face to finish waking up. In the dining room, where Paloma and Neron were waiting for me, I said, "The food smells great."

Neron smiled and said, "Thank you."

I was hungry but it was difficult to concentrate on eating. I was going crazy wondering what information Paloma had obtained. Finally, she broke the silence

"I talked with immigration today." She paused and glanced at Neron. "They can't renew your visa in that amount of time." She looked down at the plate and stuck her fork into a slice of cucumber. That cucumber might as well have been my heart.

"So my options are to go home or go to Jamaica and come back to Havana with a new visa."

She nodded as she slowly chewed her cucumber.

"How long will they allow me to stay in the country with a student visa?"

There was another pause. "Two months."

"Two months, two months, but when I was in Holguin, I met a Canadian that was able to stay six months on his student visa," I said in disbelief.

"Yes, Canadians are able to stay for six months. We've had some stay with us. But the thing is, you are from the U.S.," she said softly, trying to paint the picture for me.

"I should have applied for Jamaican citizenship while I was there," I thought to myself. I finished my food in silence, thinking only about going back to bed. I could always think in bed. I excused myself from the table and thanked Neron and Paloma for the food.

"Brandon, if you need anything, let us know," Paloma said gently as she placed her hand on Neron's. Neron looked at me and nodded in agreement. He knew more or less what I had been through, and I'm sure he shared this information with Paloma while I was asleep that afternoon.

I lay down and closed my eyes. That was that. I was going home. I softly hummed the tune that was now stuck in my mind. "You got to know when to hold them, know when to fold them, know when to walk away, know when to run...." I had held a losing hand for the past two months, and I continued to hold those same damn cards. It was time to fold them, swallow my pride, if I had any left, and walk, or rather fly, away. I made up my mind. I was going home. I could see my family earlier than expected, and Cuba would slowly become another pleasant memory. After the tears stopped, I went to sleep.

Scooping Up Chips

✦

Day 57
Friday, October 10, 2003

Something didn't feel right. Last night, the decision to go back to the U.S. felt okay, and I had slept well, but this morning was different, and I recognized the feeling. Rubbing the sleep out of my eyes, I put the pillow against the wall at the head of the bed and leaned my back against it. I lit a cigarette and remembered this feeling. When I first arrived in Jamaica, I had quite a few problems. Let's just say there were people in the community that didn't receive me with open arms. Many people in my community had never seen a white man so there was a lot of hatred that may have dated back to the time of slavery. The small white population in Jamaica lives in the ritzy parts of Kingston, Montego Bay, Ocho Rios, and Mandeville. I was robbed at knife point twice in Kingston. At my job site I was taunted and threatened. When an extremely bad experience happened, I would decide to leave. Then I would have this feeling. The feeling I was feeling that morning in Havana. It would make me remember all of the good things I had taken from the past experiences and all the unique ones I would be giving up if I scooped the chips off the table and walked away.

I had lived two months in Cuba, and my experiences were beyond description. I knew Carlos and his family better than I knew my own family. My heart was wrecked, but I would not trade my experience with Carmen for anything. My Spanish was not good, but in only two months it had grown so that I could communicate many things. I had to decide if this was the end of this experience or if there was more. I took a long drag on the cigarette and flicked the ash into the ashtray.

Paloma said good-bye to Neron, and the front door clicked shut. I put the ashtray back on the small wooden table and showered, thinking of nothing except keeping the soap out of my eyes.

In the dining room, Neron was enjoying his cafecito. He looked up at me and smiled. "Sleep well?"

"Yes, like a rock," I answered, pulling out a chair and sitting down.

"Do want to eat breakfast?"

When I answered, "Yes, please," Neron rose out of his chair and went into the kitchen. I heard him put something in a microwave and set the timer. He walked back into the dining room carrying a plate with two small bananas and a glass of orange juice. He set them in front of me and went back into the kitchen. I heard a ding, and he brought back a ham and cheese sandwich and a glass of coffee and milk.

"Thank you, Neron." He smiled and sat back down.

"Neron, do you have a telephone book?"

"Yes, what do you want to look for?"

"Air Jamaica Airlines."

"I can look for it after breakfast." He smiled and lifted the last bite of bread to his mouth and washed it down with the final swallow of coffee and milk. Neron took his dishes into the kitchen and came back wearing thick, brown-framed glasses. I assumed he only wore them for reading. The phone book was under the phone in the back corner of the living room. Sitting at an old and elegant wooden desk, he quickly found the number in the yellow pages and dialed.

When I returned from putting my dishes in the kitchen, Neron said, "There wasn't an answer. I don't think they open until nine o'clock. I will try back then." Neron paused, and I turned around. "Have you decided what you're going to do?"

I was heading back to my room. I stopped and turned around and looked at Neron.

"No, not yet. It's not easy."

He shook his head in agreement and went back to flipping pages.

Back in my room, I looked at my return ticket to Jamaica and counted my money. I had plenty for my ticket to Nebraska.

I was lying in bed when Neron said the office was open until four o'clock. I looked at my watch. I couldn't believe that it was already nine o'clock. I got up out of bed and went into the living room.

"Do you want to go to the office now?"

"Yes."

"I can walk with you and show you what road to take." He took off his glasses and put them into his pocket. I could see in his eyes that he wanted to go with me.

"Yes, that's good, if it's no problem."

He went into his room and put on a short-sleeved button shirt. He left his shirt out of his pants. We left the apartment and headed down the street. The streets were now buzzing with activity. We headed south down the street. On the same side of the street as Neron's apartment, just two blocks down, was the Omnibus Station. This was where the Viazul bus I had taken the day before would have come. No wonder it was easy for him to find Neron's apartment. We crossed the street and walked through a small park. We turned west, and Neron pointed out the *Biblioteca Nacional José Martí*. The streets were wide and full of old vehicles and lots of new ones.

When we arrived at the *Plaza de Revolución*, Neron pointed out the large monument to José Martí. At the base of the monument was Calle Paseo. Neron said that the Air Jamaica office was in the *Hotel Meliá Cohiba*, where this road ended. It ended at the *Malecón*.

I had read of this famous Cuban landmark and was excited to see it. Neron explained that the *Malecón*, built at the beginning of the 1900s, is a seawall or dike more than 4 miles long, built to protect the city of Havana from large waves. The road along the *Malecón* is the favorite east-west connection for drivers in Havana. A covered sidewalk along this road is a favorite place for young and old lovers to walk hand-in-hand. The wall itself serves as a giant bench for fishermen and wave-watchers of all ages.

He said that it was about a mile and a half, but a nice walk with beautiful houses. I shook his hand and told him thank you.

He smiled and patted me on the back. "Good Luck."

I crossed the street and moved across the large concrete lot in front of the monument and headed down *Paseo*. The houses were incredible, although many of them looked like they were now the location of businesses or embassies. The street was divided by a large green area in the middle with large trees and benches. I reached the hotel and found the office. I went inside and another beautiful Cuban woman signaled for me to come to her desk.

"How can I help you?"

I stared at her. What was I going to do?

"How much does a ticket cost to Jamaica?"

She punched some information into the computer. "When do you want to leave?"

Mentally, I was saying, "Throw the chips on the table." I answered, "Tomorrow morning."

She looked up at me and then back at her computer. When she finally told me the price of a one-way ticket, I handed her the money. She asked for my passport, and I gave it to her.

Taking a deep breath, I thought that I had finally made a decision. One second later, I was thinking about how easy it would be to buy a return ticket to Havana. In Jamaica I could cash in my open ticket and go to Omaha. However, if I came back to Havana, in two months I should be able to learn Spanish fairly well. My parents could send me money from the Peace Corps readjustment fund if I ended up short.

"Here is your ticket and your change," the clerk interrupted my confusion.

"Thank you."

As I exited the office I heard the doors slam shut behind me. I was busy staring at my ticket, wondering what I would do. My thoughts of returning to Cuba were lessening until I heard commotion coming from across the street. I looked up from my ticket and saw children kicking a soccer ball along the *Malecón*. I knew that I had to be just like this amazing sea wall. I had to protect myself from the great waves of fear and disbelief which were trying to erode my dreams. I was scared of what I would choose. I took a deep breath and put the ticket into my pocket.

I headed back up *Paseo* to the monument. I stood on the street and called up towards Neron's balcony. He walked out, looked down, and greeted me with a smile. Opening the front door, he asked, "*¿Pues?*"

"I leave tomorrow."

Neron turned and gave me a hug.

"It wasn't easy. I want to learn Spanish with all my heart." He never asked me when I was coming back.

"Do you want a *mojito*?"

As we sat and drank our *mojitos*, a rum drink with lime juice and mint, I hoped I would make the right decision.

Round Trip to JA

✦

Day 58
Saturday, October 11, 2003

"May I join you?" Startled, I looked up from my *Time* magazine to a familiar face I had never seen before.

"Certainly," I answered. "I'm just waiting for my plane. Sometimes the wait gets long."

"I hope I'm not bothering you but I like to practice my English when I can." His tone and smile seemed familiar.

"It doesn't sound like you need practice. Have you lived in the States?" I realized that I had been thinking about my father before he walked up, and he did look amazingly like my dad. His skin was darker, he was not quite as fat, and he had much better hair. But he was about the same age and height, and he wore my dad's glasses. None of my uncles looked as much like my father as this guy did.

"I went to school in Colorado for awhile in the 1960s," he said. "Graduate school. My English always feels a little unnatural so I like to practice. Sometime when I have a couple of hours in an airport, I find an American, and if he is 'amable,' we talk."

"I'm friendly," I answered. I thought about telling him I was from Canada but from the look in his eyes, decided it would be as pointless as lying to Dad. "What flight are you waiting for?"

"Air Jamaica to Havana. It leaves at four."

"Really? That's my flight too."

"So you are from the U.S. and you are going to Cuba. That is not so common. May I ask why you are going?"

"Going back, really. I flew over from Havana this morning to get my visa renewed. I'm studying Spanish."

"*¿Dónde nació en los Estados Unidos?*" he asked, testing my Spanish.

In Spanish, I easily told him that I was born in Nebraska, and he asked where. He laughed when I told him. He remembered Ogallala, the town I was born in, because in the sixties he traveled through it to North Platte from Denver with a friend.

"A small world," I said. "And what is your business in Havana?"

"I own a bar there. I do some consulting for some friends who buy things from Europe. I'm just getting back from Munich. It will be good to get back home. Was it hard to get permission to study in Havana? Since the U.S. government maintains the embargo, Americans are not very popular."

When I told him my story, he listened, and nodded when I told him how they would not let me study in Holguin in September.

"Of course they could not let you study!" he exclaimed. "You came to Cuba the same time the Latin Grammy Awards were to be held in Miami. Bush had to pay back the Miami Cubans for their help in the last election and to get their help next year. Have you heard Los Van Van?"

I nodded. I knew that their bandleader, Juan Carlos Formel, was one of several Grammy-nominated musicians who had not been allowed to attend the Latin Grammys.

"The order to change their visas had to have come from the White House. Of course, they blamed the musicians for not applying soon enough, but his band had toured in June. It was simple pay-back. Do you know how *Radio Mambi* had gathered a crowd to threaten violence if there was a recount in Miami? Those Cubans in Miami are capable of anything."

"You do not sound like you care for your countrymen who live in Miami," I remarked as I offered him a cigarette.

He shook his head. I wasn't sure whether he was thinking about Cubans in Miami or the cigarette. "I quit smoking a few years ago. I want to watch my children grow up. I have three children and seven grandchildren, all in Havana. The oldest grandson will be a doctor in two years. The youngest, a girl, is learning to walk. Here, look at their pictures."

I took the wallet and slowly looked at each wonderful smile. "They are beautiful. You don't want to talk about your countrymen in Miami?"

"Almost one-half million Cubans in Miami. I have many friends in Miami, and most of the people in Miami from Cuba are good people, but the politics permeate everything. I haven't been in Miami for over ten years. Too many of them want to come back to a Cuba that I hope is gone forever. In the early '60s, parents were allowed to send their children to the States, in an operation some called '*Pedro Pan.*' Who knows why. One of the children teaches in Minnesota or some state up north. He wrote a book recently. He called it *Waiting for Snow in Havana*. If you read it you might sense the type of people that I am glad are no longer running Cuba. His father was not proud of Cuba, only of Spain. He would not even let his children listen to Cuban music, and now he writes as though he misses Cuba. Let him stay forever where he doesn't have to wait for snow." He smiled apologetically for the angry tone and asked where I was staying in Havana.

I told him about Neron and Paloma. Neron woke me up at 5:30 that morning so I'd have plenty of time to get ready for my flight. I showered and enjoyed the smell of coffee while I made my bed. In the kitchen, the ham sandwich with cheese was waiting for me. I ate it methodically, each bite washed down with a swallow of café con leche. Neron marveled at my discipline. After the sandwich, Neron served freshly squeezed orange juice and two miniature bananas. They are yellow on the outside when they are ripe and white on the inside. The flesh is sweet and denser than a regular banana. Paloma laughed at me when I called them *fungo*. She said that only the Easterners called them *fungo*. In Havana they were called *platanitos*. Each bite reminded me of the first time I kissed Carmen.

I explained to Ricardo how much I enjoyed my new family. "Every time I eat with Neron, my worries fade away. The atmosphere at the table makes me feel like family, but the preparation and display of the food makes me feel like I am a rock star dining at the Ritz Carlton."

Then I told Ricardo about Neron's songbirds. The male bird, bright blue, always ate the cucumber and string beans without letting the female bird have any. Then she would get really mad and chase him around. I also told him about the beautiful women who had gotten off the bus that morning as I watched the line form for coffee at the bodega across the street. The sign said "*Escuela de Lenguas Extranjeros*" but the women looked more like models than students.

"Yes," Ricardo said. "Many people say that Cuba has the most beautiful women in the world. Did you find any special woman while you were in Holguin?"

Trying not to think about Carmen, I told him that they were all special. I also didn't tell him about my struggle with whether or not to return to Cuba. I did not tell him that when I arrived in Montego Bay earlier that morning, I was still figuring the price for a ticket to Omaha. That morning in Havana, a little after seven, I had to wait at the Air Jamaica desk for some soccer players and referees to check in before I could get my seat. They were flying over to Kingston for a scrimmage. As I boarded the plane I had a strange feeling. For the first time I had the sensation of flying without a destination. I wasn't flying to Jamaica to visit friends or play in the sand. I was flying to Jamaica to leave Jamaica. This feeling of confusion stayed with me as we flew over the beautiful blue water between Cuba and Jamaica. I tried to focus on the immediate world around me as I waited for MoBay to come into sight. I thought about whether or not I could open the emergency door. I thought about whether or not the tuna salad sandwich might have been a better choice than the cheese sandwich, and of course, I wondered if the beautiful stewardess had won any beauty contests.

As we touched down, my first thought was that the cost of a ticket to Omaha, Nebraska, was only two hundred dollars more than a ticket back to Cuba. The few clothes I left in Havana were not a big deal. However, I had made up my mind by the time I reached the terminal. I would return to Cuba. I would learn as much Spanish as possible in the time I had.

I went through customs, and the gentleman still wanted to look through my small bag for Cuban cigars. My bag was only large enough to squeeze in a pair of socks and maybe half of one of Fidel's favorite cigars. I made it through customs and was off to Immigration. The immigration officer wondered why I didn't have a departure ticket and at the same time noticed that I had worked in Jamaica for quite some time. I told her in my best Jamaican patio, *"Me nah ave no depacha ticket caw me naw kno ow long if we tek fe da too a we fe get marid."* She laughed and told me to buy a ticket as soon as I could. I made a beeline to the departure office and bought a ticket to Havana, Cuba. It was about eleven o'clock in Jamaica, and the plane departed for Havana at 4:00. To kill time I bought a *Time* magazine, with the stars of *Friends* on the cover, and had a patty and a cigarette. The patty reminded me that I had not talked to Carlos for awhile so I dialed his number in Holguin.

The phone started to ring. I hadn't told Carlos I was going to Jamaica so I needed to tell him that I had to leave the country and was thinking about what to do.

"Hola." Juanita answered the phone.

"Hola, Juanita. ¿Cómo estás? ¿Está Carlos?"

"Cómo no. Un momento."

When Carlos said hello, I told him I just had a patty for him.

There was a pause, and he said, "You're in Jamaica?"

"Where else can you buy a patty?" I asked, remembering how much Carlos loved patties. I don't know if Carlos liked the seasoned meat best or the crisp pastry-like crust that enveloped it, but he wished Cuba had them as well.

I told him that I was embarrassed to spend so much money to study Spanish.

"If this thing is in your heart, Brandon, then it's the right thing. Call me next week. We have to get together soon. Carmen misses you."

"Tell her 'hi.' Tell her I miss her more." I hung up laughing.

That's when I met Ricardo. It was great talking to him. Before we went to separate seats on the plane he made me write down directions for finding his bar and told me, "I enjoyed talking to you. I want to know how your Spanish class is going. I sell the best *mojitos* in Havana. Come drink one with me. I can practice English, and you can practice Spanish."

I nearly bounced onto the plane that afternoon. I finally had a Spanish course, and I was in the capital city, living in a great house. I also had met a new friend.

Back on the ground in Havana at José Martí International Airport, there was one scary moment in Immigration. After waiting twenty minutes to get to the officer, he looked carefully at my visa and sent me to the back of the line. I waited several minutes until another officer, evidently the boss, came back to talk to me. He was a bit friendlier, and after asking what I was doing and where I was staying, he stamped my new visa.

After a beer to celebrate, I paid fifteen dollars for a ride back to Neron's in an early '90s Mercedes Benz taxi. It was a little after nine. Hoping that Neron was watching the TV by the balcony, I yelled up at the open window.

After a shower and *cafecito*, I lay in bed wondering what Neron and Paloma thought about me. Did they think I was a stupid gringo who just spent over five hundred dollars to get a stamp on a piece of paper? Did they think that I was a young man who wanted to accomplish something that burned in my heart, and five hundred dollars was a small price to pay to fulfill a dream? I hoped that they thought the latter of the two. I also knew in the upcoming months I would show them the love and dedication it takes to learn their language. When I leave they will think of me as a young man who loved Cuba and Spanish, and someone who fulfilled a dream.

Mateus

✦

Day 59
Sunday, October 12, 2003

Neron and I were sipping our *cafecitos* and talking when Paloma came into the room and asked how my flight to Jamaica had gone. "It was okay," I answered with a grin. "Now I have two months to see how much Spanish I can learn, so I had better try to talk Spanish with you."

She started talking in Spanish, and I could follow enough to know that she was complaining that it was not fair for Canadians and everyone else to be able to study for six months if I could only study for two. Neron and I continued chatting for nearly an hour. Besides talking baseball with this obvious fanatic, we talked about what he had done while growing up. He said that he graduated from the University of Havana with a degree in chemistry and had worked for a United States company making cosmetics. "They stressed efficiency all the time," he said, stopping for another sip of *cafecito*.

"That has not changed. Now we have a store called Wal-Mart that has turned efficiency into a science," I said.

After Neron finished explaining how Cuba had the best chance of winning the Copa del Mundo baseball tournament this year, a new boarder joined the conversation. He said that Neron was probably right but that he would be cheering for Brazil anyway. Neron introduced him to me as Mateus, a Brazilian from João Pessoa. He had arrived today and was also starting a Spanish class. He was two or three inches taller than me and looked like a GQ model. I remembered how Antonio Banderas looked in the movie *Zorro* and decided that this guy was even better looking. He and Neron started talking in Spanish about baseball, and I hoped that I wouldn't be in the same class with him.

The *Copa del Mundo* tournament was beginning that evening with games in several cities. If I would have been in Holguin I could have watched the United States take on Mexico.

195

"Then Mateus brought a book from his room to show us the beauties of João Pessoa. His hometown is renowned for having the most per capita green space of any city in the world. It is situated on the easternmost tip of South America. The pictures of beaches, flowers, and colonial architecture were beautiful.

Later, I sat on the balcony of the house and looked at the busy activity of the street. There were a lot more cars on the road than in Holguin. There were no carriages pulled by horses. I didn't see guys sharing a bottle of rum or squealing pigs going down the street tied to bicycles. There were a lot of old American cars, but there were also a lot of newer Japanese and European cars. Absorbing the sun's warmth, I vowed to study every waking hour of the two months, but my mind kept wandering back to Holguin. I hoped I could sneak out for one weekend before the two months were over. It was great yesterday, talking to Carlos, but mostly I was thinking about someone else. I missed her, but I really wouldn't know what to say to her. I just wanted to hold her.

The Workbook

✦

Day 60
Monday, October 13, 2003

I tried to follow the conversation between the short pudgy teacher and the students. Although I recognized many of the words, I couldn't follow any complete thoughts. The teacher, probably approaching fifty, enjoyed herself as she asked the students questions, stretching their Spanish. The thick, red-framed glasses moved constantly as she nodded, shook her head, or changed expressions, correcting gently with a warm laugh when a student used the wrong tense, or helping with a smile when a student wasn't sure of themselves. Only Spanish was allowed. I watched her work, wishing that I was ready to understand, wondering why they placed me in an intermediate class where everyone knew much more Spanish than I did. I was sure that I should be called a beginner.

Still listening, I started looking at the faded workbook she had handed me before class started. I got the feeling that she didn't like the students who started a week late. "Comenzarás en página diez y siete," she said disapprovingly.

Not ready for rapid Spanish, I asked the only other male student in the class what she had said.

"She said that you will begin on page 17," Chris from Canada answered.

"Thanks. *Me llamo Brandon.*"

The ink on the cover of the workbook was hard to read. I could barely make out *La Universidad de Habana* and a picture of Mary with her arms open, ready to embrace. The sixty or so pages were held together by four industrial-size staples along the left hand side. Although the ink on the cover was faded the workbook had not been used. Evidently the toner in the copier was low the day that the university printed it. I flipped through sixteen blank pages until I found the lesson on the preterite and the imperfect. While my first sixteen pages were blank, I noticed that Chris's book was full of answers, corrections, and notes scattered along the margins.

This morning I woke up early, and since I couldn't get back to sleep, I sat on the balcony and watched the streets come alive. First, the *cocos*, bright yellow coconuts with handlebars, started purring both ways down the street. The *cocos* were three-wheeled motorcycles that served as taxis. The driver sat in front of a shell with one or two seats. Occasionally a *camelo* used our street, a semi tractor pulling a pink or blue soviet bus with a large hump on each end. More than two hundred people could be sardine-packed into one bus.

When Neron got up to prepare breakfast, I startled him as I stood up to come into the kitchen. "You're very anxious to get started," he said.

I am excited," I answered with a little laugh. "If I only have two months I need to get started early." I was finally going to do what I had yearned to do since the day I first stepped out of the plane in Havana sixty days before. I was starting my Spanish course.

"They will test you this morning," he said. "I think they will place you in the intermediate group."

"I don't know. There are a lot of basic things that I need to learn."

"I think you are ready for intermediate, but we will see." He poured the coffee in the cup and handed it to me. "Are you ready for breakfast?"

"Yeah."

When Mateus joined us, he asked Neron about *La Copa del Mundo*. On the first day of the tournament both Cuba and the U.S. were winners. Brazil's first game was scheduled late tonight. When Mateus waited for his food, he talked in English about the United States and a book he was reading. The book pictured the United States as a decaying society full of discrimination and pregnant girls, where everyone was obsessed with drugs and guns. I just listened politely with no comment. There was no point in describing the U.S. I knew, and it was too late to tell him that I was from Canada.

It took about fifteen minutes for Paloma to escort Mateus and me to the university. The building with our class was old and classical with gigantic columns running up the front. We went up a few flights of stairs and then walked along a large horseshoe-shaped balcony with classrooms jetting off and a large courtyard down below. This is where I would be studying for the next two months. Paloma introduced us to two ladies who gave us a placement test. I thought I did poorly but they placed me in the intermediate class. Mateus, as expected, went to an advanced class. He had studied Spanish for a year before coming to Havana and his native Portuguese was very similar to Spanish.

Before starting the day, the teacher introduced me to the class. There were six women and Chris. Two of the women were from Japan. The others were from

Norway, Germany, Switzerland, and the Bahamas. They had all studied several years of Spanish in their native country.

I talked to Mateus at the ten-thirty break. He was excited about some French girls in his class. He thought he could talk them into eating with us after the class ended at twelve thirty. I smiled without a commitment.

I tried harder the last half of class to understand what was being said. I especially focused on the instructor's explanation of the workbook assignment. I vowed to do every assignment and work on the empty pages at the front of the book. Mateus grabbed me after class, introduced two very attractive French women, and invited me to eat with them. I declined politely, saying I needed to study. The giant hospital next to the university was my landmark so I didn't get lost on my way back to the apartment.

Neron, watching the news on TV, asked me how my day had gone.

I told him that they put me in the wrong class. He smiled and explained what I could fix myself for lunch, crackers, like in Holguin, but with butter instead of mayonnaise. Along with the crackers, there were little bananas and coffee and milk.

I ate and studied while Neron took a nap. He woke up when Paloma came home from work and prepared a great meal of chicken in spicy barbecue sauce, with a heaping pile of *congri* and a fresh salad. Mateus came back from lunch just in time to eat with us. Then he headed back to meet some other ladies for a movie. He invited me, but again, I just wanted to study.

Midnight Mangoes

✦

Day 61
Tuesday, October 14, 2003

"I like the mangoes the same way you do. But the secret is that when the mangoes are that ripe, they become *midnight mangoes.*" I started to speak in a stage whisper. "You need to eat them under the cover of darkness."

My spy voice made Meka, the student from the Bahamas, laugh. "What do you mean by *midnight mangoes?*"

"It means you need to eat the mangoes at midnight, when it is so dark that you cannot see the mango," I explained, leading her to one of Carlos's favorite punch lines.

I walked into the classroom early that morning, but Meka had arrived first. She was sitting alone, rapidly flipping through her large dictionary and some other reference books. When I entered, she looked back and smiled. "Did you get your homework done?" My heart sped up a little because Meka looked so much like a beautiful Jamaican Netball star that I had a secret crush on while in Jamaica.

Some of the first pages of the workbook dealt with the present form of regular verbs that end in *-er, -ar, and -ir.* I was going to show off, but had no idea how to conjugate '*hacer*,' the verb for 'to do,' so I stuck to English. "Yes, I did. Did you get it done?"

"Yeah, I got it done, and now I'm just checking to make sure that I did them all correctly." The simple cotton dress, with a blue floral pattern, did nothing to conceal her striking, athletic body.

"I'm sure you did."

She glanced back and smiled again. "You're from the U.S., right?"

"Yeah, and you're from the Bahamas?"

"That's right," she said. She told me her name, and I introduced myself. Her shoulder-length hair was starting to curl at the roots. I could tell that it had been awhile since she had it straightened.

Then I asked her why she was in Cuba.

"Well, I work on the island of Grand Bahama for the Bahaman Tourist Board," she explained. "My job is to answer questions that prospective visitors may have. I've traveled to the States a few times, mainly Atlanta and Baltimore. I enjoy visiting the States but after a while I start to miss my favorite food, the Haden mango. I love to eat them when they are super ripe, and they are starting to fall from the tree. However, the only problem is the worms."

That was when I started to tell Carlos's joke, but the other students and teacher arrived before I could deliver the punch line. The teacher asked one of the Japanese girls about walking to the university. First, she had to answer in the preterite because she had finished walking to the university. Then she had to use the imperfect because the question was about what she was doing while she was walking. As I was listening I recalled a night in our apartment in Holguin when Carmen tried to explain the difference to me. My heart hurt. Was that only one week ago?

At the break, Meka approached me and demanded to know why she should eat her mangoes in the dark.

"The reason," I answered dramatically, "that they are called *midnight mangoes* is because the only thing worse than seeing a worm in your mango is seeing half a worm." She laughed and nodded. Carlos's joke had a strange simplicity that made sense to everyone.

Ricardo's Bar

◆

Day 62
Wednesday, October 15, 2003

The skinny bartender walked up to me and asked me what I wanted.

"*Un Indio*," I replied. *Hatuey*, pronounced "HOT—way," was a native who led several strikes against the Spanish settlers in the early sixteenth century. The Taino Chief was depicted on the dark bottle with a Sioux headdress. Apparently the bartender understood what I wanted and soon headed back with a brown bottle of *Hatuey*. The light lager taste was similar to Red Stripe in Jamaica and reminded me of how much I missed Carlos.

After breakfast that morning I told Neron that I wouldn't be in for lunch. I continued to turn down Mateus's invitations but had decided to find Ricardo. Also, I knew that struggling in class would make me thirsty. Following Ricardo's instructions, I followed *Avenida Universidad* around the east side of the university. Then the same street turned northwest toward the ocean. I walked about four more blocks after the turn and found the address between *Club La Red* and *Cine Yara*. On the outside of the building there was no indication that this was a bar at all. I walked past it twice before trying the door. The only indication that there was a business was a small sign next to a small drive-through-size window advertising "*Tortas: Jamón y Queso*," (Ham and Cheese Sandwiches). Inside, a bar ran along one wall. Half a dozen tables, each with four wooden chairs, filled the rest of the space. The walls were painted blue and covered with colorful posters of Switzerland, Sweden, and other European countries. The bar and the wooden bar stools were red. The bar seemed to be well stocked.

The first beer went down quickly, and I asked for another. Sipping it, I watched the bartender squeeze the juice from two limes into a glass with raw cane sugar. Then he added a shot of Carta Blanca, a white rum. After a squirt of soda he stirred in several mint leaves. It looked exactly like the *mojitos* that Neron had given me on Sunday.

When the bartender was done with the drinks, I asked, "¿*Está Ricardo?*" "*No. No está ahorita. El viene más tarde. Pero él siempre está en la noche. Usualmente ayuda a preparar las tortas en la tarde. Como a las seis. ¿Qué necesitas?*" he rattled off.

Like during the class, I understood several words but they just didn't come together into complete thoughts. There were just too many words I didn't know. I understood that Ricardo would come later, probably at six. I knew that the man was suspicious and asked what I wanted. I pretended I understood, thanked him, and answered that I just wanted to talk.

As I walked back to Neron's, I thought about my conversation with Ricardo in Montego Bay and Mateus's book about America. I had grown up in America. I had never seen a gun except those used for hunting. I had never met a pregnant girl outside of marriage. Jamaica, America's idea of paradise, was full of violence and poverty. Cuba, America's idea of violent repression, was the most relaxed wonderful place I had ever been.

Then, as always, when I was alone, my thoughts returned to Carmen. Because these thoughts caused pain, I began to conjugate. *Beber*—to drink. *Yo bebo*, I drink. *Yo bebí*, I drank. *Yo bebía*, I was drinking. *Caminar*—to walk. *Yo camino*, I walk. *Yo caminé*, I walked. *Yo caminaba*, I was walking. *Querer*—to love. I quit conjugating because my whole mind was full of the most beautiful woman in the world, and I missed her.

Back against the Wall

✦

Day 63
Thursday, October 16, 2003

Nothing made sense. I felt like I could learn more listening to a dog bark. The only word I understood all morning was "*listo*," but that one word didn't make any sense. Especially when the Japanese girls answered questions, the teacher smiled and said, "*Listo.*" I had used the word several times in Holguin. When we were going out, Carmen would ask me if I was ready. "*¿Listo?*" If I was ready I would say, "*Sí, estoy listo.*" I guess the teacher meant that she was happy that they had been ready with an answer. The *professora* asked me three questions. The first I completely messed up. The other two I just shook my head. I had struggled and struggled with the workbook the night before. This morning when I checked with Meka, I discovered that I had everything backward and had messed up most of the work.

Walking home after class, I wondered why they had put me into an intermediate class and why I thought I could learn Spanish. I remembered my first week in Jamaica, when we were staying at the University of the West Indies in Kingston. They were explaining safety rules and cultural differences before we were sent off into our communities to start a month worth of training. There was a basketball court outside of our dorm rooms at the university. A couple of fellow volunteers and I decided that we should go out to play basketball with some of the Jamaican students. After a couple of hours playing, the word "*blood-claat*" was being used more and more frequently. The following day I decided to bring the word up in our cultural meeting/language training. I found out that "*blood-claat*" was not a medical term. It is an expletive, such as "*Tek yuh blood-claat ands ov me,*" which translates into "Take your fucking hands off of me!"

Back at the apartment I told Neron that I didn't think I could learn Spanish in such a short time. "What does '*listo*' mean?"

Instead of answering my question, he asked, "Do you know the black bug that jumps?"

"Sure, cricket in English, just like the game they play in Jamaica. It's '*grillo*' in Spanish, isn't it? *Grillo* is a funny word. If they are teasing skinny girls they call them '*grillo*,'" I answered, feeling a little bit smart for the first time all day.

Neron was impressed too. "You are '*listo.*' As you probably know, it means ready, but it is also used to tell someone you think they are smart. You are smart, and you study hard. It is good that the time is short, and you are in a hard class. People learn best when their back is against the wall."

Listo

✦

Day 64
Friday, October 17, 2003

My first week was ending. Preterite and imperfect verbs were nearly behind us, in the past. Next week our main topic would be the future tense of verbs. I had consistently arrived at least twenty minutes before class to compare notes with Meka and get ready for the lesson that we would be covering that day. Both Meka and I knew that the future tense would be next in the workbook, and Meka let me in on a little secret.

"She's going to ask you what you will do next week."

I paused and looked up from the sentences I was completing by filling in the proper conjugated verbs. "What?" I asked.

"The teacher is going to ask you what you will be doing next week. She always overlaps one topic into the other. Last Friday she asked us what we did during the week. We had to answer in the past so we had to use the preterite or the imperfect. I think that it is her way of seeing if we know anything about what we will be studying. Because of where you sit, I know that she calls on you first and then works her way around the classroom. Just be ready."

As we reviewed the homework my palms began to sweat. I glanced forward in the notebook and had some rehearsed answers ready. After all of the homework questions were answered the teacher cleared her throat and turned to me. I knew it was coming.

"Brandon, *¿que quieres hacer la semana próxima?* (What do you want to do next week?)

I took a deep breath. Meka looked back at me, and we both smiled.

"*Yo estudiaré. Yo tomaré cerveza. Yo hablaré español. Yo comeré platanitos y yo dormiré un poco.* (I will study. I will drink beer. I will talk Spanish. I will eat little bananas, and I will sleep a little.)

The teacher smiled and said, "*Muy listo.*"

Common Sense

✦

Day 65
Saturday, October 18, 2003

Ricardo saw me order a *mojito*. He walked quickly to me, his hand outstretched, and grinned. "I knew you would find me. Have you started your class?"

"I've got one week done. It's hard but I will learn a lot in two months. The teacher works us hard," I responded, gripping his hand. "I found this place Wednesday afternoon and drank *Un Indio*. The bartender said you would be in today."

"I'm glad you're here. We can talk. This table is private. My crowd will all be watching Cuba beat Italy in the *Copa del Mundo*." He led me to a corner table, with a green tablecloth of rich Guatemalan weave. We sat in silence while I sipped my *mojito*. Finally, he said, "As we were parting last week you asked what I thought about...." He paused and then put his hand to his chin, the common sign for Fidel Castro Ruiz. "Your question has made me think about this. It is not an easy question. I think you should answer first. What do you think about...?" He stroked his chin.

"I'm from the U.S. I don't know anything," I tried speaking my confusion. "I do know I love Cuba, even if it is poor and some things don't seem right. I have been to Jamaica, some Caribbean Islands, Central America, and of course the U.S. In many ways, right now, life in Cuba is better even if everyone is poor. People feel safer here than in Jamaica. People accept life and live. People are generous with the little that they have. Children are given opportunities here that the poorest children in other countries are not given. If this is because of what he (I stroked my chin.) has done, then I think he has done okay. I am impressed that someone as great as Nelson Mandela admires Fidel. That tells me a lot. Plus, I know that as a leader in the beginning of the revolution he went through a lot. Major defeats. Time in jail. He didn't just talk, he put himself on the line. But mostly, I just don't know. Will you tell me what you think?"

207

"I don't think history is about individuals. I think history is about the people, "el pueblo" in Spanish. History books talk about the leaders, but I think usually the leaders happen because of history and not the other way around. Do you understand what I am saying?"

"A little bit. Please go on."

"What do you call your war from 1776 against the British?"

"The War of Independence."

"And the fourth of July, what do you celebrate?

"Independence Day."

"Yes, the thirteen Colonies declared their independence, and it is still your most important national holiday. Well, from 1520 until 1959, Cuba was a colony. In the 1500s the native Cubans fought hard but by 1570 there was no pure native on the island. In Latin America, the pope said that killing the natives was wrong, but having them work while they were taught was okay. This was permission to take Indians as slaves and work them to death." Ricardo stopped talking for a minute.

I sipped my drink and waited. Finally I asked, "Why are people like that?"

His smile was grim. Good question, but I don't have an answer. Anyway, Cuba was a colony of Spain until Teddy Roosevelt drove them out in 1898. Cubans had been at war with Spain for 400 years and would have won without help in another year or two. The Americans came and took part in one battle and proclaimed victory. The U.S. flew their flag over "*mi país*" for three years. Then a Texan designed a new flag. We were declared independent, but we were just a United States colony. We produced sugar and cigars for them at prices that they set. Then we became a playground for the rich, especially the rich gangsters."

Ricardo was becoming more passionate and talking loud enough that the others in the bar had stopped talking and were listening. He was afraid I might have been offended and spent the next few minutes quietly apologizing for his passion.

"No, that is okay," I said. I just want to learn. I am a citizen of the U.S. but I am angry too at how my government treats the rest of the world. I am not offended. I feel honored that you speak honestly with me."

In the restroom I started to wonder if they weren't a Russian colony until the Special Period. When I asked Ricardo, he laughed aloud. "You do ask good questions."

"Thank you," I said. "I just am trying to understand."

"You know about the Bay of Pigs? You know how many times the U.S. government has tried to kill Fidel? He took land, money, and power away from many rich people. He sent all the priests home to Spain. It is hard to stay alive and stay in power when so many people with passion and money want you to be dead. He had to deal with Russia to survive, but we were never a colony."

"But didn't you have to do what Russia wanted in order to keep them here?"

"It was very complicated. We gave them sugar, cigars, and a presence close to the United States. They sent us money and ugly cars. We provided a place for them to train their young men and build ugly buildings. The Russians are good people. It was complicated."

"But then they left, and Cuba now is independent."

Ricardo sighed, almost painfully, and continued, "Yes, independent. Poor, but free. *La Lucha.* The struggle for independence. Some days I think we will win. Some days I think we will lose. But in a war people die. People do whatever it takes to win. We are still struggling to be independent. Bush preaches democracy. In the rest of poor Latin America, that is a horrible joke. Democracy does not work where people can't read. Democracy doesn't work where a few people control all the money, especially if they are tied to American corporations. The American corporations don't care if gangsters control the streets, people have health care, or if kids go to school. They will keep people in power that protect their right to own the other country."

Ricardo realized he was getting passionate again, stopped, and looked apologetically at me. "I agree. Go on."

Silent, thinking our own thoughts for awhile, Ricardo finally continued, quietly. "I just thought of an interesting connection between our struggle and your War of Independence. Do you read very much?"

"Not as much as I should."

"I love to read. I am reading this week a new book about an old book. Paulo Freire, a Brazilian educator, wrote a very important book in the '60s titled *Pedagogy of the Oppressed.* It called for teaching reading to the poor through raising the *campesino*'s consciousness about being oppressed. All the revolutionaries of the '60s and '70s read it. His new book, about that book, is titled *Pedagogy of Hope.* In this book Freire continually refers to common sense, what people already know, as the starting point for true education. I just realized that this term is the title of the writing used by the revolutionaries in the United States in the 1770s, *Common Sense* by Thomas Paine. Let me show off a little and quote my favorite line. 'Society in every state is a blessing, but government, even in its best state, is but a necessary evil.'"

When Ricardo finished, he gave me another *mojito* and excused himself, saying he'd be working evenings every day but Tuesday. He apologized for practicing his English but not my Spanish. I listened to the salsa music mingled with

Spanish conversation. Listening carefully, I could pick out a few words here and there. It reminded me of picking through a can of mixed nuts and taking out the cashews.

Later, strolling slowly through the quiet streets, I marveled at what Ricardo had told me. I knew I could learn much more from him if I ask the right questions. I was sitting in front of a rich *caldosa*. I could skim the liquid off the top of this Cuban stew or I could delve a little deeper and get the good stuff from the bottom. Cuba, more than Jamaica, was the country of my heart, and I wanted to learn everything I could about "*mi país.*"

Missing Carmen

✦

Day 66
Sunday, October 19, 2003

Paloma sat across the room from me watching her favorite telenovela on the slightly newer color television. Neron sat in the opposite corner of the room watching the *Copa del Mundo* on the other television. Cuba was still undefeated in pool play and several points ahead of Canada. It was an old black and white, and the picture would roll from the top of the screen to the bottom. Neron would occasionally hit it but it didn't stop rolling. I looked back down at my verbs. I put down my pencil and rubbed my temples. I had been trying to work for over an hour but I couldn't concentrate on conjugations. I could only think about Carmen.

My mind would drift. Drift along with the waves of the greenish blue Caribbean Sea. The affectionate water holding me, warming my body and my senses until I was completely relaxed. That is the way I felt when I looked into her bluish sea-green eyes. It was hard not to drift off when I thought about the way it felt. The way my body would tingle with passion just from the slightest touch of her hand. She could say so many things to me just from the touch of her hand and the glow in her eyes. Those nights when I would walk out onto the balcony and the moon would shine through the hanging begonias to cast its light on what I considered my world.

There were times when I would sit at the table in Damita's kitchen and watch Carmen prepare dinner. The contrast of her beauty with the dilapidated surroundings was like looking at a pearl in a jar full of marbles. She was out of place. It's tough now to think back and remember the foolish thoughts that I had throughout those days. Did I really think that I could be with her? I mean forever? It was just another stupid dream for a naïve farm boy from Nebraska. Did I really think I understood what life is or what life is about because I spent three years in Jamaica? I looked down at the mangled and taped dictionary. I don't

211

remember how many times Carmen had thrown this thing at me but it had survived.

Some people say that heartache, like losing friends and lovers, is easier to overcome each time it happens. This is at times true and at times not. Sitting at the table in the apartment with the workbook open, I pondered whom I had lost. When you have become that connected to someone, they become a part of your soul. Random sounds, smells and memories take you back to the time when you felt completely happy. Then there are the thoughts about what was left behind. There are the "what if's." You do, however, find new ways to cope with the memories. You take up new hobbies or new relationships, or find something to flood your mind and drown out all the thoughts. I could have gone on pondering this forever, things I did to lessen the pain. I removed my hands from my temples and picked up my pencil. I had Spanish verbs to conjugate.

I couldn't decide if I should sneak back to Holguin some weekend or not. I couldn't get my mind around any way to be with Carmen for any length of time. Going back would just open all the wounds. I conjugated until the sun went down; every blank was full. My head was full of pictures of Carmen, even after I went to sleep.

Canadian Chris

◆

Day 67
Monday, October 20, 2003

My forearms were resting on the marble railing on the second floor. I looked down on the beautiful courtyard, the fountain and the flowers. I exhaled the cigarette smoke and watched it climb past the third floor balcony and into the blue sky. Chris came over and leaned against the railing about four feet from me. Chris was from Canada, and he was the only other male in the class. He was built about like me, maybe a little thinner with glasses. We had exchanged a little information, but no real conversation. I knew he attended a Theological University in Canada and that this was his third time in Cuba. I also knew that he was engaged to get married when he got back to Canada. Last week he had proudly shown me the picture of a blond with short hair, a big nose, and a weak smile. I told him she was beautiful.

Last week he had been excited by Canada's three wins in the *Copa del Mundo*. This morning I kidded him about how badly Cuba had beaten Canada last night. Then I asked him, "Chris, why are you in Havana? Just to learn Spanish?"

"This trip is just to learn Spanish, and to support the Cuban leaders of our Evangelical Church here. I can't help too much though since my Spanish isn't good enough to give talks or lead discussions. The first two times I came I made sure that several bicycles that were donated to us by a manufacturer in Montreal got to the right people."

"Do you plan to come back after this trip?" I asked.

"I want to continue Evangelical work in Latin America, but Megan needs to finish school first. I will start seminary next fall. We will go where ever Jesus leads us."

I envied Chris. He had a plan and someone to share it with. I had no plan, and the one I wanted to share with was locked into a country where I couldn't stay.

213

I was like Chris in so many ways, and in other ways we were total opposites. I think that part of me likes to have a plan and never stray from it. I need to have that control. That control over my future allows me to never have to worry about sharing my feelings. However, when I think back at all of the things that I have experienced, I realize the things that I cherish most were sporadic glitches in my seamless plan. I planned to do Peace Corps, but I never factored in Carlos and so many other wonderful things. I planned to study in Cuba, but I never dreamed that I would fall in love with someone. When I plan something out, I don't factor in pain, joy, love, hope, and hurt. Maybe if I did I would miss out on a lot of things. Chris had things planned out. I had things planned out far enough to know that I was planning on finishing this cigarette. In college in South Dakota I had a daily planner. Days, weeks and months were planned out. Since I left over three years ago, I didn't worry about planning. Things happened when they happened. I think when I started living like this, I started living.

La Lucha

✦

Day 68
Tuesday, October 21, 2003

So little time and so many verbs. It's nice to grow up with a language. I didn't have to learn to add -ed, it just happened. Children conjugate as well as their parents by the time they are three or four. Today, in class, I used *luchar* (the word for struggle which Carlos continually used to describe life in Cuba) to demonstrate the conjugation of an -ar verb. This inspired the teacher to ask about the war in Iraq. I used my standard defense. "*El gobierno es en una guerra con Iraq y yo no sé por qué. El pueblo, como yo, no es en una guerra. Yo no soy en una guerra. Yo no puedo entender mi gobierno.*"

The class seemed satisfied with my explanation that the U.S. government was at war but I wasn't and that I didn't understand what my government was doing.

At least I hoped they were satisfied. I didn't know what else to say, and the class went on, with Meka conjugating her favorite *-ir* verb, *vestir*, to dress.

The night before when I was conjugating *luchar*, I remembered everything Ricardo told me about Fidel Castro Ruiz. I started thinking about the struggle he faced, the struggle the Cuban people have every day, and the struggle they will have in the future.

Besides talking about Cuba and its history as a colony, Ricardo also talked about Castro's struggle. How he was the illegitimate son of a very rich landowner in the Holguin province or a province near Holguin. The son of a maid, who his father later married, Castro identified with the workers on his father's sugar cane plantation, even encouraging them to strike until his father paid them better.

Most Cubans remained poor, with long hours and back-breaking work. Workers barely earned enough money to house and feed themselves and their families. They lived on beans and rice and wore tattered clothes. Extended families shared one small, cramped house, most without running water or electricity.

Access to healthcare was limited. People died from diseases that could have been cured with simple antibiotics.

"Did you take part in the fighting in 1959, on one side or the other?" I asked him.

He was silent, for at least two minutes, and I waited, listening to the salsa music from the bar's very nice sound system. Finally, he said, "I was a teenager and worked for the revolution. I was a youth leader. But when the killing started after Batista left the country, I didn't work for the revolution any more. I just went to school and studied. My father had some dollars that he used to send me to Colorado. He had a friend in Denver that helped."

"It must have been an exciting time," I offered when he finished.

"Exciting. Scary. Confusing. Very confusing. Hard to understand what happened. Even now, I read the books about that time, about Ché and Fidel. It seems a story from someplace else."

Now, on Tuesday, remembering Ricardo's words and struggling as the class worked with the future tense, I continued thinking about the verb *luchar*. The future tense for *luchar* is *luchará*. I know I need to use the future tense, but instead, I usually rely on what Carmen taught me. Just like in English, we can use the present tense of go with an infinitive to speak of the future. In English a person can say, "I will struggle" or "I am going to struggle."

I am sure that "*Fidel y el pueblo de Cuba va a luchar mucho años más.*" (Fidel and the Cuban people are going to struggle for many more years.)

Sugar, Soldiers, Tourism, and Teachers

✦

Day 69
Wednesday, October 22, 2003

When it involved conversation with Ricardo, I expected tough topics and hard-to-answer questions. Tonight he didn't surprise me when he asked, "Why do you think the U.S. continues to insist on the embargo?"

I looked down and stirred my *mojito*, stabbing at the sprigs of mint sitting on the bottom. I remembered discussions about the embargo with Carlos, under a coconut tree with a bottle of rum, behind our apartments in Jamaica.

When I didn't answer, he prodded me. "Is it because our government is communist, or is it because of the human rights violations?"

"Ricardo, I am young. I wish my country would leave other countries alone. I know nothing, but here is what puzzles me. One word always comes to my mind when I think about the embargo, China. I mean, essentially, Cuba and China are the same, right? Same political structure. Same human rights violations. Except I can travel to China and the U.S. trades with this communist, human rights-violating country. Why?"

Ricardo grinned at my passion and shrugged, signaling me to continue.

"Cuba, of course, is a lot closer, but more importantly, Cuba has said to the U.S. government, 'We will not let you push us around,' and that has really pissed off a lot of arrogant Americans who think that they should run the world."

"I like the way you think," he said as he stood up to help wait on a group of celebrants that had just come in off the street. I had arrived at the bar a little after nine, finished with my preparation for tomorrow's Spanish class. The bar was full of people because Cuba was playing Brazil in the first championship round of the *Copa del Mundo*. With his hand on my shoulder, he continued, "I close at midnight. If you can relax and enjoy the music until then, I'll answer any questions

217

you have over some *mojitos* made from some special rum I save for special friends."

"That would be great. I'll try to think of some really hard questions."

After a while, I moved to the bar where Ricardo mixed drinks, and we chatted about whatever came to mind. I started entertaining him with Carlos stories. He laughed so loud when I told him about Carlos dropping the bananas on me that everyone stopped talking and looked at us. He kept mixing drinks, and I asked him how he felt about Bush listing Fidel with Saddam and the guy from North Korea in his war on terrorism.

"Cuba is not a terrorist threat. All of us know what would happen immediately if we threatened the U.S. Besides, we all have family in every city in the States. That is all nonsense."

I agreed and said, "That question was too easy. Here's a harder one. If the embargo ended, how soon would the Cuban economy be healthy?"

He chuckled. "That is a good one, with many possible answers. I'm not sure I have a good answer. If you have time, I have some ideas I'd like to talk about. In some ways our economy right now is the healthiest in Latin America. Your friend Carlos was in Jamaica, working as a teacher. What other country can export teachers, nurses, and doctors? Is our economy worse than theirs because no banana company is making a lot of money here?"

"And soldiers. Cuba also exports soldiers," I mentioned.

"Not any to speak of right now. In the '70s our presence in Angola certainly made the difference in driving out Portugal and starting a new government. The U.S. oil companies continue to buy the government it wants so the country is a mess, with too much corruption. The son of a close friend came home from Angola shaking his head about the irony. He was in Africa risking his life guarding oil wells owned by an American company against troops armed by the American government. Things are complicated."

"Are there any simple solutions?" I pondered.

"Of course not, but the real question is, "Will any real solution be acceptable? Have you ever heard of Deming or Sengé?"

"No. Are they Cuban?"

"Deming is a hero of mine," Ricardo handed me a fresh *mojito*, "but he is a statistician from the United States. He is most famous for what he did in Japan. People give him credit for Japan's economic recovery after World War II. More recently he worked with Ford before they built the Escort and Taurus. He wrote a book, *Out of the Crisis*, but that book has been mostly ignored. He tells how things must work together in a system to allow for change."

"And the other guy?"

"Sengé, like Deming, understands that there are not simple solutions. Everything is part of a system, and every action within a system affects the other parts of the system. He is a professor at MIT. I'm recommending a second book tonight. Sengé wrote *The Fifth Discipline* to describe how systems work. For a book on management from MIT it is pretty easy to read. He believes that when people start thinking in terms of systems, positive change will happen. I believe that to be successful economically, Cubans must take this path."

"You are talking way over my head," I said. "Give me an example."

He sipped his drink and prepared an answer. After a minute, he cleared his throat and began. "In Cuba, people are not eating as well as we should. We have a lot of land and a perfect climate. We should be supplying our people with enough food, and we should export tropical fruits. There is no excuse. It's one of the things that makes me angry. I see the farms in Colorado and California. I see how much food they get out of the desert in Israel. We could grow so much food that everyone is always full. Why don't we? We know how to produce sugar, but it is nearly worthless, and we don't know how to produce artificial sweeteners. We know how to produce tobacco, a poison that nearly killed me, but we don't seem to be able to raise enough grain to feed chickens."

"And you say that your country has to find a better system?"

He relaxed and smiled, "Good people are working on it, and people are learning, but farming is hard work and complicated. We have to train a generation of people to be true agronomists and to realize that production takes a complete system with continual checks and corrections. Right now, though, it is a mess."

"How did it get to be such a mess?"

"Spain, and then the U.S., forced us to produce nothing but sugar. Even our relationship with Russia required sugar. Our economy depended entirely upon the price of sugar. Three times in the last century, the prices, controlled by the U.S., went from less than five cents a pound to up above twenty cents, one time up to thirty-five cents, then back down to single digits. A country cannot exist like that."

"With Russia gone," Ricardo stroked his chin instead of saying Castro's name, "...decided that tourism could replace sugar as Cuba's main source of money. That's when he let the dollars come in, and that's another mess."

Watching the waitresses serve the crowd, I remembered the parade in Holguin and laughed to myself. "In Holguin I thought of an idea that would make Cuba self-sufficient in electricity."

"What is that?" Ricardo wondered.

I told him about my idea of hooking the young women up to generators and playing music. He laughed and excused himself to take drinks to a table that was getting a little loud. I relaxed and watched the game. Later, after Cuba had beaten Brazil, 4–3, the crowd went home, and Ricardo locked up the bar. He poured more rum from his special bottle and carefully mixed fresh drinks. We talked about sugar, systems, and change until four in the morning.

Music, Not Politics

✦

Day 70
Thursday, October 23, 2003

As the class was ending, Sra. Mendoza announced that we each were to do "*un exposición*" on the last day of class, the next Friday, October thirty-first. This presentation would be between ten and fifteen minutes long. We could choose any topic we cared to share with the rest of the class. Of course, it had to be entirely in Spanish. By Monday, we had to decide on our topic.

As I walked home, enjoying the palm trees and tropical flowers, I started thinking about what I could talk about for ten to fifteen minutes. Certainly not history or politics. My two conversations with Ricardo at his bar had me thinking too much about those things, and I looked forward to lying in bed thinking about something else. After coming home from Ricardo's the night before I couldn't sleep. His info about Angola and Venezuela filled my mind. Instead of counting sheep I counted sacks of sugar. In order to stop thinking about that, I thought about Holguin. I wondered if I would ever get back to Holguin and see Carlos or Carmen again. That was worse than thinking about Cuba and "*la lucha.*"

Thinking about Holguin led to thinking about Jamaica and the great times with Carlos. Jamaica had its own struggle. I thought about the children in Kingston who couldn't go to school, fighting to be chosen to wash windows so they could buy food. I had spent three years in a rural community where the lack of a basic infrastructure made any progress nearly hopeless.

The two major political parties in Jamaica, the Jamaica Labor Party (JLP) and the People's National Party (PNP) are like two gangs who provide guns and pay-offs to their supporters. "The PNP Zone" or "JLP—Enter at Your Own Risk" graffiti was written on walls to show the strong political allegiances of the communities. I was harassed for wearing clothes that represented one party or the other. JLP is green and PNP is orange. My red bike was a problem to JLP sup-

221

porters because it was something like orange. The craziness went to which beer you drank since it disturbed true followers if you drank Heineken in the PNP zone or Red Stripe on JLP turf. Although I lived in the rural part of the country, political loyalties still tie communities together or divide them. It seemed to me that both parties only sold empty promises to line their own pockets. Both would make sure that U.S. corporations and tourists were happy and that the majority of Jamaicans would remain uneducated and hopeless.

Smaller political groups battled the two dominant parties. In the summer of 2001 the Jamaica Defense Force held a garrison community in Kingston's The Tivilli Gardens for seven days. I attended a wedding in Kingston during that week. Because of the random shootings the taxi drivers stayed home. The bride, the groom, and I caught a ride out of Kingston with the priest, hoping that none of the craziness would stop us on our ride back toward Spanish Town.

Most houses in Cuba go unpainted because of the cost of paint. Approaching an exception, freshly painted in a dark blue, my favorite song by Shakira, "*Estoy Aquí,*" drifted through the steel grate, onto the street. I suddenly knew what I would do for my presentation. I grew up on country music in New Mexico and Nebraska. I loved the music from Jamaica and from Cuba. Music was much better that economics, politics, or history. I probably wouldn't be able to sleep but I would at least have something different to think about.

Entrepreneurs in Training

✦

Day 71
Friday, October 24, 2003

"You got me in trouble with my wife, talking so long on Wednesday," Ricardo greeted me, grinning.

"That's too bad, my friend," I answered. "Since it is Friday night I came prepared to talk until dawn."

"Not tonight," I promised *La Señora* that I would let Marcos close and that I would come home early."

"That's life. I have plenty of studying. The teacher gave us a new assignment yesterday. I have to talk in Spanish for ten to fifteen minutes. I'm going to talk about music, but I have a lot of work to prepare what I'm going to say. You're busy again tonight so we won't have much time to talk."

"Yeah, maybe time for only one question, an easy question."

"Well, since you told me that what happens depends on paradigms and systems, I guess my question is, 'Which system will Cubans choose after...?'" I stroked my chin.

Ricardo laughed his big laugh. "Sit down. Do you want a beer or *un mojito*?"

"A beer thanks. *Un Indio.*"

Walking to our table, Ricardo told a waitress, who was beautiful like all Cuban women, to bring the drinks to his private corner table. When we were seated, he began, "What happens next? What a question. Nobody knows what happens next. That question is easy to answer. '*Yo no sé.*'"

"I know that you don't know, but you have an idea which way it might go. Enlighten me, and I will listen."

Sipping his *mojito*, he decided how to arrange his answer. "I think if Fidel lives long enough the future is okay for us," he began. "If not, the U.S. will take over again. They will say we are democratic but it will feel like we are a colony. Too many people in Miami want us to be a colony again. They chose to live under the

223

Stars and Stripes. They would like Cuba to be a part of the U.S. so they can stay under the Stars and Stripes."

"How could that happen?"

"There will come a time when Fidel is gone, and the people will vote. What will they choose? Will money from the U.S. buy the election? It depends on what happens to the land when power changes hands. Do you think the U.S. corporations have forgotten what was taken from them when we nationalized? Do you not think that Cubans in Miami have maps of property that they believe still belongs to them?"

"But would the people in Cuba now accept that?" I asked in alarm.

"I need to check on some things in the kitchen. Then I will tell you the possibilities I see. Please excuse me. Mare will bring you another beer."

When Mare, tiny, with an exquisite face and big smile, brought me un *Indio* I asked in my best Spanish if she was still going to school.

"*Sí, estoy en la universidad,*" she answered, suddenly shy, talking to the American.

I asked what she was studying at the university, and she told me that, like Ricardo, she was interested in business. She said that maybe she would get to go to Germany to study if her grades were good enough.

In a few minutes, Ricardo returned and started immediately. "I see three main possibilities. The first one, I don't want to talk about, I just want to mention because I have read history, and I know it is possible. There could be a very bloody civil war. We have a well-trained army that I believe will defend our independence from the U.S. Wars are not logical, and anything can start one. It frightens me. I pray it will not happen, but I know it is possible."

"You are right, of course, but like you say, let's not talk about that. What are the other possibilities?"

"It is possible that Cuba will once more become an economic colony of the U.S. If we return to private ownership of the land, foreign money will buy everything of value, and corporations will take advantage of a willing work force unprotected by unions or minimum wage. Health care, nutrition, and education will again be for those with money. Like the rest of Latin America, the poor will get nothing.

"Another possibility, the one I dream of and work for, can only happen if Fidel lives long enough for the world courts and the U.S. Congress to recognize the present nationalization as legitimate. Then I believe that Cuba will become the model the world admires and that the rest of the third world can follow to true independence and prosperity."

I considered this for a moment, sipping on my cold beer. "I don't see much prosperity."

"You've been in the country for over two months. Have you noticed the black market?"

I laughed and told a whopper, "I have no idea what you mean. No one I know would consider buying anything from any place but a government-approved store."

He laughed. "You would do well in the black market. You lie with a very straight face. Now my book recommendation for the evening. A journalist named Corbett just finished a book published last year. The title is *This is Cuba*. It is about the black market. The subtitle is "An Outlaw Culture Survives." It has a lot of good stories and insights, but I think he misunderstands some important implications. He writes much hard truth that we in Cuba need to deal with. Anyway, you have seen the black market. Is the black market a secret? Do the police or CDRs try to stop it?"

Remembering the black market in Holguin, which involved everyone, including the leaders of the CDR, I laughed. "Everyone knows. Everyone uses it. I'm a gringo, and I know."

"It is my belief," Ricardo continued with his most professorial air, "that the black market will prove to be the source of our economic recovery. Schools can train teachers and doctors and then, after some experience, they can be good. Right?"

I nodded.

"Entrepreneurs, on the other hand, must be crafty problem solvers who understand business in a way difficult to teach in school. Right now, in the streets of Havana and across the country, thousands of men and women are learning the science and art of marketing. Some are building great little businesses. We are training the best business people in the world, and when the embargo ends and trade opens up, they will be ready. Opportunity will come from every direction."

"And some, like Mare, will get extra training, and be prepared for management," I added with a smile.

"Oh, you talked with her. She is brilliant. She will be a leader in the new Cuba." He noticed my empty glass and asked if I had time for another.

"No. No. No. I have to go home, and I don't want you to get in trouble again."

He slowed down his speech but had to finish. "Our entrepreneurs will deal with everyone in the world, the Japanese, Koreans, Germans, everyone. We will convert to bio-diesel so we will never have another Special Period. We will have an economy that works, and we will still take care of every child."

"Do you really believe this is possible? Do you really think this is the most likely outcome?" I asked.

"I hope, but I don't know. I am a little bit religious. But I don't think even God knows. God created us so we could decide about things, and one of the things we decide is the future. I believe God holds our hands and hopes we make good choices, but the future is up to us."

"Up to us to decide the future. That's scary. That's very scary," I mused. Then I asked, "*¿Cómo se dice 'scary' en Español?*"

The Brazilian Ambassador's House

◆

Day 72
Saturday, October 25, 2003

"Cuba is going to win! Cuba is going to win!" Neron yelled as he watched replays from Thursday's *Copa del Mundo* game. Cuba beat Tapei to put themselves into the finals. The championship game was set for tonight against Panama. Neron, along with most Cubans, had a little more bounce in his step this morning. I was happy for them but my focus was studying Spanish. I had sacrificed too much money and stress to go home empty-handed. I continued to work through empty pages in the front of the workbook whenever I was too frustrated with the new assignment. Two things distracted me. Whenever the female bird tried too hard to get her share, the male bird raised a fuss, chasing her around the cage. The other thing was that Neron interrupted me more and more to talk about the embargo. From the *Granma*, a popular Havana newspaper, he translated articles into English for me that gave examples of how Cubans were hurt by the embargo. He wondered why only the U.S. and two or three other countries continue to vote against everyone else in the world to keep the embargo in place. He assured me that fewer than five countries would vote with the U.S. in justification of the embargo. I was busy conjugating verbs for my homework so I didn't have much time to debate whether the embargo was good or bad. Or maybe I knew what the embargo was doing and was embarrassed by it.

At dinner Mateus interrupted the talk about the *Copa del Mundo*. "Brandon, I know you just want to study Spanish, but tonight I really need your company."

"*No problema*," I said with a grin. "What do you have planned? French girls?"

"Really? You will give up studying for a night?" he teased. "Tonight we will be guests at the Brazilian ambassador's house."

I looked doubtful, and he assured me it would be fun.

The ambassador's home was a large Spanish style adobe house with a red tile roof. Feeling very much out of place, I followed Mateus through the great wooden doors. Without hesitation, Mateus led me onto a patio where the ambassador and his guests were drinking and talking. The ambassador, a short heavy man with a large moustache, stood to greet us. Mateus introduced himself and thanked him for his assistance in arranging the opportunity to study in Cuba. Then he introduced me as a fellow student from the United States. The ambassador spoke to me in English, welcoming me to his home, but the rest of the conversation was in Portuguese. Mateus sat down and answered questions fired at him by the ambassador.

I wandered back into the main part of the house and helped myself to a couple of shrimp off a platter and dipped them into a thick red sauce. A tall, thin man followed me in from the patio, introduced himself as Humberto, and offered me a beer. I chose a *Cristal* and sank into a large couch near a platter of shrimp and cocktail sauce, relaxing to the erotic Brazilian music. Humberto set down his beer to shake my hand. He had a half eaten carrot in his other hand.

Humberto explained that he was a Brazilian diplomat. His dark-rimmed glasses caught most of the perspiration running down his forehead. His loud untucked sweat-stained shirt looked like he had just returned from a *discoteca*. He was a little bit taller than I was, but it was difficult to tell how much taller because his whole body moved to the beat of the music which filled the house.

"So my American friend, what do you think about Cuba?" he said as he dunked a shrimp into the sauce.

"Cuba is a beautiful place, and the people are very nice." I raised the bottle of *Cristal* to my mouth and took a long drink.

"That is what a diplomat would say," he laughed musically, "but I honestly agree with you. This is my third trip to Cuba, but I don't get to spend much time here. Because I am a diplomat…" He paused for another shrimp. "Because I am a diplomat I travel frequently and don't spend much time in one place."

"I would like to travel to everywhere," I said with some excitement in my voice. "Maybe I should be a diplomat."

Humberto and I spent the evening listening to the music, drinking *Cristal*, and talking. He asked, and I told him some about my family and my time in Jamaica. Mostly he talked about himself, his family, and his adventures as a diplomat. Finally, much later, when Mateus found us, Humberto turned suddenly serious.

He grabbed a napkin from the table and slowly wiped his mouth. His swaying slowed, and as he finally came to a statuesque pose, he said solemnly, "You are a good young man, Brandon, and you would be a fine diplomat. But there is something you should know. A foreign diplomat is a homeless person who is paid to lie for his country." He picked up his beer and swayed his way back onto the patio.

Sounds

◆

Day 73
Sunday, October 26, 2003

The Cuban baseball team won the *Copa del Mundo*, beating Panama, 4–2. During the celebration, the Cuban team raised a banner that said, "*No al Bloqueo*." The message was intended for the world, as a vote on the embargo was scheduled in the United Nations during the week. Only the United States, Israel, and the Marshall Islands were expected to vote in favor of '*el bloqueo*'.

Since my decision on Thursday to talk about music, I had considered and discarded several ideas about the exact form my presentation would take. One of the ideas I discarded first was any idea of singing to the class in Spanish. It would have been entertaining but in the same way that watching a car wreck is entertaining. Unable to settle on an idea, I spent the morning getting my homework done for Monday and Tuesday, conjugation of verbs in the subjunctive. This type of homework helped me understand English better.

Napping after lunch, I returned to Jamaica in my dreams and heard again the roosters crowing each morning and the smacks of the dominos against the table on Friday night. The sounds stayed with me when I woke up. It's not just music that's universal, but many sounds too. Some sounds, like the smacks of dominos are unique and help define a culture, while others are timeless and cross boundaries, like the crowing of a rooster.

In Jamaica: The horn of the market bus winding down the mountain road early Saturday mornings, the roar of the hurricane winds, and the frying pan sizzle of rain on the zinc roofs. In Holguin: The sound of squeaky cheese and squeaky wheels, the early morning calls of the lechero and panadero. From my own life: Alarm clocks ringing in the college dorm and the sound of falling snow settling to the ground in woven silence on my grandfather's ranch in Nebraska. These sounds connect us by stopping our inner dialog and beg to be included in our thoughts. Sound itself is part of the meaning. It is also the passionate bridge to our innermost feelings and to the feelings of our families and friends.

I knew this would work for my presentation. I would start with music, familiar and unfamiliar, and talk about how it defines a culture but also knocks down barriers between cultures. Then from country music, reggae, and salsa I would lead the class to crashing waves and crying babies. Passionate and excited that warm Sunday afternoon, I had no premonition of how little my presentation would matter by the end of the week.

Carmen's Voice

✦

Day 74
Monday, October 27, 2003

I couldn't sleep because Carmen's voice kept me awake. It kept saying, "*Yo puedo ir con ti*." Her voice was sweeter than any sound I was going to talk about on Friday. Sometimes her voice said, "*Tú puedes quedar conmigo siempre en Holguin*." Her voice was lying. She couldn't go with me, and I couldn't stay in Holguin. I wanted to sleep but her voice kept me awake. Her voice and the hungry desire to hold Carmen instead of the pillow. It is strange, wanting to hear someone's voice and at the same time hoping never to hear it again.

Earlier that evening, Paloma called me to the phone, and with a sexy smile, said, "It is a *señorita* with a wonderful voice."

"*Hola*," I spoke into the phone.

"*Hola, Brandon. ¿Cómo estás?*"

The wonderful voice brought shivers to my body, shivers of happiness and pain. I didn't want to talk to her, not now. I was finally starting to think of her only every other second of every day. Trying to rid her from my being was like trying to drain the blood from my body.

"*Estoy bien*," I said, my voice shaky. "*¿Y tú?*"

"*Bien*." She sounded happy to be talking to me. I wish I could figure out what I was feeling.

"I got your number from Carlos, and I wanted to call you. How is your Spanish class going?"

"The class is good. I think that I am learning a lot."

"I miss you, Brandon."

"I miss you too."

"I rode by *La Begonia* earlier today. Do you remember that is where we went on our first date?" Her voice reminded me of her energy and passion, the energy and passion that haunted me when I tried to sleep.

"I wish that you were here. I loved being with you."

That was the last thing I remember saying to her. I don't really remember the rest of the conversation. I know that it lasted about ten minutes. Her last words, before good-bye, told me to take care of myself.

It was painful and joyful talking to her. I guess it had been so long since I had been in a relationship I forgot how good it feels and how painful it can be. I wanted to be holding her and not the stupid phone. I remember I told her that I didn't think I would be able to go back to Holguin because of the visa. She told me not to worry about it and just to study Spanish as much I could.

After the phone call the day continued as usual. Neron talked only of the *Copa del Mundo* and the embargo. Mateus mentioned that he would be leaving at the end of the week as planned, but some of his friends from France were also leaving. Immigration had come to their apartment and simply told them to leave the country, with no other explanation.

Neron said there had to be some explanation because none of his boarders had ever had anything like that happen. Paloma, always the entertainer, with a French accent said something about movies. The men laughed, but I didn't understand until later when Mateus explained that some Frenchmen had gotten in trouble for filming naked girls. He didn't think his friends were involved in those things, but he wasn't sure.

In bed, sleepless, my conversation with Carmen kept playing through my head, bits and pieces that I didn't remember until she said, "*Adiós.*" There were so many things that I wanted to say to her but I knew that they would cause us more pain. Things like, "I love you, and I don't want to leave this country without you. I have finally felt love again."

I wanted desperately to go to Holguin. Friday afternoon I could get on a truck hauling people east and wake up in Holguin. I could spend all day Saturday and find a ride back on Sunday. My visa wouldn't allow it, but no one would know…but what if I was caught? What problems would that create for Carlos, for Neron and Paloma? I'm sure I would end up like the Frenchmen, ordered to leave Cuba.

I grabbed the pillow and brought it into my chest, squeezing it tightly. My eyes burned and tears would not put out the fire. I realized again how content I had been with her. How did I know? I knew because the real joy and happiness I felt with her was exactly equal to this pain, this pain that diminished my enthusiasm for breathing.

How Much is a Baby Worth?

◆

Day 75
Tuesday, October 28, 2003

"It is so easy to call other people evil," Ricardo talked passionately. I was surprised because Ricardo was usually so calm and rational, looking at both sides of things, but tonight he was erupting. Bush had made another speech about the evil leaders in the world. Of course, Bush included Castro. "Do you know what evil is?" he asked me.

I shook my head, wanting him to keep talking, wanting him to give me answers.

He drank most of a *mojito* in one gulp and said, "I have thought about this for many years, and I believe these two things are most evil. Killing children and not teaching children." He stopped, and we sat in silence.

I tried to think about what he was saying but, since talking to Carmen yesterday, my mind was full of her. I had a few more days to get ready for the exposition, and I wanted to do well enough that there would be a possibility of me going up to 'avansado,' the next level of Spanish. That meant putting Carmen back out of my mind. I couldn't concentrate with her in there.

After class I had walked to the *Malecón* because I had read that today marked the anniversary of Camilo Cienfuego's death, and children were walking down to throw flowers for Camilo into the ocean. I had seen the newspaper but the sight of tens of thousands of school children walking down to the *Malecón* with flowers in their arms was more than I expected. My first question for Ricardo that evening was about Camilo's history.

He told me that Camilo was born in Havana and wanted to be an artist. He was too poor to continue in art school so he went to work in a tailor's shop. In 1953 he left for the U.S., where he participated in various anti-Batista activities. He was arrested by American immigration authorities in 1955 and deported back to Cuba. Later, he was beaten at a student demonstration in Havana. He

234

returned to the U.S., where he learned of Fidel's promise to liberate Cuba. He traveled to Mexico and was one of the last volunteers to be accepted for the Granma Expedition. After the battle of Alegría de Pío, Cienfuegos was among the dozen revolutionaries who managed to reach the Sierra Maestra Mountains. With the success of the revolution, Cienfuegos became the military chief of Havana and later the revolutionary army's chief of staff. In October 1959, Castro sent him to Camagüey to arrest Huber Matos, who had been plotting a counter-revolution. A week later, as Cienfuegos was returning to Havana, his Cessna aircraft plunged into the sea. His remains were never found.

Ricardo was nearly in tears as he finished telling about Camilo. Then he exploded into his discussion about evil. After a few minutes of silence I ventured, "Is capitalism evil?"

"No. Economic systems aren't evil. I always meet people that wonder how I can support Castro with all the people he has been responsible for killing. Most of the people killed and in jail are adults. It is sad but we are at war until our government is recognized by the whole world. I think of the babies that died every day before our revolution because of hunger and sickness. Each baby must be worth the same. Their deaths were silent, and no one said anything. Killing babies is evil. Hitler was evil. When Nixon bombed Hanoi to incite more peace demonstrations, that was evil."

"What? He wanted peace demonstrations?"

"Just my theory. Nixon got many votes in 1968 because of the demonstrations in Chicago. Violent demonstrations scare voters. I don't think he was dumb enough to believe that bombing Hanoi would really change the war, and it's hard to believe he did it just for the joy of slaughter. He believed that most Americans would support him if the peace demonstrations turned violent, and he could label the demonstrators, here's that word again, evil."

"I know people who believe communism is evil," I persisted, trying to get him to talk economics rather than evil.

He smiled at my stubbornness, relaxed, and talked in his professor-tone again. "You can't get me to talk about capitalism and communism. They are just labels people use with people who don't agree with them. Neither system is evil, but either system can neglect the children. I think our system is doing better for children than any other system in Latin America.

"My family has more things than most people in Cuba, but we live in a small space, and we follow the rules. We have enough, and we are happy. I am proud to be a soldier in our strange war for independence. I think we will win. I come from a family with some money, and my children would have been okay in the old Cuba. I could leave Cuba. I could take my family anywhere in the world, but many families are not so lucky.

"You know that I am always reading," continued Ricardo. "I love to visit libraries wherever I go, and there are always new books about Cuba. One I found lately was written by an American journalist who wanted to talk to...." Ricardo stroked his bare chin and smiled. "The name of his book was *Waiting for Fidel.* He interviewed a man, a little older than me, in Santiago, who was an uneducated laborer. This man knew that without the revolution his children would have also been uneducated laborers, in cane fields or in factories. He brags to this writer that two of his children are veterinarians and one is a government translator."

After my first drink I stood up and reached across the table. "I wish I had more time to talk but today I must go back to my apartment to work on my presentation."

"That's too bad. I was just getting started." He laughed and shook my hand. "One more, I think, would be good. I will be flying to Europe tomorrow and may be gone for at least two weeks. You have made me think about many things and I feel like talking. One more, and then go study."

"*Bueno.*" I sat back down and slid my empty glass across the table. "*Uno más.*"

He took our glasses back to the bar. I relaxed and absorbed the soft rhythm of salsa. Ricardo returned and sat down, but seemed in no hurry to resume the conversation. I sipped the fresh drink and waited.

"Do you remember that last week I mentioned a Brazilian educator, Paulo Freire?" he asked.

I nodded, smiled, and waited.

"One day, Friere asked a group of *campesinos*, peasants, if they would starve two of their children in order to give a third child a good education. Of course they said no. He pointed out that God probably wouldn't either and that it probably isn't God that is responsible for the fact that some babies in this world are safe and well-fed while some babies are sick and hungry."

"This is the second time you have talked about God. I thought communists didn't believe in God."

"Some days I believe in God, but I don't think God lives in the Church. Only a devil would live in the Church the Spaniards sent to Cuba." Ricardo continued teaching. "I know that it is an important issue for Americans who worry about godless Marxism. They just don't understand our history. They don't understand the Church's role in Latin America. The Church endorsed slavery. It helped Spain maintain power. The beliefs in God's will was used by European kings to justify doing whatever they wanted. The Catholic Church that Fidel closed at the beginning of the revolution was the same. In '59, when the Catholic Church was closed, eighty percent of the priests were born in Spain. The Church taught people that they must accept the given order. It taught that God created some people poor and some rich. In all of Latin America, poor people use the phrase, "*Si Díos quiere*" or "If God desires" to explain their poverty. Is it God's will that some babies are born into families with Mercedes and other babies are born with only a 50–50 chance of having a first birthday? Was it God's will that children were sick and didn't have schools? Are some people's babies worth more than others? That is the fundamental question."

Then seeing that my glass was empty, he said, "I had better let you go study. Thank you for listening to an old man. I enjoy our talks." He paused and then smacked the table. "You must meet my family. When I told Elena about our conversations, she told me that I must bring you to meet her."

"I would love to meet your family. How long will you be gone?"

"If my schedule doesn't change, I'll be back on the tenth. I hope we can talk more when I return. I have to go back to Europe tomorrow and do more business. Then I am flying to Moscow. I will drink vodka with some old friends there. Then I will fly to Japan before I come home. Cuba must be ready to do business with the whole world. So I should be back in two weeks, but usually my schedule changes."

"I'll come by the tenth to check," I said.

"The first Saturday after I come back you must spend with us. I have a small boat, and we will go fishing."

"That would be great," I told him, not knowing that my time in Cuba was almost over and that I would never go fishing with Ricardo. Excusing myself, I walked home slowly, wondering about God and how much babies are worth.

Just Go Away

✦

Day 76
Wednesday, October 29, 2003

A knock at the door interrupted my preparation for Friday's class presentation. I assumed it was a delivery for Neron. Opening the door I almost dropped the pencil that was still in my hand.

"*¿Sí?*" I managed. It startled me to see the immigration officers in their official brown immigration uniforms. There were two men. One was older and thinner with a very neat goatee. The other was built like an NFL lineman. They looked much more serious than the officers that came by weekly to make sure that only two people were staying in the house. The regular officers had always dressed casually in jeans and polo shirts.

"*¿Está Neron?*" asked the older officer.

I sighed with relief when they asked for Neron. I told them he was sleeping.

"*Y usted es....*" He paused to look down at a paper on a clipboard, and my heart stopped.

"Brandon Valentine?"

"Yes." I relaxed. I don't have to be afraid. They are just bringing back my passport and visa. Finally. It had been over two weeks; the time that Paloma said it would probably take for them to process it into a student visa.

"*¿Se habla español?*" the older officer asked.

"*Un poco. Soy estudiante.*"

He nodded and said, "We can speak English then. Can we come in?"

I opened the door the rest of the way, allowing them to come in. They sat down at the table.

"We have been told that you have a visa being changed into a student visa, is that correct?"

"Yes."

"As soon as you get back your visa and passport you need to leave the country."

"Excuse me, I don't understand."

They looked at each other, and the big man spoke very softly, "When you get back your visa and passport, you need to leave the country."

"But why do I need to leave? My visa is being changed into a student visa."

"We have been told to tell you that you need to leave."

"But what have I done? I don't understand."

"We can't tell you anything more because we don't know anything more. We just know that you need to leave."

I leaned my head back and glanced up at the ceiling and sighed.

I wasn't necessarily asking them another question. It was more directed at the ceiling I was staring at. "Why?"

"You can tell…" He paused, glanced down at his papers, and continued, "Paloma that she can check at the office on Monday for the passport and visa. It may be ready by then."

They got up from the table. I got out of my seat and walked them to the door. They opened the door and left without a goodbye.

Tears were dripping on unconjugated verbs when Paloma came home. She walked over to the desk, like she always did. But before she could say, "You're studying a lot," I looked up at her. Her face changed as she asked, "What's wrong?"

"I have to leave."

"What? What happened?"

I don't know why the thing that popped into my head did, but it did, and I said it.

"It's my brother."

"What happened?"

"He was in a car crash, and he is in the hospital. My mom is worried about her children right now so she wants me to come home."

She patted me on the back and told me that she would go to see if the passport was ready tomorrow. I finished my exposition and went to my room. I was confused. I didn't know why I was being sent home, and I didn't know why I lied. I didn't know why I couldn't just learn Spanish. The truth was complicated and confusing. The truth would have made everyone uncomfortable, and no one could fix anything. The lie was easier.

Por or Para

◆

Day 77
Thursday, October 30, 2003

Meka, dressed in a blue T-shirt and white shorts, was, as usual, very attractive, perky, and waiting to chat. I thought that if I had pursued her a little that she might have been open to a romance. I had kept our relationship friendly because I had assumed until yesterday that I would find a way to get back together with Carmen before I left Cuba. Now was too late for any romance in Cuba. I was headed back to the States and tomorrow would be my last chat with Meka.

This morning, after saying good morning, she asked, "Do you understand when to use '*por*' or '*para*'? I always feel like I'm using the wrong one."

"I know what you mean," I answered, pretending to care. "I know that they are both prepositions that mean the same as 'for,' but when I listen for them, I just get more confused."

"Me too, but no one corrects me no matter which way I use them. I guess they understand what we mean even if we're wrong, so it doesn't matter."

I smiled and nodded, thinking that to me, this morning, nothing mattered. I considered telling Meka that I was leaving, but I didn't want to deal with that. I would get through the next two days and then disappear. I could tell the class the same lie that I had told Paloma, but dealing with the lie with Neron and Paloma was hard enough.

Unable to sleep last night, I dreaded this long horrible day. I was nervous speaking in front of any group. I was numb from yesterday's order to leave Cuba. The two feelings together were killing me.

I was leaving Cuba **for** the United States. ¿*Por* or *para*?

I wanted to be with Carmen again **for** awhile. ¿*Por* or *para*?

I would give almost anything **for** the chance to make it different. ¿*Por* or *para*?

Carlos would want to do something **for** me. ¿*Por* or *para*?

Meka was right. It didn't really matter. The world would turn and the waves would never stop crashing into the *Malecón*.

My Presentation

✦

Day 78
Friday, October 31, 2003

Chris walked to the teacher's desk that had been cleared for our presentations. Each student would use her desk as the podium from which we would display the skill in Spanish we had acquired in her class. Chris removed three pieces of paper from one of his notebooks. Each sheet, front and back, was covered in a small black handwriting. I sighed in relief. Chris would take up the whole class time and I wouldn't have to do my presentation. That would have been a great relief despite the hours I had spent in preparation. Reverently, he introduced us to the romance between himself and his fiancé. As a conclusion, he played a solo on his trumpet. His exposition set a high standard and was brief enough to leave us all plenty of time.

Meka's exposition was about growing up in the Bahamas and, of course, she used all of the verbs perfectly. Whether she was talking about her childhood or what she planned to do in the future, she was flawless. I was third from last, and each of the other students talked about their country. I realized that they all missed their home or family very much. It was ironic that I would be leaving within a few days and didn't want to go.

"*Sonidos*" was the title of my presentation. I talked about the sound of waves crashing against rocks. The sound of rain slapping tree leaves. I explained that sounds let you know that you are alive. They can evoke pain, happiness, joy, and laughter. Voices, music, and sounds of our environment create the world we live in or the world we want to forget. I told about country music from my home in Nebraska. The modern country music of Alan Jackson, Garth Brooks, and George Strait. They wrote and sang great songs about loving, living, and growing. Like most music, it encompasses life.

I talked about Reggae music and Salsa and Merengue. Jamaican Bob Marley and his great song, *One Love*. Everyone relates to music, and music brings everyone to life, across borders and around the world.

I did a little research for my presentation and included these gems. In ancient Greece, Plato noted that "music makes better people," and a philosopher named Schopenhauer gave the opinion that "music is the bath of the soul."

The class loved my exposition. Señora Mendoza kissed me on the cheek as she handed me my certificate of completion and wished me success in the advanced class. This reminded me that there would be no advanced class. For awhile I had forgotten that everything had changed. I did not bother to tell anyone that I was going home next week or lie about my brother's accident. I acted as though nothing had changed. I survived the class with a smile on my face and then went home and cried.

Wandering

✦

Days 79 to 83
Saturday–Wednesday, November 1–5, 2003

The seas crashed into the *Malecón* and the mist enveloped me. I found myself sitting there, motionless, day after day. I watched the sea surge and retreat, waves endlessly marching toward the city. My mind focused on the waves. After each crash, I listened for Carmen's voice, but I heard nothing. The waves would return and crash against the rocks and leave the echoes of my voice crying her name. The cool mist wrapped around me but there was no comfort.

In the house I ate and pretended to listen to the conversation. I didn't sit around and chat. I repeated the story about my brother's accident when Neron or Paloma asked. When Mateus flew back to Brazil on Sunday, I repeated the same lie. I lay on my bed or walked.

I wanted to feel the same feeling I felt when I left Jamaica. I wanted the bad things to drip away and leave me with the clean feeling of pain. I told myself that I needed to stop thinking about Cuba. That season had past. The only thing certain now was my life back in the States, but I could not form a picture of what that might be. I gazed out into the sea and waited for the pain, but there was no feeling. My mind felt like some monster was scribbling calculus equations on the back of my brain. Nothing made sense to me. Was I coming or going? Did it matter?

Lying to Carlos

♦

Day 84
Thursday, November 6, 2003

"*Hola Pedro. ¿Cómo estás?*" I was glad Carlos's brother-in-law answered the phone.

"*Bien, Brandon. ¿Y tú?*" Pedro answered, recognizing my voice.

"*Estoy bien. Y Mariella y Salvador. ¿Cómo está tu familia?*"

"*Todo está bien. ¿Cuándo regresará a Holguin? Todos quieren verte.*"

"*Yo no sé cuando voy a Holquin. ¿Está Carlos?*"

"*Sí. Aquí está.*"

"*Brandon, ¿cómo estás?*" Carlos asked, his voice full of his usual enthusiasm.

"*Mal.*"

"Why? Are you sick?" Carlos's voice filled with concern as he changed to English.

"I'm leaving Cuba tomorrow. Paloma just gave me my passport, and I will fly out tomorrow. I'm going home." My eyes filled with tears. I knew what I had to tell Carlos but the pain was real and excruciating.

"Why? What happened?"

The telephone line was stiff with silence. Finally I told Carlos the same lie I had been telling for a week in Havana. "My brother was in a car accident, and I have to go back to the States."

"Oh no, my friend, is your brother alive?"

"Oh, yes. I think that he will be alright, just some broken bones. But my mother is worried, and she wants all of her children with her."

"I'm sorry, Brandon. I'm sorry for your brother, and I'm sorry that your experience here went the way that it did." After more silence he continued. "I wanted to celebrate your birthday here. I wanted to celebrate Christmas here in Cuba with you. I wanted you to help me shave many more pigs before you left. You never even went to the beach."

There was more silence until I interrupted it. "Carlos, don't worry about what we didn't do. I had a great time here in Cuba. I had a great time with you. Remember all our times in Jamaica, drinking rum, eating cane, drinking coconut water, killing chickens, and picking fruit? I have great memories, and I thank you for being part of them."

I was smiling, as I remembered. There was more silence. I'm sure that Carlos was playing some of those moments out in his mind, and I hoped that he was smiling too.

"Carlos, how is everything going with your visa and your passport?" I asked.

"Everything is going good. I think that everything is going to work out."

There was more silence.

"How is Carmen?" I asked, wanting to know but at the same time not wanting to know.

"She misses you, and she comes over to the house almost every day asking if I have talked to you."

I closed my eyes in pain. I knew this hurt Carlos because he worked so hard to make everyone happy. I knew he would be angry at himself for not making my time in Cuba work out better.

"Carlos, I will call you when I get to the States to let you know how everything is going. I need to get all of my things together. I thank you again, my brother, for everything, and good luck with the passport."

"Brandon, I hope that everything is alright, and say hello to your family for me. Take care of yourself. *Adios, Brandon.*"

"*Adios, Carlos.*" I heard the line click. I listened to the silence for awhile before hanging up the phone. So many words unspoken. So much silence. For me, something had died, and the silence represented this death. What was it? Was it a dream or hope that I had? Would I ever see Carlos again? Would I…?

Back in my room I lit up a cigarette and stared up at the ceiling. It's November, and I will possibly see my family tomorrow. I shivered slightly. It's November. Damn, it's going to be cold in Nebraska.

Leaving My Heart

◆

Day 85
Friday, November 7, 2003

I was tired of floating on my back, and I had decided to give up and drown in self pity. I looked down as I passed over Cuba. Cuba with Carlos, Belicia and Galeno. Cuba with Neron and Paloma. Cuba with Ricardo. Cuba with Damita and Carlosito. Cuba with Carmen. Would I ever see Cuba again? Straight from Havana to Miami would have only taken forty minutes, but I had to fly to Jamaica in order to fly to Miami because I was a U.S. citizen. A citizen of the only country in the world that forbids its citizens to visit Cuba.

I was still trying to figure out why I had lied to Carlos last night, the same lie I had been telling Neron and Paloma all week. My brother was still in the hospital, and my family needed me. Why did I lie? Carlos wanted to help me but I didn't think he could change anything. I had been told to leave so I was leaving. I didn't want him to think that he was unable to keep a promise to a friend. That would have killed him.

In Miami, the immigration officer glanced up at me and then back down at my passport. He flipped through it noticing the visa stamps from Jamaica.

"What were you doing in Jamaica?"

"I was a Peace Corps Volunteer."

He smiled and said, "Welcome home," as he offered his hand.

I shook his hand, smiled, and said, "Thank you." I was home, but my heart was in Cuba.

Epilogue

✦

Tuesday, December 31, 2003

The once wide, sun-drenched interstate from Wyoming into Montana was now a skinny, one-car track in the snow, and it was hard to see the track. My little black Nissan pickup labored over drifts. I felt like I was pushing a tinfoil-wrapped shopping cart in a hurricane. I had entered the "Big Sky State," which should be nicknamed the "If You Don't Have a Four Wheel Drive Vehicle Stay Out State." I wasn't in Cuba or Jamaica anymore, but if it ever did snow in Cuba or Jamaica I know that there would be someone out along the road selling snow chains. I was afraid to stop, so even though I was only going ten miles per hour I kept going. The blizzard I had been trying to outrun had finally caught up with me, and I just hoped that I could reach Billings alive.

I left Omaha the day after Christmas without looking at a weather report. I was going to start a job in Missoula, Montana, on the 20th of January.

On Christmas morning my dad asked, "So what time tomorrow do you plan on taking off for Montana?"

"Sometime after breakfast."

My dad smiled and said nothing. In his eyes I could read all of the questions that his smile didn't say. "Why are you leaving for Montana when your job doesn't start for a month? Why are you leaving your family who loves you and wants to spend time with you? Why don't you look at the weather channel to see if you are going to run into a storm? Why can't you relax and play with your little brother and sister who missed you while you were in Jamaica and Cuba?" His eyes asked, but he knew that I didn't have answers so he didn't ask out loud.

I had arrived in Omaha Friday night, November 7th. For the next six weeks I stayed busy. I played some basketball with my little brother and sister. We raked the lawn and picked up leaves.

I visited my home town in western Nebraska and talked to high school class-mates. I didn't feel like I belonged. They couldn't understand about third-world poverty, so I gave pat answers that they accepted, and I didn't really talk about

Jamaica or Cuba. My friends had changed in their own way. One of my friends would always want to drink all night the last time I saw him. Now he politely excused himself early because he missed his two-year-old daughter.

I started looking for jobs when I got home, and one of my goals was graduate school in Missoula, Montana. I applied for a job with airport security in Missoula and was hired to start work in late January.

I still don't know why I left Omaha the day after Christmas. Maybe I was tired of lying on the bottom bunk in my little brother's room playing over in my mind the long list of things I wished I hadn't said throughout the day. Maybe I had to leave because I was sick of myself. Maybe I was tired of feeling like a guest in my own home. When I closed my eyes in the shower, I wondered why I felt that way when my parents were so warm and open.

My parents, both teachers, have Christmas vacation with the children. Coming back from mall shopping one day with Mom I said, "You know if I didn't have to be here, I wouldn't be." Taking her eyes off the road for a split second she looked at me with shock and hurt. I wanted to unsay the words but I knew that was impossible. In many ways the words weren't true. I loved my parents, and I had missed them. The familiar parts of my old life felt good but I just didn't feel like I belonged. I had been living surrounded by body-shriveling poverty for more than three years. Now I am surrounded by obesity and over-indulgence. Visa and MasterCard give everyone everything, and no one has to give away anything they would like to keep.

In Cuba, especially in Holguin, I saw that anytime anyone saw someone in need they gave away from what little they had and expected nothing in return. It wasn't a situation where someone has a ton of rice so they give a cup away to help someone and to make themselves feel good. It's a situation where someone has a "little," and they have decided that the word would still work as "litle" so they give away one "t." A true gift and true love are things you give when you don't expect anything in return. I had really witnessed Christmas in September when I was living with Carlos.

I don't know if it was all of those things I was running away from but I had to leave Omaha or stay and think about them. It was easiest to take off without thinking. But stuck in the blizzard, frightened that I might not get out of it, the warm tears running down my face felt good. I realized that my parents had tried to give me true love along with all of the rest of the presents. I accepted all of the gifts that didn't matter and refused the most important gift of all.

Finally, through the blowing snow, I saw the blue flashing lights of the Montana Highway Patrol and then the lights of Billings. The interstate was closed and the Patrol was directing people to motels with empty rooms. I called collect from an outdoor pay phone, while I waited my turn. Thankful to be alive, I realized that the struggle on the interstate had been fun. I wondered why.

Mom answered the phone, and we talked awhile. I said good-bye and then added I was sorry. She said that I didn't need to worry about it.

"I love you, Mom, and tell Dad I love him too."

"I will. I love you too."

I think that was the first time in my life I was able to say "I love you" before my mom did. My breath drifted up until the wind and snow pierced it and blew it away. I wondered what shape of snowflake my breath would eventually form.

The road report was passed around like a daily newspaper for the next three mornings. Each day it said, "I-84: Closed. No travel due to blizzard conditions." Finally, on the fourth morning, when I picked up the coffee-stained report, the message had changed. "All roads are snow-packed and icy." It didn't say closed, so they must be open.

I thought about the icy, wind-whipped trail that I had guided my little pickup down a few nights before. My adventures weren't always painless but in time the good memories always outweighed the bad. I packed my bags, my little truck started on the first try, and I was back on the road.

978-0-595-39335-
0-595-39335-7

CPSIA information can be obtained
at www.ICGtesting.com
Printed in the USA
FSOW01n1218131115
13391FS